THE MEN
WHO WERE

SHERLOCK HOLMES

THE MEN WHO WERE SHERLOCK HOLMES

DANIEL SMITH

Michael O'Mara Books Limited

This paperback edition first published in 2024
First published in hardback under the title *The Ardlamont Mystery*
in Great Britain in 2018 by
Michael O'Mara Books Limited
9 Lion Yard
Tremadoc Road
London SW4 7NQ

A CIP catalogue record for this book is available from the British Library.

This product is made of material from well-managed, FSC®-certified forests
and other controlled sources. The manufacturing processes conform to the
environmental regulations of the country of origin.

ISBN: 978-1-78929-629-7 in paperback print format
ISBN: 978-1-78243-847-2 in ebook format

1 2 3 4 5 6 7 8 9 10

Image three on page 4 of the picture section: Sir George Reid, Sir Henry Duncan
Littlejohn, 1826–1914. President of the Royal College of Surgeons, Edinburgh,
National Galleries of Scotland.

Cover design by Natasha le Coultre
Designed and typeset by Mark Bracey
Printed and bound by CPI Group (UK) Ltd, Croydon, CR0 4YY

www.mombooks.com

For Rosie, Charlotte and Ben

Contents

	Prologue	11
1	The Holmes Connection	15
2	Fates Entwined	32
3	A Gentleman and a Scoundrel	40
4	A Tangled Web	50
5	Partners in Crime-Fighting	68
6	The Body in the Woods	83
7	An Exact Science	96
8	The Third Man	106
9	A National Sensation	119
10	Two Men in a Boat	135
11	The Smoking Gun	145
12	A Second Opinion	158
13	The Element of Doubt	166
14	The Jury Returns	178
15	For a Sheep as a Lamb	190
16	The One that Got Away	202
17	A Dog with a Bad Name	212
18	The Veiled Lover?	223
19	Aftermath	235
	Bibliography	242
	Acknowledgements	247
	Index	248

'... the lowest and vilest alleys in London do not present a more dreadful record of sin than does the smiling and beautiful countryside ... Think of the deeds of hellish cruelty, the hidden wickedness which may go on, year in, year out, in such places, and none the wiser.'

Sherlock Holmes, 'The Adventure of the Copper Beeches'

Prologue

It was no day to go hunting. Thunderclaps punctuated the incessant beat of the rain, lightning streaked across the sky and a Scotch mist hung over the land. But the three intrepid stalkers were not to be deterred.

At a little after 7 a.m., they left the comforts of Ardlamont House – an oasis of Georgian splendour rising up amid hundreds of acres of rugged terrain on the Cowal Peninsula. The group was led by Alfred Monson, who had been living at the property since the beginning of the summer. His companions were a man known as Mr Scott, who had arrived at Ardlamont two days earlier, and a dashing young army lieutenant, Cecil Hambrough. Hambrough was just twenty years old and Monson – a respectable rector's son with impeccable connections – had been engaged by Cecil's father to tutor the young man some three years earlier.

They were, perhaps, an unlikely looking group. Hambrough was the standout physical specimen. He stood over six-foot tall, strong and well built, with a firm jaw, blue eyes and a crown of blond hair. As the newspapers would later put it, he had 'beauty of the Saxon type'. Monson, meanwhile, boasted an authentically aristocratic pedigree and was in the prime of life. Thirty-three years old and in fine shape, clean-shaven and well turned-out, he radiated an aura of intelligence and civility.

11

Scott, on the other hand, was rather less imposing. Introduced to the locals as an engineer from London, he dressed neatly enough – a bowler hat sat proudly on top of his head – but he nonetheless seemed a little rough around the edges. There was something imponderable about Mr Scott, so that those who encountered him on this trip were unsure as to quite what to make of him. Perhaps it was his lack of ease in the grand surroundings of Ardlamont, his slightly straggly moustache or the way he dropped his aitches. Whatever it was, he did not seem to fit the then commonly held image of a gentleman.

Mrs Monson, her three young children and their governess had left Ardlamont by boat for Glasgow early that morning. The three men had all risen shortly afterwards despite their previous night's misadventure. A moonlit fishing trip on Ardlamont Bay had only narrowly avoided tragedy when the boat that Monson and Hambrough had taken out sprang a leak. The two were forced to swim for their lives. Yet, despite the danger they had faced, they – along with Scott, who had remained on shore – returned to the house in good spirits, toasting their safe return long into the night.

When Wright the butler got up just after seven, he had found Hambrough in the dining room and served him a glass of milk and a biscuit. A little later, Monson, Hambrough and Scott left for their morning's sport. They walked along a road by the house, then climbed into a field and from there entered the surrounding wood. They were spread out in a line as if intent on beating for rabbits.

Around nine o'clock, Wright encountered Monson and Scott back in the house, standing at the dining-room door. Neither of them had their gun, but Scott was carrying several rabbits that he said Hambrough had shot. Then Monson told Wright that their young companion had also shot himself. 'In the arm, sir?' enquired the butler nervously. No, came the reply. In the head. He was, Monson explained, lying out in the woods. Quite dead.

Guided by Monson, the appalled Wright went to view the scene of the calamity, picking up Whyte the gardener and Carmichael the coachman along the way. They discovered Hambrough's corpse on top of a dyke by a ditch. His head was leant against his left shoulder, blood oozing from a wound behind his right ear and soaking into the ground behind. His right arm lay at his side, while his left rested across his chest. 'What should we do?' asked Monson agitatedly.

'We had better send for a doctor,' the butler replied, stony-faced.

Then Wright, Whyte and Carmichael contrived to move the body in a rolled-up rug out of the woods and back to the field, from where it was driven by cart to the house. Back indoors, Wright helped dress the body ahead of the arrival of the local GP. It seemed like the right thing to do – a nod to decorum in the face of the tumult prompted by such a grisly and sudden death.

Among aficionados of the then blossoming genre of crime fiction, the mysterious death of Cecil Hambrough might have evoked memories of a story featuring the most famous literary detective of all time, Sherlock Holmes. Two years earlier, the *Strand Magazine* had published Arthur Conan Doyle's Holmes adventure 'The Boscombe Valley Mystery'. It featured a young man who reported the death of his father – in whose company he had recently been – his 'body stretched out upon the grass' in a wood. But whereas the son was quickly arrested on suspicion of murder and the location of death treated as a crime scene, at Ardlamont there was an assumption that Cecil Hambrough's death was an accident. With scant regard for the preservation of potential evidence, so began one of the most notorious cases of the Victorian age – an enduring mystery that wreaked havoc in the lives of all its main actors and a good many others besides.

Prominent among them were two upstanding citizens of Edinburgh, both of them leading figures in the medical world and pioneers of forensic science – Dr Joseph Bell and Dr Henry Littlejohn. Moreover, these two were, as chance would have it, the chief inspirations behind the creation of Sherlock Holmes. Brought in to investigate the case far later than Holmes would have ever appreciated, they nonetheless proceeded to deliver vital evidence as to what had gone on at Ardlamont. The death of Cecil Hambrough would pitch the pair into a furious battle between reason and knowledge on the one hand, and doubt and the dark heart of man on the other. It was a real-life playing out of the struggle that Doyle had Sherlock Holmes wage countless time over his illustrious fictional career.

A mystery as perplexing as any Holmes ever faced, the Ardlamont affair established Bell and Littlejohn as the definitive link between the imagined, gas-lit world of 221b Baker Street and the thrilling frontiers of real-world criminal investigation in what was the first golden age of forensic sleuthing. This being real life, however, the stakes were – for everyone – far higher.

1

The Holmes Connection

'The world is full of obvious things which nobody
by any chance ever observes.'

Sherlock Holmes, 'The Boscombe Valley Mystery'

In 1893, Sherlock-Holmes-mania was in full swing. In fact, it seemed like the whole world was in thrall to the world's first and greatest consulting detective, with one notable exception – his creator, Arthur Conan Doyle.

Doyle's fractious relationship with his detective-son was rooted in the author's hope to be regarded as something more than a scribbler of crime stories. His great desire was to create epics of historical fiction – a sort of Walter Scott for a new generation. The Holmes stories came almost too easily to him – well-paying trifles that distracted him from more serious works like *Micah Clarke* and *The White Company*. As he rattled off tale after tale of Holmes's exploits for the avid readership of the *Strand Magazine*, his frustration at being pigeonholed grew. If only the damned magazine would not throw so much money at him to write more of the potboilers.

Like a deranged criminal, Doyle saw only one way to free himself from the tyranny of his fictional progeny. He planned to throw Sherlock to his death down an Alpine waterfall – an act he would execute before the year was out. Holmes was to plunge to his seeming doom over Switzerland's Reichenbach Falls in the story 'The Final Problem'. It would be a literary event of extraordinary magnitude, rendering countless readers bereft. Indeed, when the story was published, crowds of young men gathered at the *Strand*'s offices in London wearing black armbands as a symbol of their mourning.

Yet just as Doyle was preparing to consign his most famous son to history, the two men upon whom Holmes was most closely modelled were about to explode into the public consciousness as players in the most talked-about real-life murder trial for years, that of Alfred Monson. To add to the fevered interest, one of them – Joseph Bell – had recently been 'outed' as the primary inspiration for Baker Street's most beloved resident. That a similar connection had not been drawn with Henry Littlejohn is testament to the unfussy way in which Bell and Littlejohn joined forces to investigate their real-life cases. So how had the lives of Bell, Littlejohn and Doyle become interweaved?

Their combined story begins at Edinburgh University in 1876, when Doyle took up his medical studies there while Bell and Littlejohn were two of the most respected men on the faculty.

Bell had been born in Edinburgh in 1837 into an esteemed medical family. That he would pick up the professional mantle was all but inevitable, but his natural feel for medicine (as both a practitioner and teacher) was still breathtaking. He finished his formal studies at the university's Medical School in 1859 and subsequently served as house surgeon to Professor James Syme, the great pioneering surgeon of his generation. Then, at the age of just twenty-six, Bell was tasked with organizing classes in systematic and operative surgery at the university.

Remarkably, given this blistering start to his career, he kept up the pace for years to come. Mid-century Edinburgh was a hotbed of progressive medical practice and social reform, and, as the likes of Syme reached the end of their working lives, Bell became a leading figure in moving things on again. Not only were his students trained to the highest levels, but he also sought to refine and improve the systems in which medical professionals worked. He was, for instance, a great mentor of nurses, recognizing their importance in the delivery of the best medical care rather than viewing them as lowly skivvies as had hitherto been their more usual fate. In his desire to elevate the professional standing of nursing, he became a friend and confidant of Florence Nightingale, even dedicating his book – *Some Notes on Surgery for Nurses* – to her in 1887. Among his many other achievements, he was elected president of the Royal College of Surgeons in Edinburgh, campaigned to have women admitted to the city's Medical School, was the first surgeon at the Royal Hospital for Sick Children (an institution that opened in 1860 after years of campaigning by Bell and a number of his colleagues, not least Littlejohn), and still found time to edit the *Edinburgh Medical Journal* for almost a quarter of a century. Away from medicine, he was a devout churchgoer, a justice of the peace and a deputy lieutenant (that is to say, the hand-picked assistant of the Queen's personal representative in the local county). In short, he was a doer on a grand scale, driven by a genuine desire to improve the conditions of his fellow citizens.

Nor was Littlejohn any less energetic, despite being the older man by some eleven years. He, too, was an Edinburgh native, but his pathway into medicine was a much less obvious one. His father had been a master baker and Henry, the seventh of nine children, might have got lost in the crowd. But his passion for medical knowledge won through and he graduated from the city's university in 1847. He then spent a year working on the continent before returning to his hometown as assistant pathologist at the Edinburgh Royal Infirmary.

In this role, Littlejohn became intimately familiar with death in many, varied and often gruesome forms. It was a natural move, then, when he became Edinburgh's police surgeon in 1854. This was a post that made many demands on his time. He was not only responsible for the medical welfare of all police staff and prisoners, but was also among the first ports of call for officers investigating serious incidents – whether accident or criminal act. He was regularly called upon to carry out forensic investigations – in an age when forensic medicine was in its infancy – and to conduct post-mortems. He was, as well, a familiar face in the Scottish courts, offering evidence as an expert witness on everything from catastrophic rail accidents to sexual assaults and child murders. Present at virtually every significant criminal trial conducted in Edinburgh in the second half of the nineteenth century, he gained a view of Scotland's underbelly that few could rival and even fewer envied.

His work as police surgeon gave him a significant public profile in the city, and his fame only grew when in 1862 he was appointed the first Medical Officer for Health for Edinburgh, charged with promoting the health and safety of the general public. The role had been created in part as a response to the collapse of a tenement building the previous year on the city's high street that had left thirty-five people dead. For a man already stretched by his position with the police, Littlejohn attacked his new job with extraordinary vigour. Indeed, he was about to carry out much of the work for which he would become best known.

In 1865, he published a landmark study, *Report on the Sanitary Conditions of the City of Edinburgh*. Despite its driest of titles, the review sparked a revolutionary overhaul of the Edinburgh landscape. Littlejohn painted a vivid picture of urban poverty and decay, of a city beset by overcrowding and crawling with filth – all of which, as he comprehensively showed, led directly to the spread of poor health. His account was the spur that the local authorities needed to pass the 1867 Edinburgh City Improvements Act – a piece of legislation that ushered in slum clearances, the construction of a new and infinitely better drainage system, and the building of the wide, grand streets that mark out Edinburgh even today as a particularly elegant and appealing metropolis. In a way that only a handful can legitimately claim, Littlejohn changed the face of the city in which he lived.

A catalogue of other notable achievements followed. For example, he took the fight to those infectious diseases that had long beset the city's poor, who had historically been condemned to live one on top of another. Not only did he establish a permanent hospital for those suffering with infectious diseases, but he also spearheaded a change in the law that made it compulsory to notify the authorities of every case of potential contagion. He was also the chief adviser to the Board of Supervisors, an organization that from 1873 was the city's main authority for public health. And if all that were not enough, he served as chairman of the Scottish Society for the Prevention of Cruelty to Children and founded the Scottish Burial Reform and Cremation Society. Yet perhaps the greatest proof of his effectiveness is to be found in the raw statistics – the city's mortality rate fell from 34 per 1,000 people in the 1860s to 14 per 1,000 by the turn of the century.

Both Bell and Littlejohn, then, were great public servants and medical trailblazers – the sort of men upon whom empires are built. But for the young Doyle, they were also inspirational teachers capable of extraordinary feats of mental gymnastics. Bell in particular regularly lit up his lectures with dazzling demonstrations of deductive reasoning, which Doyle copied down and adapted into the character of Sherlock Holmes. Littlejohn, on the other hand, lectured on forensic science in the university's extra-mural school, breathing life into a subject that, by Littlejohn's own estimation, had been largely ignored up to that point.

Littlejohn was a natural-born entertainer. Even as the years advanced, he maintained a lithe and youthful appearance and was an easily identifiable figure around the city in his trademark top hat and frock coat. He was also blessed with an infectious sense of humour and an impish glint in the eye. He liked to terrify unwary onlookers, for example, by positioning himself between tram stops and then launching himself at a carriage as it sped by. It was a routine that he executed so often that the tram drivers knew not to slow down as he came into view, secure that he would safely scramble on board even as eyewitnesses feared a tragedy was about to play out.

His showmanship translated into the lecture theatre, too. An expert in the fields of pathology, toxicology and assorted other medico-legal subjects, he began lecturing in medical jurisprudence (that is to say, the law as it relates to medicine) from 1855. Beginning with barely twenty students, by the 1880s his talks had gained such a reputation that they regularly attracted crowds upwards of 250. Calling on his first-hand experience of police investigations and criminal trials, he filled his addresses with the most up-to-the-minute ideas and theories – he was, for instance, a great champion of the then nascent science of fingerprinting and was an early advocate for the use of photographic evidence. His vast knowledge was conveyed with both humour and colour, as he continually sought new ways to enliven his lectures. Trips to court and visits to actual crime scenes were a particular highlight for both Littlejohn and his students.

While Doyle never publicly confirmed he had been present at Littlejohn's lectures, it is all but unthinkable that he would have missed the opportunity to attend these talks in medical jurisprudence and forensic medicine at the Surgeons' Hall. Not least, Littlejohn was great friends with Bell, and Bell was Doyle's foremost mentor while he studied in Edinburgh. Even if Doyle had not found his way to Littlejohn's sessions of his own accord – unlikely as that seems – Bell would have been sure to have sent him on his way. And while Littlejohn was perhaps the more flamboyant of the two teachers, Bell was renowned for his own theatrics that illuminated the student days of Doyle and a great many of his contemporaries.

Bell's sharp features, flash of neat white hair and penetrating blue eyes saw him regularly likened to an eagle. It was a strangely appropriate comparison, given the preternatural way he could swoop upon truth and fact as if they were his prey. Bell was of the firm belief that a doctor should hone his powers of observation so that apparently even the most trivial detail might assist in diagnosis. He practised quite as well as he preached, and his deductive set pieces became the stuff of legend.

One of Doyle's contemporaries, Dr Harold Jones, wrote years later of how Bell went about encouraging his charges to 'use your eyes … use your ears, use your brain, your bump of perception, and use your powers of deduction'. On one memorable occasion he ushered a patient before a group of students and urged a particular pupil to diagnose his medical condition. The unlucky fellow flailed about for the correct answer, concluding that the man suffered from disease of the hip joints. Bell leant back in his chair, his chin resting on hands pressed together at the fingertips. 'Hip – nothing!' he began, in a tone guaranteed to deflate the ego. 'The man's limp is not from his hip but from his foot. Were you to observe closely, you would see there are slits, cut by a knife, in those parts of the shoes where the pressure of the shoe is greatest against the foot. The man is a sufferer from corns, gentlemen, and has no hip trouble at all. But he has not come here to be treated for corns, gentlemen. His trouble is of a much more seriousness nature. This is a case of chronic alcoholism, gentlemen. The rubicund nose, the puffed, bloated face, the bloodshot eyes, the tremulous hand and twitching face muscles, with the quick, pulsating temporal arteries, all show this. These deductions, gentlemen, must, however, be confirmed by absolute and concrete evidence. In this instance my diagnosis is confirmed by the fact of my seeing the neck of a whisky bottle protruding from the patient's right-hand coat pocket … Never neglect to ratify your deductions.'

Another of his party tricks was to pass a test-tube of amber-coloured liquid among his class. It was, he informed them, a powerful drug with an extremely bitter taste, and in order to assess each student's powers of observation he wished them to sample it one by one. But, he told them, being a fair man, he would not demand of them that which he wouldn't do himself. He promptly dipped a finger in the potion, put his finger in his mouth and pulled an appropriately pained face. Every member of the group then followed suit, so that the room was soon filled with faces set in an array of contortions. As Bell surveyed them, he began to laugh quietly to himself. 'Gentlemen, gentlemen,' he said. 'I am deeply grieved to find that not one of you had developed the power of perception, the faculty of observation which I speak so much of, for if you had truly observed me, you would have seen that, while I placed my index finger in the awful brew, it was the middle finger – aye – which somehow found its way into my mouth.'

Such was Bell's confidence in his own observational abilities that he was prepared to trust his powers even in the face of apparently incontrovertible evidence. He told the story, for instance, of how he had once drawn a few preliminary conclusions about a patient in front of a room of attentive students. He informed the assembled throng that the rather short man who had walked in with something of a swagger was most likely a bandsman in a Highland regiment. The swagger, Bell stated, was characteristic of a piper, while his general demeanour suggested a military background. Given his relative lack of height, a position as a bandsman seemed most logical. When he asked the patient to confirm whether or not he was correct, he was temporarily floored when the man said he was actually a shoemaker. Bell, though, remained convinced that his initial appraisal had been right and asked a couple of his assistants to keep the man in a side room. Having dismissed the class, he went to the patient and asked him to remove his upper clothing. Immediately he spotted a small, blue letter 'D' branded into the skin beneath his left breast – the sign of a deserter. The patient's evasiveness about his military career was immediately explained away.

Bell and the student Doyle quickly established a rapport, with

Bell's techniques making a profound impression on the young man. Bell recollected one consultation, for instance:

> He was amused once when I walked in and sat down. 'Good-morning, Pat,' I said, for it was impossible not to see that he was an Irishman. 'Good-morning, your honour,' replied the patient. 'Did you like your walk over the links to-day, as you came in from the south side of the town?' I asked. 'Yes,' said Pat, 'did your honour see me?' Well, Conan Doyle could not see how I knew that, absurdly simple as it was. On a showery day, such as that had been, the reddish clay at bare parts of the links adheres to the boot, and a tiny part is bound to remain. There is no such clay anywhere else round the town for miles. Well, that and one or two similar instances excited Doyle's keenest interest, and set him experimenting himself in the same direction, which, of course, was just what I wanted with him and all my other scholars.

In turn, the doctor was greatly impressed by the student and would recall of the young Doyle: 'I always regarded him as one of the best students I ever had. He was exceedingly interested always upon anything connected with diagnosis, and was never tired of trying to discover all those little details which one looks for.' That Bell considered him not only among the elite of that period's intake of medical students but nothing less than a protégé was confirmed when he selected Doyle to serve as his outpatient clerk. This gave Doyle the opportunity to study the master's techniques at close hand, and the more he saw, the more impressed he became. As Bell would remember it: 'Doyle was always making notes. He seemed to want to copy down every word I said. Many times after the patient departed my office, he would ask me to repeat my observations so that he would be certain he had them down correctly.'

Doyle left Edinburgh in 1880 and briefly served as ship's surgeon on an arctic whaling vessel, during which a fall overboard almost resulted in his death. A second voyage on a cargo and passenger ship destined for West Africa was no less eventful – the vessel was battered by storms, Arthur fell victim to a typhoid epidemic and even as the ship returned to the relative safety of Liverpool Docks its hull was ablaze. So, it was hardly surprising that he next opted for the rather more genteel life of a general practitioner in Southsea, near Portsmouth, on the south coast of England. Yet life as a doctor was not all that he wanted it to be. For one thing, business was not so good that he could set aside his financial worries. Given Doyle's own family background – his father was an illustrator whose career was blighted by alcohol abuse and psychological problems – money was an important consideration for him. When he submitted a tax return in 1883 showing that he had earned insufficient money to make him liable for tax, the tax office returned it emblazoned with the comment 'most unsatisfactory'. Doyle resubmitted it with his own additional observation: 'I quite agree.'

Alongside the lack of financial security that his work afforded him, Doyle's desire to earn a living as a writer burned bright. He had already enjoyed some success, having a story published for the first time while still a student (in *Chambers's Edinburgh Journal*). By 1885 he was playing with the idea of turning his hand to detective yarns. He was a fan of the genre – particularly the legendary investigator Dupin created by Edgar Allan Poe – and though detective fiction was yet to find literary respectability, he sensed he might have some aptitude for it. Bell kept swimming into his thoughts as he formulated his ideas for a detective novel. 'I thought of my old teacher Joe Bell,' Doyle would write, 'of his eagle face, of his curious ways, of his eerie trick of spotting details. If he were a detective he would surely reduce this fascinating but unorganized business to something nearer to an exact science.'

Within a year, Doyle had taken the kernel of an idea – an idea with Joseph Bell at its heart – and turned it into the first Sherlock Holmes story, the novella-length *A Study in Scarlet* that appeared in *Beeton's Christmas Annual* in 1887. Holmes would get a second airing in another novella, *The Sign of the Four*, in 1890. But it was when Doyle turned to the short-story format, publishing in the *Strand* from 1891, that the Holmes phenomenon exploded. Before long, Doyle was the best-paid writer in the land and there was guaranteed interest in anything to do with his literary offspring. That included the question of whether he was based on a real-life individual.

If Doyle had wanted to keep the cat in the bag, he was peculiarly unsuccessful in doing so. When the first twelve short stories were collected in a single volume, *The Adventures of Sherlock Holmes*, published in 1892, he dedicated it 'To My Old Teacher, Joseph Bell', who in turn favourably reviewed it for the *Bookman*. It did not take a super-sleuth to draw a link between the writer, his creation and his old mentor. Several months earlier – in a May 1892 interview with one Raymond Blathwayt for the *Bookman* – Doyle had provided another hint as to the identity of the inspiration behind Holmes. Doyle told Blathwayt: 'Sherlock Holmes is the literary embodiment, if I may so express it, of my memory of a professor of medicine at Edinburgh University, who would sit in the patients' waiting room with a face like a Red Indian and diagnose the people as they came in, even before they opened their mouths.' In the same month, Doyle wrote to Bell to confirm that he had been immortalized in print. His letter read:

My dear Bell,
It is most certainly to you that I owe Sherlock Holmes and though in the stories I have the advantage of being able to place him in all sorts of dramatic positions, I do not think that his analytical work is in the least an exaggeration of some

effects which I have seen you produce in the outpatient ward. Round the centre of deduction and inference and observation which I heard you inculcate I have tried to build up a man who pushed the things as far as it would go – further occasionally – and I am so glad that the result has satisfied you, who are the critic with the most right to be severe.

The evidence was also there in the stories themselves, for those who were familiar enough with Bell's modus operandi. Just consider the similarities between one of Bell's recorded demonstrations of deduction and an exchange between Holmes and his equally brilliant brother, Mycroft, in the 1893 story, 'The Adventure of the Greek Interpreter'. In Bell's case he was, in the usual manner, presented with a patient about whose background he knew nothing. Their conversation went as follows:

Bell: Well, my man, you've served in the army.
Patient: Aye, sir.
Bell: Not long discharged?
Patient: No, sir.
Bell: A Highland regiment?
Patient: Aye, sir.
Bell: A non-commissioned officer.
Patient: Aye, sir.
Bell: Stationed at Barbados.
Patient: Aye, sir.
Bell: You see, gentlemen, the man was a respectful man but did not remove his hat. They do not in the army, but he would have learned civilian ways had he been long discharged. He has an air of authority and he is obviously Scottish. As to Barbados, his complaint is elephantiasis, which is West Indian and not British.

While Doyle did not directly lift the episode for use in 'The Greek Interpreter', the echoes are clear. To set the scene, Sherlock and Mycroft are sat together in the bow-window of the latter's exclusive London club:

'To anyone who wishes to study mankind, this is the spot,' said Mycroft. 'Look at the magnificent types! Look at these two men who are coming towards us, for example.'

'The billiard-marker and the other?'

'Precisely. What do you make of the other?'

The two men had stopped opposite the window. Some chalk marks over the waistcoat pocket were the only signs of billiards which I could see in one of them. The other was a very small, dark fellow, with his hat pushed back and several packages under his arm.

'An old soldier, I perceive,' said Sherlock.

'And very recently discharged,' remarked the brother.

'Served in India, I see.'

'And a non-commissioned officer.'

'Royal Artillery, I fancy,' said Sherlock.

'And a widower.'

'But with a child.'

'Children, my dear boy, children.'

'Come,' said I, laughing, 'this is a little too much.'

'Surely,' answered Holmes, 'it is not hard to say that a man with that bearing, expression of authority, and sun-baked skin, is a soldier, is more than a private, and is not long from India.'

'That he has not left the service long is shown by his still wearing his ammunition boots, as they are called,' observed Mycroft.

'He had not the cavalry stride, yet he wore his hat on one

side, as is shown by the lighter skin on that side of his brow. His weight is against his being a sapper. He is in the artillery.'

'Then, of course, his complete mourning shows that he has lost someone very dear. The fact that he is doing his own shopping looks as though it were his wife. He has been buying things for children, you perceive. There is a rattle, which shows that one of them is very young. The wife probably died in childbed. The fact that he has a picture-book under his arm shows that there is another child to be thought of.'

Sherlock is evidently Bell to the nth degree. A wily newshound from the *Strand* called Harry How was the first to positively make the connection in June 1892. Doyle immediately warned Bell that his cover was blown and that he should expect a deluge of attention, including 'lunatic letters from Constant Readers who would request his assistance in rescuing maiden aunts from certain starvation in sealed attics at the hand of homicidal neighbours'.

Quite what Bell made of this unexpected new fame is not clear. To friends and family, he suggested he found it all rather wearisome and some of the sillier aspects of Holmes-mania probably tested his patience. However, he did not find it so troubling that he wouldn't give interviews to the press on his links to the great detective. He also agreed to write the introduction to an 1892 edition of *A Study in Scarlet*. Behind the scenes, too, he continued to fuel the Sherlock beast, responding to Doyle's plea to help him with plots. One storyline involved a murderer who used germs, with Bell implying he knew of a real-life case that followed much the same lines. Doyle rejected it on the principle that the public was not yet ready for such a horrifying tale (although he would explore the theme in the 1917 story, 'The Adventure of the Dying Detective'). 'Doyle's the clever man. It's nothing to do with me,' Bell told one interviewer of his part in the creation of Holmes, though this was evidently nothing but false modesty.

Then, at the peak of interest in the Ardlamont case, Bell decided to go public with revelations that he was not merely the medical alter ego of Holmes but had been involved in true-life criminal investigations for decades. 'Well, for twenty years or more I have been engaged in the practice of medical jurisprudence on behalf of the Crown,' he told a journalist from the *Pall Mall Gazette*, adding, 'but there is little I can tell you about it. It would not be fair to mention that which is the private knowledge of the Crown and those associated therewith ...' So, the real-life inspiration for Holmes had even more in common with the detective than had previously been suspected. 'Any deductions and inferences, and so on which I have been the means of placing at the disposal of the authorities are simple and commonplace,' he explained in a typically understated way. He went on to discuss how the powers of observation Doyle had seen so many times within the university setting could be used to progress a police enquiry:

> The vast importance of little distinctions, the endless significance of the trifles. The great majority of people, of incidents, and of cases, resemble each other in the main and larger features. For instance, most men have apiece a head, two arms, a nose, a mouth, and a certain number of teeth. It is the little differences, in themselves trifles, such as the droop of an eyelid or what not, which differentiates men.

Finally came the explanation for how he had come to be an instrument of the police – his relationship with Littlejohn: 'I must explain that Dr Littlejohn is the medical adviser, and he likes to have a second man with him. He is a very intimate friend of mine, and it so happens that for more than twenty years we have done a great deal together, and it has come to be the regular thing for him to take me into cases with him. But I have no official connection with the Crown.'

It is curious that Doyle so readily acknowledged the influence of Bell in the invention of Holmes but never went on record to credit Littlejohn while the latter was still alive. It simply does not make sense to think that Littlejohn did not feature prominently in Doyle's imaginings as he conjured with the idea of a literary detective. Bell was Doyle's primary coach and counsel in Edinburgh, most certainly, but Bell and Littlejohn were true friends – in their later years Littlejohn presented Bell with a large silver cup inscribed 'in memory of a constant friendship' – and as not only a favoured student of Bell but his assistant as well, Doyle could not have failed to come into contact with Littlejohn on a regular basis. As a student of crime and criminal investigation, Doyle would surely have actively sought out contact with the man who was, after all, the official police surgeon and the leading light in Scottish medical jurisprudence. On top of that, he must have known that Bell was also a regular companion on his police work. In short, Littlejohn could not be anything but the other principal model for Holmes.

Where Bell provided the blueprint for Holmes's logical deductions, Littlejohn was the prototype for the renegade forensics pioneer. As Harold Jones revealed in an article for the long-defunct *Tit-Bits* magazine in 1900: 'while Joseph Bell is the original Sherlock Holmes, another Edinburgh professor "had a finger in the pie", so to speak. While Joseph Bell gave Doyle the idea of the character Holmes, the man who, unknowingly perhaps, influenced Doyle in adapting that character to the detection of crime, was Sir Henry Littlejohn.' Yet, Doyle's only recorded nod towards the police surgeon came in March 1929, in a little-reported speech to an audience of Edinburgh graduates residing in Nairobi. According to a report in the *East African Standard*, Doyle ruminated on the unsatisfactory methods of detection exhibited in so much of the crime fiction he had read in his youth before reflecting that 'neither Joe Bell nor Littlejohn would have gone about things in that way'. It was their methods, Doyle told his audience, that first induced him to write a detective story from the point of view of the scientific man.

So why was Littlejohn largely written out of the record, while Bell was so actively inserted into it? Might there have been some personal acrimony between Doyle and Littlejohn? A reason why Doyle would not want the police surgeon bathed in the reflected glory of his literary hero? It is a possibility. But perhaps the silence surrounding Littlejohn had more noble causes. If this wasn't an act of outright deception by Doyle, was it not instead a gentle piece of deflection? Was Bell thrust into the limelight so that Littlejohn could remain outside it? In the end, Bell was the hobbyist in terms of detection, the 'second man' in his own words or, to put it another way, the unofficial consulting detective. For Littlejohn, the stakes were rather higher, with criminal investigation much more clearly within his professional remit. If the shadow of Holmes had hung over him, it would have inevitably complicated his labours. That would surely be reason enough to have kept his association with Sherlock quiet. Bell and Doyle were both the kind of upstanding individuals who would do all in their power to ensure that the life-and-death work that Littlejohn practised on a day-to-day basis was not compromised by public hysteria over an imaginary character. But, to be sure, the ties that bound together Littlejohn, Bell, Doyle and Holmes were strong.

By the time that Cecil Hambrough lay dead in the woods at Ardlamont in August 1893, Littlejohn, Bell and Doyle had each seen and contended with much over their prestigious careers. Each of them in their own way had confronted the dankest recesses of the criminal mind, while themselves being subject to public scrutiny. Yet not even their combined intellects and imaginations could have foreseen the drama that was about to unfold.

2

Fates Entwined

'… you do occasionally find a carrion crow
among the eagles.'

Sherlock Holmes, 'The Adventure of Shoscombe Old Place'

In 1890, Cecil Hambrough had every reason to feel optimistic about his prospects. Born Windsor Dudley Cecil Hambrough in 1873, he was the son and heir of Major Dudley Hambrough. Young, handsome and full of lust for life, he would one day – so he believed – take over as head of his wealthy and revered family.

The Hambroughs came from the Isle of Wight off the English south coast, where they had lived in the grand, gothic Steephill Castle a little outside the booming seaside resort of Ventnor. If that extraordinary building, with its imposing square battlement and high round tower, looked like it was built centuries earlier, it was in fact of rather more recent vintage. Although the Steephill estate had passed through various aristocratic hands over the years, the main accommodation had always been a cottage – albeit a rather splendid one. Then, around 1830, the estate was bought by John Hambrough, Cecil's great-grandfather, who had made his fortune in banking and through a series of wily property deals.

Hambrough knocked down the cottage, along with several other buildings, to make room for the castle of his imagination. Oak panelling and extravagant carvings adorned the walls of the library and study, a stained-glass window illuminated a grandiose billiard room, and in the dining room an oversized marble chimney piece rose up through a polished pine ceiling. Outside, the driveway was spanned by an arch into which were carved Hambrough's initials, along with those of his wife, Sophie Townsend. Hambrough had made a success of his life and he was not about to hide his light under a bushel – it was said that the castle had cost a quarter of a million pounds (over £11 million today) and took over two years to build.

But tragedy was to stalk the family. Hambrough would never get to see the product of his labours, since he went blind shortly before the castle was finished in 1835. Nonetheless, Steephill soon became a focal point of island life, attracting many illustrious visitors – among them Queen Victoria and Prince Albert, and Elisabeth, Empress of Austria, who rented the castle in the summer of 1874. She so loved her time on the island that she commissioned a London jeweller to create a cup for the winner of the annual Ventnor Steeplechase. The inaugural champion was a mare called Beauty, whom Dudley Hambrough (Cecil's father) had once owned but had sold on in the belief that she was too slow. It would not be the last time he would back the wrong horse.

By then, John Hambrough had been dead eleven years, with Steephill passing to Dudley when he came of age in 1870 (his father – John's son – a renowned botanist called Albert, had died in 1861). Dudley also inherited some property in Middlesex (the Stanmore estate) that provided an additional income and retained a prospective interest in the Pipewell estate in Northamptonshire, on the assumption that his ageing, widower uncle died childless. But where John Hambrough had been so financially astute, Dudley was completely inept. Intent on maintaining the family's social position, he haemorrhaged money in order to be seen in the right places with the right people. A major with the Isle of Wight Rifles, part of the

Hampshire Regiment, he also served as a magistrate, but his principal source of income was the money generated by Steephill. In all, he got about £4,500 per year, at a time when most families made do on not more than a few hundred.

But still Dudley could not make his money stretch. As a mover-and-shaker – he was, for example, the first captain of the Royal Isle of Wight Golf Club – he could see no way to rein in his spending. By 1885 he was a crushing £37,000 in debt (some £2 million in modern money). In a last-ditch attempt to get his finances into some sort of order, he mortgaged his life interest in Steephill – his lifelong entitlement to the rents that the estate generated – to the Eagle Insurance Company for £42,000. It was all to no avail. Within twelve months, he had borrowed another £2,500 but it was not long before he fell in arrears with the repayments. With no more credit lines to be plumbed, Hambrough found himself in a true fix. In 1890, his creditors foreclosed and took over his life interest in Steephill.

This was, of course, bad news for the family. Dudley and his wife, Marion, had no choice but to take up temporary tenancies in a series of gradually more depressing addresses in London. Meanwhile, life rumbled on. Dudley was determined that Cecil should follow in his military footsteps but the boy was at that difficult age, flighty and prone to distraction. He had always been kept on a short leash by his parents, who had opted not to send him to school but instead had him educated by a certain Mr Jackson of Ventnor. The boy was not a particularly good student, preferring to be out with his dogs and horses, hunting, fishing and shooting, rather than being stuck indoors. Only his love of botany encouraged him to pick up a book at all. Naive and somewhat guileless, he was nonetheless ready to cut the apron strings as his teenage years rolled by. Moreover, if the parents wanted to instil in him a sense of duty and responsibility, their personal circumstances seriously undermined their authority. In the end, they decided that some outside influence was needed, so they set about finding Cecil a tutor to prepare him for life as an army man.

Mr and Mrs Hambrough also had it in mind to send their two daughters to school on the continent. All of this was far beyond them financially but Dudley was Mr Micawber-esque in his faith that 'something will turn up'. It was an attitude that did little to sharpen his financial acumen or make him a better judge of character. Instead he had an unfortunate tendency to attach himself to anyone who seemed to offer him a way out of his troubles. As often as not, their words of encouragement were inspired by self-interest rather than altruism.

Yet all was not lost for the Hambroughs. Far from it. The family might have been impecunious but hope abounded in the son. Under the terms of his great-grandfather's will, the Hambrough estates were held entail. That is to say, they were passed from generation to generation on the male side so that no one generation might sell the estates outright. An individual could choose to lease his interest for the duration of his life but, upon his death, the property would revert to his male heir. For Dudley and Cecil this was vital. Although Dudley had forfeited his life interest to Eagle Insurance, on turning twenty-one Cecil would theoretically be able to leverage credit on the expectation that he would in due course take over the estate. Father and son could even choose to legally disentail, so as to be able to sell the properties outright and start afresh. There was certainly the prospect that, with some careful management, Cecil could come into some serious money – even enough to dig his father out of the mess into which he had got himself. All Cecil needed to do was stay alive. It could not have been simpler.

Had Dudley been of a more patient disposition, his problems would surely have been solved or at least relieved. Relations might sometimes have been fraught with his boy, who no doubt felt intense frustration with his profligate parents. They were all in mourning for a glorious lifestyle now lost – at least for the time being. But things had not become so bad as to think that Cecil couldn't manage his birthright – which would have included Stanmore in Middlesex, as well as the claim to Pipewell in Northamptonshire – to restore them to something approaching their old standing.

But among his many failings, Dudley was not patient. At a time when he would have been best served by sitting on his hands, he attempted to remedy the mess of his own making. The Eagle Insurance foreclosure ought to have been the low point of his life. Instead, it was merely the starting point for a catalogue of ill-judged decisions that heaped unimaginable grief on the Hambroughs.

≈

In a story full of 'if onlys', Dudley Hambrough must surely have wondered how things might have been different if only he had never encountered the grandly named Beresford Loftus Tottenham (or Tot, as he was known to his acquaintances). A financial agent with the firm Kempton & Co., based in Westminster, he had an outward veneer of respectability. He claimed, for instance, the former Tory Member of Parliament and one of Britain's largest landowners, Arthur Loftus Tottenham, among his relations. Yet Beresford Tottenham, incorrigibly shady, was the very model of a Victorian rogue.

Only in his thirties when he met Hambrough, Tot had already crammed in an extraordinary life. After a stint with the Tenth Hussars cavalry regiment, he followed his former commander, Valentine Baker, to Turkey (Baker had been dishonourably discharged from the British army in 1875 after being convicted of indecently assaulting a young woman on a railway carriage somewhere near Croydon). There Tot became a fully paid-up member of the Ottoman army under Baker Pasha, as Valentine now modelled himself. Tottenham eased into life as a mercenary and only a year before he encountered

Hambrough in London, he was helping the Ottomans suppress an uprising in Crete. There were also rumours that he took himself off to Venezuela for a while. But by 1889 he had dreams of making money in a less immediately hazardous environment.

Setting himself up in business in Westminster, Tottenham dispensed advice to a roster of clients in the guise of a financial agent, but he was essentially a moneylender with his eye on the prize. How the pound signs must have flashed before him when Hambrough came on the scene. If he could somehow find a way to untangle the incompetent Major's financial dealings, he might yet win back Steephill for his grateful customer and earn himself a hefty – perhaps life-changing – commission in the process.

Tottenham quickly inveigled himself into Hambrough's confidence. When Dudley shared his hopes of getting a tutor for Cecil, Tottenham found himself able to offer a seemingly perfect solution. He had recently been introduced to a fellow by the name of Alfred Monson – a man, as luck would have it, who had spent the previous few years building up a name for himself as a personal tutor to the sons of well-connected families.

To an aspirational parent like Hambrough, Monson seemed like a dream. He was presented as a product of some of England's finest educational establishments, including the University of Oxford, and his uncle was Lord Oxenbridge, who would become the Queen's Master of the Horse in 1892, while his maternal grandfather had been Lord Galway. There were also familial ties to the Duchess of Lincoln, while another uncle served as an ambassador on the continent. Monson's own father was the Rev. Thomas Monson, formerly Rector of Kirby-under-Dale in Yorkshire, himself the son of a bishop. Respectability was ingrained in the family line.

Monson began working as a tutor after turning his back on what had seemed a promising civil service career as a colonial administrator in South Africa at the start of the 1880s. Self-possessed, eloquent and smart, he was ideally placed to persuade Major Hambrough that the search for a 'guiding hand' for his son was over. All at once he gave the impression of modesty and gravitas. As an acquaintance who knew him would later say, he exuded the broad-ranging knowledge of the teacher, the exactitude of the lawyer and the wisdom of the philosopher.

And if Monson's charisma and accomplishments weren't enough on their own, the presence of his wife, Agnes, was sure to seal the deal. Elegant, comely and fashionable, she was used to turning heads wherever she went. She, too, came from good stock. The daughter of a self-made mine-owner from Barnsley in Yorkshire, she was raised in the affluent village of Sherburn within a family considered pillars of local society. Her father, William, had died in 1882, leaving his wife and children in a healthy financial state. But by then, Agnes had already bound herself to Monson.

Besotted with him, in 1881 she had followed him to Cape Town (then part of the Cape of Good Hope in South Africa), where they married shortly before Alfred decided that life abroad was not for him. Once back in England, he had attempted to get a number of businesses off the ground alongside his teaching, but with little success. By the time the Monsons met Hambrough, they were living at a property called The Woodlands, near Harrogate in Yorkshire. There they enjoyed a seemingly comfortable lifestyle, socializing with the local great and good while earning a reputation for largesse. It was all just the job for Hambrough, who agreed to entrust Cecil to the Monsons' supervision.

Terms and conditions were quickly ironed out. Alfred was to be retained on a fee of £300 per year (a sum that must surely have caused the Major to wince in private) and Cecil would travel to Yorkshire to take up residence with the Monsons. After a brief stay at The Woodlands, Cecil and his guardians moved to a new home, Riseley Hall near Ripley. Monson continued to spend freely on good food and drink, and encouraged Cecil to join him in manly pursuits such as horsemanship and hunting – not that Cecil needed much urging. It was not long before Cecil came to regard the Monsons not so much as *in loco parentis* but as genuine friends. That they offered him the footloose and fancy-free existence that his own mother and father could no longer afford only cemented their appeal.

For a while, it seemed like everyone was reaping the benefits of this arrangement. Cecil had apparently fitted into Monson family life with consummate ease, they meanwhile had a new paying pupil, and the Major could rest easy that he was looking out for his son's future interests – even if the immediate strains on his finances were punishing. Yet it would not be long before the first cracks in the veneer began to show.

3

A Gentleman and a Scoundrel

'How an English gentleman could behave in such
a manner is beyond my comprehension.'

Sherlock Holmes, 'The Adventure of the Bruce-Partington Plans'

Although Major Hambrough was yet to realize it, Alfred Monson
was not a man to be taken at face value. The image he presented to
the world was a composite of truths, half-truths and outright lies –
and trying to unpick them was all but impossible. Unfortunately for
Cecil Hambrough, Monson and Tot had quickly worked out that the
boy's father was readily impressed by the right kind of accent and a
well-turned phrase, and Alfred was a man to whom smooth talking
came naturally. Already creaking beneath the many worries that
burdened him, the Major had neither the inclination nor the energy
to conduct a thorough background check on the man to whom he
was about to entrust his beloved son and heir. Monson seemed like a
good thing and that was quite enough for now.

Yet even the most rudimentary enquiries would have raised
suspicions as to the tutor's true character. Anyone trying to trace
his name in the registers of Oxford University, for instance, or any
of the country's pre-eminent schools, would struggle to find him.
Then there was the curious question of his flight from South Africa.
Why did a young gentleman starting out on what seemed like a

40

most promising career in government service simply pack it all in? Especially for the less secure and potentially less rewarding role of a privately engaged teacher? Agnes and Alfred had fallen in love while still in their teens and she had clearly believed that when he moved overseas, he intended to stay for a decent long while. Otherwise why would she go to the trouble of transporting herself halfway around the world to reunite with him? This at a time when travel for a woman journeying alone – particularly a young and beautiful one – was fraught with peril. She also was at serious risk of losing her good name by such a wanton pursuit. If Monson had rejected her, her future would have been very uncertain, her image forever sullied in the eyes of Victorian society's moral guardians. Yet they were back in Britain within a matter of weeks. What had happened to so alter Monson's assumed career trajectory? What occurred in Cape Town that made it so uncomfortable – if not impossible – for Monson to stay that he ended his stint as a colonial administrator even before it had really begun? The idea, as it was put about back in England, that he had simply grown tired of life abroad pushed the bounds of credibility – although the exact circumstances of his return have never come to light.

Regardless, for a while the Monsons seemed like they were making a decent go of life together – even if Agnes reputedly wished Alfred had not been so eager to turn his back on Africa. Once they had returned to Britain, they moved first to Retford, an attractive market town in Nottinghamshire, where Alfred was employed by a Captain Jebb to tutor his sons. The Monsons quickly became fixtures in the local smart set. To anyone meeting them for the first time, they must have seemed thoroughly honourable and decent types. But the costs of fostering friendships with those of an apparently comparable social class were already forcing them to live well beyond their means. Nor did Monson take kindly to having to worry about money, and he was no longer enjoying teaching – he felt it such a mundane way to keep the coffers filled for a man sure he was made for better things. He was constantly dreaming up schemes to make his fortune but could persuade none of his wealthy friends or acquaintances to invest.

As his frustrations grew and his commitment to his pupils fell away, Retford lost its appeal. By 1886, Monson was ready for a change of scene. That year a formidable property called Cheyney Court, not far from Castle Frome in the county of Herefordshire, came up for rental. Built in the Tudor age on land where a monastery once stood, the mansion (which had been expanded and improved many times over the intervening years – especially during the Jacobean period) was owned by the Kier family. However, James Kier, who had inherited it eight years earlier, was keen to move on. The grandeur of the building must have appealed to Monson's sense of his own worth and he shuffled his finances until he found a way to take up the lease. Cheyney Court now became Alfred Monson's private preparatory school.

But it was not long before his hopes that the school would be a financial success were extinguished. Even with an initially promising number of paying pupils, his expenditure exceeded his income by some distance. Now, though, he started to benefit from another income stream – insurance payouts following a series of fires (of which there were at last three) that took place at the house over the two years he was resident there. The worst of these, which utterly gutted the main building, occurred in 1888. Not only was the structure devastated but valuable contents, including antique furniture and works of art, also disappeared forever. The Monsons received around £2,000 for the loss of their personal property and, although there were widely held suspicions of foul play, the authorities could find no firm evidence that the tenant was responsible.

Another conflagration that happened a few months earlier cast Monson's character in an even murkier light. On that occasion, neighbours had seen smoke spewing from Cheyney Court's stable block and rushed there to lend whatever help they could. They were surprised, however, to discover that Monson had done nothing to free the horses trapped inside the burning building. 'Why the devil don't you loose the horses?' asked one man. Monson told them that he did not know where the key to the stable door was, so it fell to a group of burly locals to smash their way in with axes and save the animals. In financial terms, this was bad news for Monson. The stables were the property of the landlord, who would receive any compensation in the event of their damage. But the horses were Monson's own and their accidental destruction was the only means by which he would secure a personal payday. Monson had been a keen horseman since childhood but the evidence suggests he could set aside any sentimental attachment to the creatures if there was a pound or two to be made.

Unsurprisingly, Monson got a cool reception from his neighbours in the days and weeks that followed. By the time the final fire of his tenure had burnt itself out and taken the ancient property with it, the finger of suspicion must have been all but unbearable, even for a character as brazen as Monson. As was becoming his go-to strategy, his way out of an uncomfortable situation was simply to move on to try his luck elsewhere. Monson closed up the school and fled town, leaving behind a stack of unpaid bills to local tradesmen and shopkeepers. Reputedly, even the local vicar had become embroiled after agreeing to stand as security for about £300 in loans.

The next few years were an ongoing race in which Monson strived to keep one step ahead of his many creditors. The situation became even more critical as Alfred and Agnes began to add to their family (there would be three children by 1893). In 1887, there was a further complication when Monson's father died and with him went the small allowance that he had provided for Alfred. The Monsons ended up flitting from one home to another, performing financial sleights of hand at every turn.

Alfred, though, clung to the belief that his quick wits would eventually turn their fortunes around. Yet each failed scheme only mired him further into debt. One seemingly promising financial avenue was his interest – through his wife – in the Mount Osborne Colliery in Yorkshire. It had belonged to Agnes's father, William Day, who had taken over his brother's shares in the business back in the 1840s. Under William's steady guidance, it had turned a profit year in and year out for decades but, without him at the helm, it had fallen into disuse by 1884. Alfred and Agnes now claimed a one-eighth stake in the defunct colliery and Alfred planned to use their prospective share to raise a loan and attract investors with a view to relaunching the business. But with depressing predictability, the venture failed to get off the ground. By the time Monson was prepared to write it off, he had run up a debt of £627 to a creditor in respect of unspecified 'promotional expenses'.

The Monsons then took up a six-month tenancy on a residential property, although Alfred prematurely broke off this agreement on the grounds that the house had drainage problems. By that point he had decided to invest the money that he received from the Cheyney Court fires into another business that, on the face of it, had a credible chance of success. Monson the horse-lover (at least, when he was not plotting to burn them to death) decided to establish a stud farm and in 1889 found a suitable property to rent – Gaddesley Farm in Horley, Surrey. Using a mixture of his own capital, a bank loan and a £2,000 injection from another investor who did not yet have reason to mistrust him, Monson planned to breed and trade high-quality chargers. There was always a profitable market for such prestigious beasts among the military classes and his instinctive feel for horses ought to have stood him in good stead.

This time, though, his need to meet the immediate financial

demands upon him saw off his longer-term ambitions. Monson made the decision – reckless even by his own standards – to take out a £200 loan from a moneylender by the name of Brown. In return, he offered a bill of sale on the farm stock. Monson's fellow investor was, of course, kept entirely in the dark. When Brown turned up on the appointed day to make a claim on the promised stock, Monson was nowhere to be found. He had moved on again, leaving another furious creditor and an even more irate business partner to pick through the mess. That Monson was prepared to sacrifice a potentially promising business for the sake of such a relatively paltry sum as £200 points either to his accelerating financial incompetence or, perhaps more likely, to his growing desperation to get his hands on some money – any money – and damn the consequences.

Monson's business partner was not to be brushed off, though, and called in the police. In 1890, Monson was arrested and charged with fraud – an accusation he was to face in the land's leading criminal court, the Old Bailey in London. In the event, Monson was acquitted on technical grounds but it was a pointer to the future: he was starting to push his luck a step too far.

After the trial, the Monsons moved back to The Woodlands in Yorkshire – where they had been living since just before Monson's arrest – and to the casual onlooker seemed to be enjoying the high life. It was a bravura performance by Alfred, who was sticking with his gamble that if one appeared to be a gentleman, one could live like a gentleman even if one lacked a gentleman's bank balance. Indeed, it was his contention – shared only with a few close acquaintances – that such was the power of his family name that he could 'stock a five-floored warehouse on the strength of it'. For a while, his confidence did not seem misplaced. He bought provisions on credit from local shops and engaged workmen who trusted that a man such as he would be sure to pay them in good time. He did not even feel the need to cut back on his collection of horses, paying just enough upfront to secure local stabling.

The extravagant dinners continued, too, with Monson inviting local worthies on the basis that, as he told Agnes, he would never cultivate a friendship of which he could not make use. His guests, meanwhile, were utterly charmed by their debonair host – who always kept the food coming and the drink flowing – and his wife, blessed with undeniable beauty and good manners. What Monson could not obtain on personal credit, he paid for using a £700 overdraft agreed with the York City and County Bank. Monson could sweet-talk a bank manager as easily as any of the other marks he preyed upon – at least for the time being.

Of course, the charade could not go on forever. Within a year, there was growing disquiet among those who had supplied Monson with goods and services on account. In the end, it was the bank that lost patience first when they sent round the bailiffs to recover property in lieu of repayments on the overdraft. But when they arrived, Monson assured them that none of the property at The Woodlands was his (he was now in the habit of making many of his purchases in his wife's name as means of protecting at least some of their assets from creditors) and so they left empty-handed. Meanwhile, he told his friends and associates that he felt he had been treated utterly shabbily by the bank. Had they waited a few days, he claimed indignantly, he would have benefited from the realization of certain securities worth more than enough to cover any monies owed. For its part, the York City and County Bank did not mention the affair too loudly, judging that it did little to enhance its reputation. Cecil Hambrough – young and naive and having joined the Monson home only a few months earlier – seemingly bought his tutor's story without hesitation. Nonetheless, Monson realized that the time was approaching to set down new roots elsewhere.

The veil of embarrassed silence that descended among those taken in by this evident swindler allowed Alfred to weave a new web of deceit – this time at Riseley Hall. By now the number of properties inhabited by Alfred and Agnes since they had married was into double figures. The fees Monson was earning from tutoring, plus revenues from Agnes's separate estate (courtesy of her father), ought to have been enough to sustain a perfectly decent standard of living for the couple. But he simply would not curtail his spending.

As ever, he capitalized on his gent's demeanour to secure credit and employed staff to cater for his every need. There was a butler, a coachman, a governess for the children, several female domestic servants, farmhands and additional staff to look after the horses. He even employed a tutor for Cecil at a cost of £150 per year (with bed and board thrown in), despite being paid £300 to oversee the job himself. Monson would deny himself nothing and with precious little in the way of assets – the roll call of creditors in the background was growing ever longer – he boxed clever with his financial arrangements. He increasingly used Agnes as the front for his dealings, opening bank accounts in her name and recording possessions as hers to protect them from anyone calling in a debt against him.

Nonetheless, he could not fend off the inevitable and in August 1892 – having sold the last two horses in his possession and having had furniture in his name to the value of £35 seized by bailiffs – he was declared bankrupt. Yet even now the game was not up. Life at Riseley Hall for a while appeared to continue much as before. When a gap in the finances opened up, Tot, back in London, was happy enough to fill it – though on the clear understanding that one day in the not too distant future he would reap the rewards of his 'generosity'.

For Alfred and Agnes, however, the reality was that their quality of life seems to have taken a nosedive around this time as Monson's desperation at his situation increased. Where once the couple had entertained well-born guests at cultured soirées, the Hall now became the scene for debauched evenings of drinking and revelry. Monson could take his liquor with the best of them but held back so as to keep his wits about him – all the better to take advantage of anyone foolish enough to overindulge in his company. Agnes, though, would recall a 'peculiarly unpleasant crew' that regularly descended upon her home.

Meanwhile, Alfred, having immersed himself in a world of deceit and deception, found his trust in his fellow man correspondingly diminished – like the adulterer worried that he himself shall be cheated upon. Not even Agnes would escape his wrath, with Cecil stepping in to protect her from bodily violence on at least one occasion. Nonetheless, Hambrough stayed devoted to the couple through it all. Even when the tutor that Monson had hired proved unequal to the job, Cecil easily overlooked the lapse. He was far more interested in living the grand life of a young and lusty gent – roaming around the country during the day and carousing at night – that Alfred made possible for him. And when he tired of roistering, Agnes was there to act as a counter-balance. She was unstinting in her efforts to ensure that he felt like one of the family. A good conversationalist with an engagingly easy manner, she would now and then take a walk out with him, the pair doubtless delighting in the spectacular views offered by the Yorkshire landscape. Riseley Hall was not so much a home from home for Cecil but a positive upgrade on the life he had left behind.

Yet his position within the Monson set-up had changed in ways far beyond his imagination. The time was coming, as far as Monson was concerned, when he needed to start seeing a real return on the time and effort he had invested in the boy. When Monson committed to act as his tutor in 1890, he was exploiting a new cash cow. The £300-a-year that the Major agreed to stump up was not to be sniffed at. On top of that, there was the potential to benefit from the family's wider economic circumstances. By helping the Major restore some equilibrium to his finances, there was the opportunity for Monson to do the same for himself. His motivations for becoming involved with the Hambroughs were never noble, of course, but in the three intervening years his own position had starkly deteriorated. Now a registered bankrupt with a number of near misses with the police and in the criminal courts to his name, his faith that he could simply charm his way through life had taken a knock. It was getting harder to talk his way to new credit, and the house of cards that he had constructed over the previous dozen years was in real danger of collapse – even as Cecil remained blithely oblivious to the fact.

The pressure was on Monson to get his hands on some serious money. Not the odd £200 from a moneylender secured on a false promise, but the sort of sum that could set him up for the long term and keep him in the manner to which he had become accustomed. Such was the complexity of Major Hambrough's own financial tangle that neither Monson nor Tot harboured much hope of a quick cash-in now. But Cecil was still a promising prospect – a boy who, on reaching his majority in April 1894, would be in line to access some real wealth.

4

A Tangled Web

'… we live in a utilitarian age. Honour is
a mediaeval conception.'

Von Bork, 'His Last Bow'

Dudley Hambrough's unstinting desire to somehow recover a semblance of his former wealth and lifestyle saw to it that he, Tot and Monson (aided by a motley cast of supporting characters) embarked on a series of outlandish and ill-fated financial schemes. Their dealings were marked by evolving mutual distrust, shifting loyalties and outright dishonesty. Moreover, the substance of much of the negotiations they each entered into was illusory. Figures were routinely plucked from the air, offers made and sums of money guaranteed without their having any basis in real assets. At the heart of their various plans was a shared belief – held with far greater optimism than it surely deserved – that they might each make a tidy sum by the mere juggling of the Hambrough finances in order to open up new credit lines. Just as Monson believed his family's reputation was enough on its own to stock a warehouse, they each laboured under the illusion that Hambrough's once good name could be manipulated to make money. But did this shared sense of entitlement create a chain of events that rendered the death of Cecil Hambrough a grisly inevitability?

Major Hambrough's finances had been managed by the firm Messrs Kyne & Hammond until sometime in 1889 when they conceded that they could see no way to raise the capital to pay off the Eagle Insurance Company and save his Steephill estate. After Eagle Insurance took possession of the Major's life interest in Steephill in 1890, Hambrough and Tot then began to discuss how he might recover his stake in it. With Hambrough barely able to muster a farthing in his own name, it was a tall order. But Tot was not one to let a chance pass and he came up with what he hoped was a master strategy. Hambrough had a number of life insurance policies that Tot believed could be exchanged for new ones offering better terms for lower premiums. The Major could surrender his existing policies (freeing up, he was led to believe, some £5,000 or £6,000 of capital) and then borrow against the newer, more advantageous policies, using the money to pay off Eagle Insurance and so reclaim Steephill (and its revenue of several thousand a year).

There was a problem, though. The Major may have been only in his mid-forties but he was not in sufficiently good health to pass the medical examination demanded by the insurance companies. In due course, the health of both the Major and his son would become the subject of public speculation. The Major would always claim that neither he nor Cecil suffered any significant condition, his own failure to pass the medical being merely a temporary glitch. It would subsequently be rumoured that the Major and Cecil both suffered from Bright's disease, a condition characterized by inflammation of the kidneys and often associated with high blood pressure and heart disease. However, there is limited evidence that this was the case. Certainly, Tot did not believe that Hambrough Snr was a lost cause. He employed one Dr Hambleton on a fee of £3 a week to supervise the Major's health and get his fitness levels up. Tot also provided Hambrough with a weekly allowance of £7 to tide him over in the meantime. Hambleton, incidentally, was an acquaintance of Monson, whom he had first met around 1882 or 1883 through a colleague at a hospital where the doctor had worked.

When Tot spent on others, it was usually with a view to getting his money back and a bit more, too. In what was effectively a paper exercise, the Major granted him mortgages worth £2,500 over his assets to cover whatever outlays Tot had to make, as well as a chunk of commission. Quite what the real worth of these mortgages was given Hambrough's precarious situation is unclear, but they served well enough as a negotiating chip for Tot, and later Monson, in their dealings with other financial institutions. Nonetheless, as the months ticked past in 1890 it was clear that the Major was still not in good enough shape to pass a medical and so Tot's careful plot unravelled. By then, though, Monson was on the scene and keen to act for the Major, too.

This seems to have been a situation that initially suited everyone. Monson was, of course, employed as Cecil's tutor on £300 a year, but all must have known that there was little prospect he would see any of that until Hambrough Snr's situation was resolved. Indeed, as Monson's own finances took a turn for the worse, he became every bit as reliant upon Tot's bankrolling as the Major. Perhaps that is why he took on the challenge of reviving the Hambrough family fortunes with far more gusto than he showed for teaching the boy. Tot, meanwhile, was able to slip into the shadows, leaving the frontline negotiations to Monson but providing the oof (his memorable expression for money) so that the other two were placed firmly in his debt.

According to the Major, he was under the impression that Monson was to act as his agent in renewed talks with Eagle Insurance – a not unreasonable assumption. However, it was not long before the dynamics of the relationship changed. For much of 1891, the Major expected Monson to strike a deal that would see Eagle Insurance offer him a contract allowing him to reclaim his life interest – a contract, he believed, that would be on the table for several months in return for a deposit somewhere in the region of £600. This would, theoretically, give him the time to get his fitness levels up sufficiently to renegotiate his life insurance and then raise the required capital.

However, between May and September 1891, the Major signed over to Monson a number of additional mortgages on his assets, worth about £10,600 altogether – far beyond an ordinary agent's fee. Monson in turn used them to raise several loans of a few hundred pounds each, with the Major claiming he only saw a small percentage of that money coming his way. Furthermore, by then Monson had become the main conduit for the cash Tot provided to Hambrough. It must have been truly humbling for the Major, who was reduced to sending begging letters to a man who was meant to be in his employ. Monson responded by clearing some of the Major's low-level debts and paying for his accommodation, as well as flinging small amounts of money in Hambrough's direction – all part of a process that saw him able to dangle the Major on a string.

Critically, around this time the Major put his name to a letter permitting Monson to negotiate on his own behalf, rather than as an agent for the Major. Quite why Hambrough agreed to this is unclear, although it is likely that he received dubious legal advice suggesting that since he (Hambrough) was subject to bankruptcy proceedings, it would be necessary for Monson to sign paperwork in his own name. The Major certainly understood it as a means to an end – perhaps naively, his expectation was that Monson would undertake the legal formalities to take nominal possession of Steephill before passing the estate back to Hambrough in return for a fee. Hambrough's new solicitor, Morris Fuller, appointed in February 1892, certainly saw the danger, noting that were Monson to have the estate signed over to him in his own name, 'when the boy [Cecil] came of age, Monson and the boy would be in such a position that Monson could do what he liked'.

It was also about now that there was the first suggestion that, given the Major's problems in passing a medical, they should look at insuring Cecil instead. A plan was mooted that would have seen Cecil's life insured for £60,000, upon which enough capital might be raised to free up the Hambrough estate and leave a few thousand over for Monson. It was, however, quickly rejected by the Major and there the matter seemed to lie.

By the end of 1891, Monson's powers of persuasion had seen him reach an agreement in principle with Eagle Insurance to take over the Hambrough estate – in accordance with the rights the Major had assigned to him – but by then Monson had a lawyer, Mr R. C. Hanrott, with aspirations of his own. Hanrott had recently endured a run-in with the law, having earlier in the year faced charges (later dismissed) of conspiring to defraud a certain Sir Eustace Piers and the shareholders of Ormerod, Grierson and Co., a long-established Manchester engineering firm. When Monson was unable to pay the required deposit to Eagle Insurance, Hanrott moved to take over the agreement in his own name. Monson began legal proceedings against his solicitor and the courts duly found in his favour, forcing Hanrott to reassign the contract to his client. However, Monson still lacked the necessary funds to furnish the deposit so struck a new deal that gave Hanrott a 25 per cent share of the deal. But the agreement, forged amid mistrust and bad will, was dead by the middle of 1892, the funds for the purchase never materializing.

Major Hambrough was by then done with Monson, his faith that his son's tutor might see him right utterly exhausted. His correspondence tells us that the Hanrott sideshow confirmed his growing suspicions that Monson was out for himself. Where once it had seemed that the tutor yearned merely for a sizable commission by renegotiating the Major's financial affairs, it was now evident that he had his eye on taking over the estate wholesale – a step too far even for the gullible Major. The schism had been building for several months. For instance, in February 1892 the Major instructed his solicitor, Mr Morris Fuller, to send a letter demanding a full breakdown of the monies Monson had spent in the interests of the Hambroughs. Monson gave the request short shrift. In an antagonistic reply, he suggested to Fuller that he ought to consider the merits of representing the Major given that Hambrough was an undischarged bankrupt who could be subject to criminal proceedings for racking up yet further debt. This was not strictly true – while the Major was facing bankruptcy proceedings he was never declared bankrupt and so, while operating within an admittedly grey area of the law, he was not in breach of it. It was also somewhat rich for Monson to be casting such allegations, given that he himself would be declared bankrupt just a few months later.

Monson also threatened to stop the albeit limited funding he was providing to the Hambroughs, suggesting that he could see the Major thrown out on his ear from the rooms on London's Jermyn Street that he was then inhabiting. Fuller, though, saw no reason to turn his back on his client, instead seeking to find a workaround with Monson. He suggested that the tutor might continue negotiations with Eagle Insurance in his own name while the Major got his finances in order, but on the understanding that Monson would sell any agreement on to Hambrough Snr at a later date for a pre-agreed price. The Major, justifiably, remained nervous, fearing what Monson might do were he to get his hands on Steephill even under these terms.

There were other sources of tension. Hambrough Snr not only feared what Monson might intend for Steephill but believed he was losing his son to him, too. He was particularly annoyed that Cecil had not been signed up as planned to the same Hants Militia in which he himself had served. Instead, in May 1892, Cecil joined the West Yorkshire Regiment in direct contravention of his father's orders. The Major felt thoroughly hoodwinked. Monson was supposed to be buying Cecil's uniform for the Hants regiment when he claimed his London tailor could not fulfil the order. The Major thus agreed to allow Monson to take Cecil to York to buy the uniform there. Instead, it was on this trip north that Cecil signed up with the Yorkshires. As the Major's ire grew, so Cecil reduced his contact with his mother and father, instead encamping with the Monsons. Invitation after invitation to visit his parents in London was rebuffed, and allegations of misconduct against Monson rejected by the impetuous son. On 24 March, Cecil wrote to his father that 'I cannot see any good in coming to town. I could not do any good, and should only be an extra expense to you, and, goodness knows, money is scarce enough ...' A few days later there was another missive:

My dear Father,
I am truly sorry if I have added to your troubles, and can only say that I had no intention of doing so. I think you greatly mistake Mr Monson's intentions. I am sure he has not misrepresented things to me, and I cannot see what nefarious ends he has in view. He has always been straightforward to me. How has he attempted to defraud you? He has only tried to save the estates from being sold by the Eagle. If it had not been for him Hanrott would have bought them. I can assure you I mean no disrespect to you whatever. I am only doing what I am sure is for the best. I would sooner not leave my studies now, but in the holidays I should very much like to come and see you. The Eagle, as you are aware of, have foreclosed, and have got the foreclosure made good by the Court of Chancery, so it is impossible to upset it. Mr Monson is going to pay off so as to cut off the entail when I come of age. If he does not succeed, and it passes into other hands, even when I come of age I do not see what could be done. I do not see how anything can be done at all except through him, so I think it is bad policy, if nothing else, to quarrel with him. I shall never forget how good both you and my mother have been to me.

I am sure this grieves me very much. But you know I must have an education; I cannot go about utterly ignorant all my life.

Undeterred, the Major continued his attempts to, in his own mind, liberate his son from Monson's grip. On 20 June, he wrote:

My dear Cecil,
Your training with the Yorks Militia will now be over in a few days, I am writing to tell you that it is our wish that you should join us here, and not return to Riseley. On no consideration whatever can I permit you to continue your studies under Mr Monson. Your mother and I have our own very good reasons for our decision in this respect, one of which is the gross and unpardonable deception which was practised upon us with regard to your joining the Yorkshire Regiment. We have made our own arrangements as regards you until you are of age; though, of course, we shall be anxious and willing to meet your wishes so far as lies in our power and our duties as your guardians will permit.
I am arranging an allowance for your education and maintenance, which will enable us to give you everything necessary for your comfort, not, of course, permitting of extravagance.

But Cecil had no intention of swapping his life of freedom and pleasure with the Monsons for the strictures and deprivations that his parents offered. By now, the Major was speculating as to how Monson had brought Cecil so thoroughly under his spell, even suggesting that the tutor had used hypnotism to subdue the boy. The Major's animosity ramped up as the year went on. In October 1892, he wrote directly to Monson, informing him that 'I have once more written to my son requiring his presence in town, and will thank you to see that my wishes are obeyed,' adding that Cecil would continue his studies 'but certainly not with you'. Monson replied: 'I beg to say that I am not your son's keeper', echoing the sentiment from a letter he had sent back in July: 'I hereby give you notice that I am not custodian of your son, as you seem to suggest in your letter. Your son is perfectly at liberty to go when and where he pleases, as far as I am concerned.'

Meanwhile, heartfelt appeals to Cecil himself ('You are killing mother and causing untold trouble,' read one telegram) continued to fall on deaf ears. In November, the Major went as far as to threaten legal action against anyone attempting to obtain money for Cecil without parental authorization. 'I do not understand what you have further found out against Mr Monson,' Cecil flashed back, 'but after he has done everything for me that he possibly could I think that it would be extremely mean of me to come away as you propose.' His father's suggestion that his son's 'most unjustifiable conduct' was 'not of [his] own thought or desire' may well have only fanned the flames of Cecil's discontent. The Major apparently saw no risk in consigning the young man eager to carve his niche in the world to the role of a dupe.

The net result of all these machinations was that by the middle of 1892 there were two competing alliances going after the Major's former life interest. On one side was the Major himself, Dr Hambleton (who had assumed a role something akin to the Major's trustee), and a solicitor called Prince, who had been brought in as a replacement for Fuller. On the other was Cecil and Monson, with Tot the spectre in the background, drip-feeding money to Monson (and via him, to Cecil and the Major). Following his bankruptcy in August 1892, Monson needed the oof from Tot as much as the Major needed his handouts from Monson. It was clearly an unhealthy state of affairs – Monson and the Major, daggers-drawn and both intent on keeping up a standard of living that would collapse without the largesse of their puppet-master, Tot.

Around this time, a new and rather mysterious figure entered the scene – Adolphus Frederick James Jerningham. Like others in this story, he came from noble lineage – the Jerninghams had held the baronetcy of Cossey in Norfolk since the seventeenth century and more recently had also claimed the barony of Stafford – but was himself low down the familial line of succession and found himself in straitened circumstances. Although only a fairly distant relative of the incumbent baronet, Fitzherbert Stafford-Jerningham, by some quirks of inheritance, Adolphus's son, William, would nonetheless become the last baronet in 1913 on the death of his second cousin once removed.

Adolphus was a civil engineer who had not practised at all since 1876. Prior to that, he had hardly a stellar career – for instance, a building company he had been associated with had gone bankrupt in 1869. As of 1892 he was living in rooms a little outside London, making do on money generated by some property in the capital that he had gained through marriage. He was unsure as to quite how much the property brought in but he hoped that he would not be reliant on it forever, since he believed he had a good expectation of 'succeeding to a position of some distinction'. It would be fair to say that Jerningham, already fifty years old, lived a life unhindered by specifics. The terms of his relationship with Monson and Cecil were characteristically vague. He first got to know Monson in early 1892 when Monson had sought to secure a loan for Jerningham. Within a few weeks he had been co-opted into negotiations for the Major's life interest. Exactly why is unclear. Presumably, his gentlemanly air – even if based on shaky foundations – persuaded Monson that he might be of some use. Even so, it seems an eccentric decision. 'I was asked by Monson to be Cecil Hambrough's trustee and guardian,' Jerningham would recall, 'but nothing was settled; I never heard that I was appointed.' Nonetheless, Monson represented him as such in assorted dealings. What Jerningham was to be offered in return for acting as a figurehead was never clear. By his own admission, there

THE MEN WHO WERE SHERLOCK HOLMES

was no prospect that he might be able to put up the money for the purchase himself and he also claimed that Monson never discussed remuneration with him. He would also reflect that Cecil 'knew very little about business and only went by what Mr Monson told him'. It was an altogether strange arrangement.

There was yet another twist in proceedings in early 1893 when Agnes Monson took Cecil to court and received a judgment in her favour for £800 for monies owed for board, lodgings and education. The suit went undefended and Agnes promptly sold the debt to Tot for £200 in cash. There is no indication that the case did anything to dent Cecil's affection for the Monsons and, indeed, there is the suspicion that he was quite happy to go along with it. For the Monsons (and by extension, Cecil), it created a nugget of new capital from Tot, while Tot was doubtless happy to absorb the hit for the time being in return for cashing in his chips later on. The more indebted he could make the Hambroughs to him, the greater the potential rewards if they could eventually recover the gleaming diamond that was Steephill.

However, the hopes of the Monson–Tot axis received a mighty blow at the beginning of April 1893 when Eagle Insurance agreed to transfer the life interest in Steephill back to the Major's consortium in a deal scheduled to be completed by 1 August. Desperation is evident in a letter sent ostensibly by Cecil (although the voice of Monson echoes through it) to Henry Richards, solicitor for the Eagle Insurance, on 29 March 1893:

> The question appears to be as to whether the directors
> will accept Mr Jerningham's offer or that of Mr Prince [the
> Major's solicitor]. I hope, however, that the directors will
> take my position into their consideration and accept Mr
> Jerningham's offer, and that they will distinguish what a very
> great difference there is between the *bona fides* of the two

offers. The one made by Jerningham, with a deposit of £5000,
is a substantial offer made by a gentleman of considerable
position, and one from which I shall benefit; while the other,
made through Mr Prince, with a small deposit, is merely a
speculation in the name of a person of no position whatever,
and with a view to making money out of me when I come of
age, ostensibly for the benefit of my father, but really for the
benefit of others. If the directors accepted the offer made
by Mr Prince I should absolutely be deprived of any further
interest in the estate to which I am the tenant entail, because,
when I come of age, I should have either to disentail or take
the consequences, which might be very serious. My father
has the benefit of his life estate, besides which he has recently
charged the estate with an annuity of £400 per annum to
my mother, which has been already mortgaged with a policy
on her life; he has also charged the estate with £5000 for the
benefit of my sisters and brother, and thus I am left quite
unprovided for, and made to suffer the consequences.
– I am yours truly, W. D. C. Hambrough.

The deal with the Major was essentially an act of goodwill by Eagle
Insurance, who could have opted to follow the letter of the law and
retain the life interest so as to dispose of it however they saw fit. A
counter-offer in Jerningham's name was meanwhile set aside, with
the possibility of taking it up should the Major fail to make the
required payments by the cut-off date. At the end of July, Monson
learned that there had been little progress on the Major's part and
saw a glimmer of a new opportunity from which Jerningham would
now be sidelined. 'I understand from a letter from Dr Hambleton
that nothing has been done by them in regard to the purchase of
the Hambrough life estates,' Monson wrote to Richards. 'Therefore
I assume your clients will be open to negotiations otherwise for

the sale, as the time mentioned was in August.' What he proposed was a deal with a completion date of June 1894, whereby his wife would pay a deposit of 5 per cent towards a £40,000 buy-out price. 'Cecil Hambrough is staying here with us,' he added. 'I do not see it concerns your clients what arrangements Mrs Monson may enter into with Cecil Hambrough, so long as you are satisfied there is a *bona fide* purchase for your clients and a substantial deposit made.' Quite where the bankrupt Monson and his wife (who at this point was reduced to pawning household items to get by) were going to raise the £2,000 for the deposit was never explained. Regardless, Richards was unconvinced and rejected the offer. Moreover, he revealed that the deal with the Major was delayed only because Eagle Insurance's secretary had been so busy that the paperwork had been stalled on their side.

Cecil and the Monsons had moved to Ardlamont back in May 1893, renting it from the owner, Major John Lamont, for £450 for the season. Edith Hiron, governess to the Monson children, also came with them, and before long the domestic staff had expanded to include a cook and kitchen maid, a housemaid, a butler and a nursemaid, not to mention gardeners, gamekeepers and other estate staff employed by Lamont. Tot granted Cecil an allowance of £10 a week and covered much of the expense incurred by the move. After life at Riseley Hall had turned sour, this handsome, out-of-the-way house on the arresting Cowal Peninsula promised yet another new beginning. Crucially, Cecil was thoroughly cocooned from his parents, the Monsons cementing themselves into their role of surrogate family. Here he could commune with nature – as he loved to do – while enjoying the personal freedom craved by most young men finding their way in the world, all while accessing the comforts of a fine and well-tended home.

Little wonder that before long there was talk of taking up an option on Ardlamont on a more permanent basis. In July, Tot travelled up from London to discuss how they might go about it. Shortly after his return to the capital, he received a message from Monson in which he claimed to have struck a deal to buy the estate in Cecil's name for £48,000. He suggested that he and Tot should factor in a further £1,000 each for their efforts in securing the property, so that Cecil would need to raise a total of £50,000 to complete the purchase. If Tot could supply capital for the deposit – a mere £250 – then they would have until June 1894 to raise the remainder. In fact, since the estate was burdened with £37,000 of debt that Cecil would be taking on in the purchase, he needed only to find a further £13,000 to cover the house price and Monson and Tot's commission.

All of this might have worked out quite nicely but for one thing – Monson had reached no such agreement with the agents of Major Lamont. Indeed, he had not even approached them with the proposal. They were in fact asking for £85,000 and later revealed that they would never have considered a figure as low as that quoted by Monson. Furthermore, even if they had done so, they would have required a down payment of several thousand, not several hundred. Nor was it the first sharp move that Monson had pulled in relation to Ardlamont. The rental, it would transpire, was secured on the signature of Cecil's 'guardian' Jerningham, who had in fact never seen the contract let alone knew that Monson had forged his signature upon it.

So, what possible motivation could Monson have had for misrepresenting to Tot, of all people, the potential purchase of Ardlamont? It is difficult to see the ruse as anything other than an attempt to defraud a further sum out of a man who was already covering most of the Monsons' outgoings. But to what end? By now, Monson had hit upon a new scheme – insuring the life of Cecil in the name of his wife. But he needed a cash injection to cover the premium. It was a precarious undertaking, made all the more complicated by the fact that Cecil was a minor and the law required that anybody taking out life insurance on another must show an insurable interest – in other words, the insuring party must prove that they will derive benefit from the continuing existence of the insured individual. This had not always been the case. Until 1774, literally anybody could take out a policy on anybody else, no matter how they were connected or indeed whether they had a connection at all. While it might have been feared that such a system would give rise to an increase in murders by those set to benefit from the deaths of complete strangers, it was actually concerns about gambling that prompted a change in the law. Laying a wager on the death of a stranger – often a celebrity – became a popular pastime for gents in the latter half of the eighteenth century. It was said that in some London clubs, such bets constituted a quarter of all wagers in the 1770s. The Gambling Act of 1774 aimed to quell such 'mischievous kind of gaming'.

Monson therefore needed to show that he, or more specifically Agnes, had an insurable interest in Cecil. This should not have been too taxing a task. Cecil had been provided with board and upkeep and had, in theory at least, received tutoring, none of which had been paid for by his father. There was a sizable bill racking up month by month, which the Monsons might legitimately believe would be met once Cecil reached adulthood and had independent means of his own. Monson and Agnes could convincingly argue that they had an interest in Cecil's ongoing existence, and that should that existence come to an end they qualified for compensation. The £250 extorted from Tot would do very nicely to cover the early premiums.

But the temptation to stretch a legitimate claim of interest was to undo Monson's early attempts to agree a policy. For instance, he approached the Scottish Provident Institution in search of £50,000 cover when he must have known he had no chance of proving such a large insurable interest. In due course, he would reduce the figure to £10,000 to, in his own words, 'cover the money actually due from Mr Cecil Hambrough on his attaining twenty-one', but never got around to proving an interest at that level, either. He then began talks with the Liverpool, London and Globe Company, asking variously for coverage of £15,000, £50,000 and £26,000. On 31 July 1893, Cecil even sent a letter to the company declaring: 'I am requested by Mrs Agnes Maud Monson to write to inform you that she has an interest in my life to the extent of £26,000. I have given her an undertaking to pay her this sum on my attaining twenty-one, if I should live until then.' 'If I should live until then ...' Those words would gain a devastating poignancy within a mere fortnight of Cecil writing them. The request, meanwhile, was rejected at a meeting with Monson in Glasgow on 2 August. 'It is a pity,' Monson told the company's secretary.

After his unsuccessful meeting in Glasgow, Monson promptly visited the nearby office of the Mutual Life Insurance Company of New York. He now adopted a different tack, seeking a policy directly in Cecil's name. In a meeting with John M'Lean, the company's district manager, Monson presented himself as Cecil's trustee and guardian. His charge, Monson said, was due to come into a fortune of £200,000 on reaching his majority and was currently intent on buying the Ardlamont estate. In order not to miss the opportunity by delaying the purchase until he turned twenty-one, so Monson said, Cecil was being advanced £20,000 by Agnes. Cecil therefore required £20,000 coverage to be actioned, subject to a medical, by 8 August – the purported day of the sale.

There was the question of the validity of the insurance policies, Cecil being below the age of twenty-one. As things stood, were he to die before attaining his majority, the policy would be paid out to his next of kin – his parents. To do otherwise required a reassignation of the policies, which would require the permission of Major Hambrough. Any reassignment undertaken by the underage Cecil on his own account had no legal status in either England or Scotland. To what extent Monson was aware of this would become a question of deep significance. Regardless, Cecil set about naming Mrs Monson as beneficiary of the policies. He wrote to the Mutual Life, requesting:

> Will you kindly deliver my two insurance policies of £10,000 each [this was how the £20,000 cover was to be structured] to Mr and Mrs Monson, as I have assigned the policies to Agnes Maud Monson for proper considerations received. Mrs Monson will therefore be the person to whom the insurance is payable in the event of my death. Kindly acknowledge receipt of this notice and oblige,
> Yours truly, W. D. C. Hambrough.

To Agnes he sent a separate note. 'I am willing,' he wrote, 'that you should hold the policies as security for all monies due to you from me, and as security against all liabilities incurred by you on my behalf, and in the event of my death occurring before the repayment of these monies you will be the sole beneficiary of these policies.'

On 8 August, the Mutual Life duly granted the two policies of £10,000 each on condition of payment of a premium of £194 3s 4d. This money was drawn on Agnes's bank account in anticipation of Tot's cheque for £250 – for the non-existent deposit Monson had claimed was due – clearing. He had post-dated it for 10 August, given he was experiencing some cash flow problems. 'I have an awful lot of irons in the fire,' he had told Monson, 'and the oof don't always turn up as expected.' It was only after securing the deal with Mutual Life that Monson travelled to Edinburgh to meet William Murray of Messrs Anderson, the agents handling the Ardlamont sale. Murray emphasised that the property was available for £85,000, while Monson explained Cecil Hambrough could not possibly go above £60,000. The negotiations ended before they had begun. What Monson hoped to achieve by the slightly surreal encounter is uncertain. Perhaps he believed it might head off any initial enquiries by the Mutual into the story of Cecil's purchase of Ardlamont. Monson could surely spin the meeting as a step in his ongoing negotiations with the estate agents. Maybe he hoped that it might also hold off Tot if he wanted to check out exactly how his £250 was being used. Indeed, at one point Monson even suggested that Tot make the cheque out to the agents before it was decided instead to put it in Agnes's name.

Clearly, though, Tot had his concerns about what his business partner was up to. Monson was certainly acting with a new level of recklessness. On 8 August, for instance, he met with James Donald of the engineering and shipbuilding firm, Hanna, Donald & Wilson, to talk over the sale of a steam yacht, *Alert*, on behalf of Cecil. The proposed price was £1,200 – money that Monson had no hope of raising. Tot seems to have smelled a rat, for not only did he post-date his cheque for £250 but he ultimately had it cancelled, although not before Agnes's bank had unsuspectingly honoured it.

The situation on 9 August was such that the Monsons were in possession of two temporary policies insuring the life of Cecil for £20,000 – policies granted on the basis of a fallacious real estate deal and paid for with a bouncing cheque. Moreover, they were essentially worthless to the Monsons until Cecil turned twenty-one and could legally reassign them. But who of Cecil and the Monsons understood this? If they knew the policies could not be activated, why the rush to obtain them? Just what did Monson believe he had in his grasp? An indemnity safeguarding his considerable investment in the young man, should tragedy somehow befall the lad? Or did he think he had set in motion the ultimate get-rich-quick scheme?

5

Partners in Crime-Fighting

'Oh, a trusty comrade is always of use ...'
Sherlock Holmes, 'The Man with the Twisted Lip'

Despite his years of dodgy dealings and nefarious plotting, as of August 1893 the law was yet to successfully call Monson to account. This was, it is fair to suppose, more the result of good fortune than criminal mastery. Monson was up to this point a run-of-the-mill fraudster who took advantage of others' good will and leveraged the widely held belief that a man of manners and bearing could be trusted. Whenever the net started to close in – as after the fires at Cheyney Court – he simply ran away and started again elsewhere. Monson showed no sign of being a Moriarty – Sherlock Holmes's great nemesis whom the detective referred to as 'the Napoleon of crime'. Instead his career was hitherto characterized by inelegant schemes and a seeming over-estimation of his own abilities. Crimes such as insurance-inspired arson hardly represented a sophisticated modus operandi and he only escaped punishment because the necessary evidence was hard to track down among the burning embers of his ambition. His abuse of credit granted by unwary men of banking and commerce was similarly basic, and only his willingness to exit a scene while the finger of suspicion had yet to turn into the iron fist of the law saved him.

By contrast, Bell and Littlejohn were several decades through careers that brought hitherto unknown skill and finesse to the detection of crime. The doughty Dr Watson once commented of Holmes that 'I could not but think what a terrible criminal he would have made had he turned his energy and sagacity against the law instead of exerting them in its defence.' Much the same could have been said of this pair. Over more than twenty years they had worked together, applying their acute powers of observation and reasoning while adopting the latest forensic innovations, of which there had been many during their lifetimes. Faced with determining how – and by whom – a crime had been committed, they would work through a logical series of steps to trace a path back from the crime scene through the various circumstances that led to it. Their method prefigured that of Holmes as he described it in *A Study in Scarlet*:

> The grand thing is to be able to reason backwards. That is a very useful accomplishment, and a very easy one, but people do not practise it much. In the every-day affairs of life it is more useful to reason forwards, and so the other comes to be neglected … Most people, if you describe a train of events to them, will tell you what the result will be. They can put those events together in their minds, and argue from them that something will come to pass. There are few people, however, who, if you told them the result, would be able to evolve from their own inner consciousness what the steps were which led up to that result. This power is what I mean when I talk of reasoning backwards, or analytically.

Littlejohn and Bell lived in an exciting age of forensic science as it developed from a fringe activity often sneered at by the courts into a vital feature of the criminal justice system. Indeed, the two were crucial to this evolution so that Edinburgh came to be seen as the capital of the discipline, in Great Britain at least and perhaps even in the world. In particular, they propelled forward forensic pathology – the skill of determining the cause of death by examination of a corpse. In so doing, they brought new esteem to the figure of the scientific (and especially, medical) expert.

Until well into the nineteenth century, the scientific expert had enjoyed a curious status. Of course, doctors had long played a role in criminal cases, giving their opinion, for instance, on cause of death. However, they did not hold special privileges as expert witnesses. Their opinion carried no more weight than, say, a medically untrained witness sharing their own ideas on cause of death on the basis of their personal observations. It was, slightly curiously, a trial in 1782 concerning responsibility for the decay of the harbour walls in the Norfolk town of Wells-next-the-Sea that led to a re-evaluation of the role of the expert witness. From then on, it was acknowledged that scientific experts might express an opinion in the courtroom, whether or not they had directly observed the facts of the case. A new industry of professional expert witnesses was thus unleashed.

The results were predictably mixed. The sight of so-called experts slugging it out in courtrooms and contradicting each other at every turn did little to foster the faith of the public. There was also the problem of the growing number of witnesses who sought to bolster the often meagre income of the scientific researcher with appearances in the courtroom. These 'opinions-for-hire' hardly assuaged public doubts about the worth of the expert witness. In 1862, the esteemed English chemist and physicist William Crookes was moved to write in *Chemical News*:

> The evidence of Experts is just now the object of general derision. Smart newspaper writers, wishing to indite a telling article, select the discrepancies in scientific evidence for a

theme; noble Lords, anxious to enliven the dull debates of our hereditary legislators, find nothing so provocative of laughter as a story about the differences of 'mad doctors'; and barristers, ready to advocate any opinion, and anxious, perhaps, for a monopoly of the 'any-sidedness', when addressing a jury, dilate with a well-simulated indignation on the fact that eminent scientific men are to be found in the witness box on opposite sides.

Yet even as the figure of the scientific expert was routinely decried, this was unquestionably a golden age for forensics. The first great British work of forensic medicine, Dr Samuel Farr's *Elements of Medical Jurisprudence*, had appeared in 1788, and from the 1790s Andrew Duncan the Elder began to lecture in Edinburgh on the subject. In 1807, his son (Andrew Duncan the Younger) became the first professor of forensics anywhere in Britain. It was not until 1831 that the first English professorship was established at King's College, London, ensuring that Scotland was a great many strides ahead of the game by then. In 1821, Robert Christison took over the Edinburgh professorship and proceeded to publish a series of groundbreaking works, including a *Treatise on Poisons* in 1829 and, in 1836 – along with Thomas Stewart Traill and James Syme – a pamphlet entitled *Suggestions for the Medico-Legal Examination of Dead Bodies*. This latter work provided a framework upon which medical experts could base their practice, bringing a rigour to the field that did much to liberate them from the disdain (both from lawyers and the public) that was threatening to overtake them. In due course, Littlejohn would count all three of its authors among his lecturers at the university. Bell even served as dresser to Syme in the early part of his career. By 1869, Syme had developed such respect for his former assistant's surgical skills that he asked Bell to take over his clinical surgery classes on his retirement. Bell and

Littlejohn were thus immersed in the culture of forensic innovation that Edinburgh had fomented since the turn of the century.

Edinburgh University – their *alma mater* – was important not only for the innovative research it supported but also for synthesizing new techniques and ideas from other centres of learning and bringing them into the mainstream. Henry Littlejohn was the most famous real-life forensic expert in the land by the 1890s because he was the personification of this Edinburgh ethos. He merged a sharp brain and expert eye with a willingness to adopt the most cutting-edge methods, all presented to the courts with unstinting professionalism. While many expert witnesses carried with them dubious reputations, Littlejohn elevated the role. Sherlock Holmes, at the same time, was bringing forensic science to the public at large in a way no academic could ever hope to emulate. That the fictional detective was employing methods often far in advance of those being used in the real world only serves to prove that his creator had been learning from the best.

Take, for instance, the emerging science of fingerprinting – a method that Littlejohn championed early in his lecture theatre. A British colonial administrator in India, William James Herschel, is widely regarded as the first to have used fingerprints as a method of identification – a practice he wanted to use in the criminal courts of Calcutta as early as 1877. Meanwhile, in 1880, a Scotsman, Henry Faulds, suggested they could be used to identify (or, indeed, exonerate) a suspect by recording prints left behind at crime scenes and comparing them against those of known criminals. Then, in 1892 an English polymath, Francis Galton, undertook a systematic classification of the different patterns evident in fingerprints, calculating the odds of two people having identical prints at one in 64 billion. In the same year, the first fingerprint bureau specifically for law enforcement opened in Argentina. But it was only in 1901 that Scotland Yard adopted fingerprint identification, and it would be 1905 before it was first used to catch a killer (in fact, two killers, brothers named Stratton who were convicted of killing a shopkeeper and his wife in Deptford, London, on the basis of a smudged print found on a cashbox). Yet Doyle had Sherlock Holmes routinely using the method to ensnare criminals from the beginning of the 1890s – fingerprint evidence is referenced in no less than seven of his cases, and was key to apprehending the wrongdoer in 'The Adventure of the Norwood Builder'.

Holmes was also a pioneer in terms of blood testing. It had long been a problem accurately to identify bloodstains, especially when there was some age to them. It was difficult, for example, to tell a rust spot from a genuine bloodstain, and then there was the question of how to distinguish between human and animal blood. (The idea of distinguishing different types of human blood was still far off.) The first reliable test for the presence of blood was developed in the early 1860s using hydrogen peroxide as an agent. Yet we see Holmes in *A Study in Scarlet* (1887) proclaiming: 'I have found a re-agent which is precipitated by haemoglobin, and by nothing else.' It was, he said, 'the most practical medico-legal discovery for years. Don't you see that it gives us an infallible test for blood stains.' By his reckoning, his test could identify blood in a solution where the proportion of blood was not more than one in a million. It is difficult to imagine that Doyle would have been sufficiently on top of the current state of forensics to write such passages were it not for his intimate interaction with Bell, and Littlejohn, too.

There is other corroborating evidence for their influence on Doyle. Littlejohn, for example, wrote and lectured extensively on poisons and toxicology. Holmes, meanwhile, told Watson: 'I dabble with poisons a good deal', while Stamford (the man who introduced Watson and Holmes) observed that Holmes would not think twice about administering a 'vegetable alkaloid' to a friend for the purpose of gauging its effects.

Littlejohn was also at the forefront of those who saw the potential of photographic evidence and especially the use of crime-scene photography. Spurred on by technical improvements in cameras and printing, photographic evidence was first used in Europe's courts in the late 1860s but the British judicial system remained sceptical for many more decades. Scotland Yard tellingly only bothered to employ its own trained photographers, rather than commercial photographers who might otherwise be snapping family portraits and the like, in 1901. Indeed, in this respect Littlejohn was so far ahead of the game that even Doyle was slow to catch up. It was only in the 1926 story 'The Adventure of the Lion's Mane' (set around 1907) that Holmes produces an enlarged print of the wounds suffered by the victim of an attack, noting, 'This is my method in such cases.' 'You certainly do things thoroughly, Mr Holmes,' his companion says. 'I should hardly be what I am if I did not,' he retorts.

The second half of the nineteenth century also saw a blossoming in the field of forensic ballistics – the study of firearms, their ammunition and functioning. This is the subject upon which Bell and Littlejohn would spend so much of their time in the final few months of 1893 in relation to the events at Ardlamont. Holmes used his own ballistics expertise, particularly his knowledge of gunshot residues, to great effect in stories including 'The Adventure of the Reigate Squires', 'The Adventure of the Dancing Men' and 'The Problem of Thor Bridge'. 'There is a test before us,' he said in the last of these stories. 'If the test comes off, all will be clear. And the test will depend upon the conduct of this little weapon.' His words surely echoed the sentiments of Littlejohn and Bell as they confronted the mystery at Ardlamont.

Underpinning the forensic practice of Littlejohn, Bell and Holmes was a shared passion for close observation. Examine the minutiae with scientific rigour, and the truth will be exposed. As Bell put it in his review of *The Adventures of Sherlock Holmes* for the *Bookman* in 1892:

Dr Conan Doyle has made a well-deserved success for his detective stories and made the name of his hero beloved by the boys of this country by the marvellous cleverness of his method. He shows how easy it is, if only you can observe, to find out a great deal as to the works and ways of your innocent and unconscious friends and by an extension of the same method to baffle the criminal and lay bare the manner of his crime.

Bell's own skills extended beyond the party-piece diagnoses with which he astounded his students. It was said, for example, that he could identify any species of bird on the wing. But he was first and foremost an observer of people. For him, forensic detection was essentially a process of logic applied to observation. 'The student must be taught to observe,' he once wrote a letter published in *Tit-Bits* newspaper.

To interest him in this kind of work, we teachers find it useful to show the student how much a trained use of the observation can discover in ordinary matters, such as the previous history, nationality, and occupation of the patient. The whole trick is much easier than it appears at first. For instance, physiognomy helps you to nationality, accent to district, and, to an educated ear, almost to county. Nearly every handicraft writes its sign-manual on the hands. The scars of the miner differ from those of the quarryman. The carpenter's callosities are not those of the mason. The shoemaker and the tailor are quite different.

How Bell must have revelled in Doyle's own abilities in this direction, which the author then passed on to Holmes. On meeting Holmes in *A Study in Scarlet*, Watson was astonished by how much this stranger seemed to know of his recent history in Afghanistan. 'Nothing of the sort,' Holmes said.

> I knew you came from Afghanistan. From long habit the train of thoughts ran so swiftly through my mind, that I arrived at the conclusion without being conscious of intermediate steps. There were such steps, however. The train of reasoning ran, 'Here is a gentleman of a medical type, but with the air of a military man. Clearly an army doctor, then. He has just come from the tropics, for his face is dark, and that is not the natural tint of his skin, for his wrists are fair. He has undergone hardship and sickness, as his haggard face says clearly. His left arm has been injured. He holds it in a stiff and unnatural manner. Where in the tropics could an English army doctor have seen much hardship and got his arm wounded? Clearly in Afghanistan.' The whole train of thought did not occupy a second.

Like Bell, Holmes was also an expert in dialectology (attempting to place a person by their accent and other distinguishing vocal traits), an attribute he also made use of when assuming one of his many disguises – a roll call that included Italians, Frenchmen and Irish-Americans, not to mention Englishmen of all classes from 'common loafers' to booksellers, seamen and clergymen. In addition, Bell put great faith in handwriting analysis, believing it possible to conclude much about an author simply by studying the nature of their handwriting. So, too, the great man of Baker Street, who in 'The Adventure of the Reigate Squires' asserted: 'You may not be aware that the deduction of a man's age from his writing is one which has been brought to considerable accuracy by experts. In normal cases one can place a man in his true decade with tolerable confidence. I say normal cases, because ill health and physical weakness reproduce the signs of old age, even when the invalid is a youth.'

Littlejohn was no less eager than Bell to inculcate his students with a sense that the devil is in the detail. To this end, he extolled footprints as a vital source of identification, particularly in the rural setting, since there 'people who commit crimes never go bare-foot' so that the question becomes 'one of comparing the foot mark with the boots of suspected persons'. Holmes was clearly on the same page, using footprint evidence in no less than twenty-six of Doyle's stories, and even writing a monograph on the subject and their use in criminal identification.

In his 1892 introduction to a new edition of *A Study in Scarlet*, Bell said of Doyle that he 'created a shrewd, quick-sighted, inquisitive man, half doctor, half virtuoso, with plenty of spare time, a retentive memory, and perhaps with the best gift of all – the power of unloading the mind of all burden of trying to remember unnecessary details'. Aside from the spare time, of which they assuredly had little, this might equally have served as a description of Bell or Littlejohn.

Notes of Littlejohn's lectures on medical jurisprudence emphasise the clear-sighted approach that he brought to his subject. He taught, for instance, a simple checklist that the forensic examiner should keep in mind when attempting to establish whether a death is the result of accident, suicide or murder. The investigator, he said, should consider:

1. The position of the body.
2. The nature of the injuries.
3. The direction of the wound.
4. The position of the instrument.
5. The marks of blood.
6. The evidence of a struggle.

Typically, he was able to bring to life such potentially abstract tools by plundering practical examples from real-life cases – his encyclopaedic knowledge of criminality and suspicious deaths surely rivalled even that of Sherlock Holmes. He would fill his lectures with such stories as the demise in 1868 of Theodore II, Emperor of Ethiopia, who was found dead from a gunshot wound received as British troops overcame his forces at the citadel of Magdala. Littlejohn reminded his audience of the need to establish the distance from which a shot is fired in such deaths. In this particular case, the pattern of singeing on the Emperor's moustache and eyebrows seemed to prove beyond doubt that he had died by his own hand. Another story of more local vintage served to warn against the instinct to jump to conclusions after a preliminary survey of the evidence. Littlejohn told of an unnamed gentleman who was suffering from delusions so that he thought he was being tried in Edinburgh's criminal courts even as he resided in Glasgow. Fancying he had received news of his conviction, he went to his private room, battered his head against his safe, drove several nails through his forehead (resulting in the complete laceration of the left frontal lobe) and then repeatedly stabbed himself with a fork. It just so happened that he had left a large sum of money to his housekeeper in his will and she would surely have found herself on trial for his murder, Littlejohn surmised, had not the man's extraordinary bout of self-inflicted violence been seen by several other witnesses.

As both professor of forensic jurisprudence and police surgeon, Littlejohn disseminated a coolly analytical approach to criminal investigation that set the benchmark for the future. Policing as we understand it today was then still in its relative infancy so that the likes of Littlejohn (with the able assistance of Bell) were vital in defining best practice. He was not merely rewriting the rulebook but virtually authoring it from scratch, encouraging a sophistication in approach where it had hitherto been all but absent.

Robert Peel famously oversaw the establishment of the Metropolitan Police in London in 1829 (really a successor to the smaller-scale Bow Street Runners who had been operating since the middle of the previous century), but again Scotland had been ahead of the game. Back in 1800 the City of Glasgow Police was established, becoming the first publicly funded professional police force in the world. Then, in 1805, Edinburgh got its own version, taking over from the Town Guard, which, since 1682, had comprised, as one writer of the time noted, 'old Highlanders, of uncouth aspect and speech, dressed in a dingy red uniform and cocked hats'. Prone to drinking and quick to resort to violence, especially when required to enforce curfews, the Guard earned the nickname of the 'Town Rats' and by the start of the 1800s they were reviled and mocked in almost equal measure. The introduction of professional police forces was certainly a step forward but, as the nineteenth century approached its end, practical policing still struggled to rise above the rudimentary. Cases were often solved only if a suspect was caught red-handed or if a confession could be extracted, or else if there was sufficient hearsay evidence to be able to convince a jury.

In a discussion with the *Pall Mall Gazette* in 1893, Bell touched upon his frustrations with the police – feelings, it is fair to assume, Littlejohn shared with him though perhaps could not comfortably voice. Bell said:

It would be a great thing if the police generally could be trained to observe more closely. The lines upon which it might be done would be to make the prize bigger for the educated man. At present the incentive to special training is not too great, I believe. The fatal mistake which the ordinary policeman makes is this, that he gets his theory first and then makes the facts fit it, instead of getting his facts first and making all his little observations and deductions until he is driven irresistibly by them into an elucidation in a direction he may never have originally contemplated ... You cannot expect the ordinary bobby, splendid fellow as he is so far as pluck and honesty go, to stand eight hours on his legs and then develop great mental strength. He doesn't get enough blood to his brain to permit of it. The only feasible scheme which strikes me would be to get a good man and give him *carte blanche* about the choosing of his assistants and the special education of them.

Again, a glance at Holmes's own utterances on the professional policeman reveals that he, Doyle, Bell and Littlejohn were cut from the same cloth. Even the bobbies Holmes quite likes are damned with faint praise. Inspector Gregory of Scotland Yard is thus described as 'competent' but not 'gifted with imagination'. Moreover, Holmes says of Gregory, Athelney Jones and the most famous Holmesian policeman of them all, Inspector Lestrade, that their 'normal state' is to be 'out of their depth'. What infuriated him most was to arrive at a crime scene after the police had already got to work. 'Oh, how simple it would all have been,' he once muttered to Watson, 'had I been here before they came like a herd of buffalo and wallowed all over it.' While Holmes was helping to change public perceptions as to what the detective was capable of, Bell and, especially, Littlejohn were spearheading improvements in real-life practice.

Bell and Littlejohn first started working together on real-time criminal investigations sometime around the early 1870s – several years into their acquaintanceship. In 1878, they cooperated on a case that brought Edinburgh to a standstill for a while – an affair that would cement their reputation among the select few who knew of their joint involvement. On 2 January 1878, a young mother, Elizabeth Chantrelle, was discovered in her bed, seriously ill from apparent coal-gas poisoning. Littlejohn was called to the scene by the woman's GP – whether in his capacity as police surgeon or as an old friend and trusted colleague is not clear – but despite their best efforts and those of the infirmary, by the end of the day she was dead. Littlejohn expressed disquiet about the assumed cause of death and, after consultation with Bell and extensive post-mortem testing, it was discovered that Elizabeth had died not from gas inhalation but from opium poisoning. Suspicion quickly fell upon her dissolute husband, a teacher of French origin called Eugene Chantrelle – in fact, a former teacher of Doyle's when the author was a seven-year-old at Edinburgh's Newington Academy – who had met the victim when she was a fifteen-year-old pupil of his. The trial, although relatively open-and-shut, caused a sensation and filled countless column inches in the newspapers, although word of Bell's involvement was kept quiet. A long while after, a former student of Bell's, one Z. M. Hamilton, recalled the morning that Chantrelle was hanged, with Littlejohn in attendance in his role of police surgeon. Hamilton reported how Chantrelle removed his hat and took a final puff on his cigar before turning to the doctor. 'Bye-bye, Littlejohn,' Hamilton reported Chantrelle as saying. 'Don't forget to give my compliments to Joe Bell. You both did a good job in bringing me to the scaffold.'

There were plenty more high-profile cases to follow. Among them was that of Jack the Ripper, who notoriously unleashed a reign of terror in London during 1888 when he murdered and dismembered at least five women. Although the case remains officially unsolved, years later Bell would allude to the fact that he and a colleague (surely it could only have been Littlejohn) had undertaken a review of the evidence for Scotland Yard. After a close study of all the available information, each then independently wrote the name of the person they considered the chief suspect. The two hit upon the same man – whose identity has infuriatingly been lost in the annals of time – and duly passed on their thoughts to the police in London. Within weeks, it is said, the murderous spree had come to an end.

The year 1889 proved another notable one for the Littlejohn–Bell partnership. In March was the trial of William Bury, accused of killing and mutilating his wife in Dundee. After initially confessing to the murder, he entered a plea of not guilty and it was a post-mortem (the third carried out on the victim) conducted by Littlejohn that was instrumental in securing a conviction. The Burys had only moved to Scotland at the beginning of the year. They had previously lived in Bow, East London, close to Jack the Ripper's hunting ground, prompting speculation that Bury might actually have been the Ripper.

In November came another trial for which the public literally queued around the block. On this occasion, it centred on the death of an Englishman, Edwin Rose, on the picturesque Isle of Arran. His body was discovered in a howff – a sort of hut hewn from rock – a little below the summit of Arran's highest peak, Goatfell. He had been missing for some three weeks when his decomposing corpse was found with calamitous injuries to the head and back. The police soon alighted on a travelling companion he had recently met, a Scot called John Laurie, as his murderer. Laurie was in many ways an unappealing character and admitted robbing Rose but vehemently denied killing him. The defence suggested death had been caused by an accidental fall. Littlejohn was again pivotal to proceedings, arguing that such a fall could not possibly have resulted in the violent injuries Rose had suffered. Laurie was subsequently found guilty by majority verdict. Again, Bell's name was absent from coverage of proceedings but his behind-the-scenes involvement as Littlejohn's 'second man' is highly likely. His anonymity would not last much longer, though – the Ardlamont mystery was just four years away and it would thrust him and Littlejohn together into the public spotlight, whether they liked it or not.

6

The Body in the Woods

'There is but one step from the grotesque
to the horrible.'

Sherlock Holmes, 'The Adventure of Wisteria Lodge'

As James Wright, the Monsons' newly arrived butler, waited at table on the evening of Wednesday 9 August 1893, all seemed perfectly normal at Ardlamont. Earlier in the day, at around three in the afternoon, Monson and a visitor had taken some of the children out for a boating trip in the bay. Cecil and Mrs Monson, meanwhile, took a walk together along the cliffs overlooking Ardlamont Point. Now seated for supper were Cecil, Monson and Agnes plus the governess, Miss Hiron, and the visitor, a man going by the name of Mr Scott. He had arrived by ferry the previous evening and Monson had driven to meet him. Scott was presented as an engineer come to inspect the yacht that Cecil was planning to buy. In due course, Monson would imply that he scarcely knew the man and that Cecil had been the one who had engaged his services. Nonetheless, they all seemed to be getting on well enough and the conversation flowed freely over dinner.

Talk turned to a potential late-night fishing trip. According to Monson, it was Cecil's idea. The boy had developed a taste for splash-fishing over the previous few weeks and he believed the waters were rapidly filling with salmon just then.

Splash-fishing involves taking a long net and fastening one end to the shore by means of a heavy stone. The other end is weighted with a second stone and stowed in the stern of a boat. One person then rows the boat out into deeper waters and back, while their companion feeds the net gradually into the sea. Eventually, the second end of the net is fastened to shore so that the boat sits within a semicircle of netting. The boat's inhabitants then start splashing the water in order to drive any fish into the net. Previously, Cecil had fished with a 150-yard net but on this night, so Monson said, the plan was to tie two together to give a full 300 yards. Not only did the act of splashing tend to cause large volumes of water to accumulate in a small rowing boat, but the effect would be magnified by having to haul in such an unwieldy net.

Having asked Wright to sit up and wait for them, Monson, Scott and Cecil headed out on their night-time escapade, but they soon ran into trouble. As it was reported to members of the household, Monson and Cecil – a non-swimmer – were some distance from shore when their boat struck a rock and they were propelled into the water. According to Monson, he himself had become ensnared by a net or an anchor rope and had nearly drowned, but fortunately he and Cecil were able to scramble on to a rock before striking back for home. Scott, who had remained on the beach, rushed to the house to get a torch to guide them to safety. Ultimately, no harm was done and the trio returned to the house at around one o'clock in the morning, where Monson and Cecil changed out of their sodden clothes before re-joining Scott in the smoking room to enjoy a few more hours of roistering.

Considering the dramatic events of that night, it was perhaps surprising that the three should decide to meet just a few hours later for their fateful hunting trip, especially given the inclement weather. Regardless, at about seven o'clock on the morning of 10 August, Monson called on George Lamont, the second gamekeeper, and requested a gun – a twenty-bore weapon, a little smaller than Monson's own twelve-bore – for Cecil. Sometime before nine o'clock, Monson, Cecil and Scott were spotted by James Dunn, a watchmaker from Newcastle who happened to be holidaying on the estate. Looking out of his pantry window, he saw Hambrough jump a wall to pick up a rabbit that he handed to Scott. A couple of minutes later, Dunn saw the group come off the road, skip over a wire fence and enter the woods east of the main house. Here they could expect to encounter plenty of rabbit and pigeon. After a few steps, Cecil veered off to the right on his own, while the other two went off to the left. Before long they were all out of Dunn's view but about three minutes or so later he heard a shot.

What happened between Dunn losing sight of the three men and Wright encountering Monson and Scott back in the house, where they broke the news that their young companion was dead? That was the question that kept a nation on tenterhooks over the months that followed. But, for now, the assumption was that there had been a terrible accident. The primary concern was to recover the body and make sure matters were handled in an appropriate fashion.

The estate gardener, Archibald Whyte, was in the company of Hugh Carmichael, the coachman, when they met Monson and Wright coming back out of the house after Monson had revealed Cecil was dead. 'Young Hambrough's shot himself,' Monson said to Whyte. 'See and find something and bring him up to the house.' So Whyte collected a rug and took it into the woods. By now there was quite a crowd around the body, which lay on top of a dyke – beside Monson and Wright were Hugh Carmichael and his ploughman father (also called Hugh), John Steven (the factor – effectively the estate manager), Stewart M'Nicol (the estate joiner) and another man called James Lyon. Between them, they placed the rug under Cecil's feet and drew it up underneath his body. He was then raised on to a cart that Steven had brought to the scene and taken back to the house, where he was redressed and put in his bed. It was now about ten o'clock.

When Steven found Scott and Monson again, they were together in the smoking room and seemed agitated. 'This is a terrible job!' the factor observed. Scott agreed, then told Steven that he had not been carrying a gun, since he was no sportsman and he thought it safest to leave firearms alone. Given the circumstances, it was a thought perhaps best left unvoiced. Monson, meanwhile, seemed unsure what he ought to do next, so it was suggested that the doctor be called. After briefly returning to his own home, Steven came back to the main house around eleven o'clock. Monson now accompanied him to where the body had been found and told him how Cecil had been walking on top of a turf wall, with Scott someway behind and Monson himself further back when he heard a shot. 'Hulloa, Hambrough,' Monson claimed to have called out, 'where are you? What have you got?' A moment later, he said, he and Scott stumbled upon the wretched sight of the boy lying shot in a ditch. 'To tell you the truth, Mr Steven,' he continued, 'I don't know where we lifted him from, but we lifted him.'

The local GP, Dr Macmillan, arrived sometime between half-past eleven and midday. Steven took him to Monson but the latter was notably reluctant to go near the body so Steven took Macmillan to the bedroom, where Carmichael was sponging Cecil's face with soap and water. The bedclothes were heavily soiled with blood. The doctor – whose experience of gunshot wounds was limited to a pistol shot on the finger, a gunshot wound through the ankle and a few minor small-pellet injuries – set about examining the dead man, commenting that had the impact been an inch-and-a-half to either side, it would surely not have been fatal. With his finger, he felt the hole in Cecil's skull and also inspected the victim's jacket, which had a little blood on the collar. He also noted the absence of any blackening or singeing around the wound and estimated time of death at about three hours previous. The body was still warm but rigor mortis had set in. After finishing his examination, he bound the head, cleaned away the blood and helped dress the body again.

The doctor, Steven, Scott and Monson then lunched together. It was at this stage that Scott said he was due for an important meeting in Glasgow and so wished to catch a boat at the earliest opportunity. The subject of the death was largely avoided, although Monson noted that had it happened in England, a coroner's inquest would proceed. Would there be anything similar here in Scotland? he wondered. Macmillan explained that the Procurator-Fiscal (the Scottish equivalent of the English coroner) would conduct a private investigation but, since this was clearly an accident, it was unlikely that there would be a post-mortem.

After lunch, Monson gave the doctor an account of what had taken place for his records. It was much the same as the narrative he had given to Steven and was corroborated in its essentials by Scott. Monson, Steven and the doctor then made for the place where the body was found. Rather macabrely, Monson also brought one of his young children with him. Monson remained agitated, so it fell to Steven to point out to Macmillan the various places of interest Monson had shown him on their earlier walk there. The doctor also told Monson that he saw no reason why Scott need stay, as he was satisfied that his report on the accident would satisfy the authorities. So, at about two that afternoon, Scott was driven in Steven's trap to catch a boat, having left a forwarding address of the Central Station Hotel in Glasgow.

Agnes Monson returned home from her own trip to Glasgow later that evening. On being told what had occurred, she immediately took to her room, too distressed to dine downstairs either that night or the following day. Tot also made an appearance the next day, staying overnight before returning to London – Monson had made sure to telegraph him immediately with news of the death. Cecil's parents, meanwhile, received a message from Dr Hambleton informing him that his son had been wounded in a shotgun accident and that he and his wife should come north without delay. Whether Hambleton had himself received the news from Monson directly by telegraph or via Tot is unclear. Regardless, Monson said he would meet the Hambroughs at Glasgow. The Major subsequently telegraphed Monson from London's King's Cross Station, asking him to send further details on Cecil's condition and the nature of the accident via the station master at Newcastle. But no such update was forthcoming. Nor was Monson in Glasgow when their train came in at six o'clock on Friday the 11th.

Having walked to their hotel, the Hambroughs retired to the coffee room where a waiter happened to have a copy of the *Citizen* newspaper. Mrs Hambrough saw her husband's face drop as he surveyed its pages. A short article was headed: 'Sad shooting accident. Young gentleman shot dead at Ardlamont.' The report continued:

> The young gentleman was crossing a dyke with his loaded gun, which he was carrying under his arm at full-cock. It is supposed that the trigger was caught by the bushes, and this, it is believed, caused the gun accidentally to go off. The charge lodged in the unfortunate gentleman's head and he was killed on the spot. His friends coming up immediately afterwards were too late to render any assistance. The sad occurrence has caused gloom over the district.

On hearing the terrible news, Mrs Hambrough screamed and then fainted. It was not until later that the couple had any direct communication from Monson, who warned them in a telegraph message: 'Prepare for the worst.'

The Hambroughs arrived at Princes Pier station in Greenock on the morning of the 12th. Alfred and Agnes Monson met them on the platform in a state of such distress that any feelings of bitterness towards them that the Major may have harboured immediately dissipated. 'This man is punished sufficiently,' he told his wife before shaking Monson's hand. The two couples arrived at Ardlamont a little before three in the afternoon, and the Major subsequently viewed Cecil's body twice – once before he was placed in his coffin, and once afterwards. Dr Macmillan felt it better if Mrs Hambrough did not join her husband in that arduous task, on account of decomposition having already taken hold.

The Major also broached the subject of insurance with Monson, who told him there was none. Moreover, on the day of the accident, Monson had given Steven a letter to read from the Scottish Provident that detailed acceptance of an insurance policy on which the deposit had not been paid. Monson had not, however, mentioned the two policies worth a combined £20,000 that had been completed. Certainly, Steven felt he had been given the impression that no viable insurance existed, and the Major was led to believe the same. As far as Cecil's parents were concerned, their boy had fallen victim to a tragic accident but there was no hint of foul play.

This view was also shared by Dr Macmillan, who duly prepared a report for the Procurator-Fiscal. He concluded that the fatal wound was 'exactly what I would expect to find from a charge of small shot fired from a distance of perhaps 12 inches'. In other words, there was every indication that the shot had come from the victim's own weapon. Given the other circumstantial evidence, the doctor had no reason to suspect suicide, and certainly not murder. 'The information above given makes it probable,' Macmillan wrote in his report, 'that the deceased was going along the wall with the gun – a short 20-bore – under his arm and his finger on the trigger, when his foot caught on something, and he plunged forward, put down his hands to save himself, thus lowering the breech, raising the muzzle, and pressing the trigger, with the result described in the first part of this report.'

On the Monday after the shooting, Cecil's body began its long journey back to Ventnor where it was to be buried. Almost everyone who lived and worked on the Ardlamont estate gathered at eleven o'clock in the morning to form a funeral procession beneath the blazing summer sun. The coffin was taken some ten miles to the village of Kames, where it was placed on a steamer. Monson had ordered the coffin from a firm in Glasgow, its silver plate inscribed:

> WINDSOR DUDLEY CECIL HAMBROUGH
> Lieut. 3rd Bat. 3rd West Yorks Regt.
> Aged 20 Years
> Died at Ardlamont from Gun Accident
> 10th August, 1893

Monson and Steven travelled with the corpse and, on arriving at the Isle of Wight, they went directly to the mortuary in Ventnor. Indicative of how far Monson had interposed himself into family business, he was insistent that the body be interred in the Hambrough family vault, but he faced opposition from the local vicar, who was unwilling to disturb the vault without the express permission of the Home Office. Monson called upon his cousin, Lord Oxenbridge, to chivvy things along and, sure enough, a wire was sent from the Secretary of State granting permission, but by then arrangements for the funeral were too far progressed to be changed. Cecil was buried in the same grave plot as his aunt at 2 p.m. on Thursday 17 August, just opposite the front entrance of the picturesque church of St Catherine's, Ventnor – a church Cecil's grandfather had built back in 1836. Many of the dead boy's family were in attendance although, as Monson told it, they contributed nothing financially to the occasion – instead, according to the tutor, he picked up all the expenses, from the funeral fees to the hotel bills. (Presumably, though, Monson was actually spending Tot's money.)

Back in Scotland, meanwhile, Dr Macmillan had received a visit from two representatives of the Mutual Life Insurance Company of New York. They left him a form to fill out in relation to the insurance policies held by Agnes Monson. The key sections ran as follows:

> State the remote cause of death; if from disease, give the predisposing cause, date of the first appearance of its symptoms, its history, and the symptoms present during its progress. [Macmillan's answer: Gunshot injury to brain.]

> State immediate cause of death. [Macmillan's answer: A gunshot.]

> If from any cause other than disease, state the medical and other facts connected therewith. [Macmillan's answer: He had been accidentally shot by his own gun through the occipital bone, the charge entering the brain in a compact mass through an opening 1 inch in diameter.]

This revelation that there were, after all, insurance policies on Cecil's life should surely have set alarm bells ringing with the doctor, but this was seemingly not the case – for now, at least. He, like a good many others in the immediate aftermath of Cecil's death, exhibited an overwhelming willingness to accept Monson and Scott's version of what had occurred in the seclusion of the woods. While this might have been understandable when there was no hint of a motive for foul play, news that the Monsons might financially benefit from Cecil's death surely demanded a reappraisal of events. There were other peculiar aspects to Monson and Scott's conduct in the immediate aftermath, too, although they barely seemed to raise an eyebrow, at first. Why, for instance, had Monson removed his own and Cecil's guns from the scene of the shooting and taken out the ammunition before telling anyone of the incident? And why had he not first raised the alarm with Hugh Carmichael, who stood in the stables watching Monson and Scott pass by on their way from the woods to the house immediately after the boy had been felled? Why, surely someone must have wondered, did Monson wait until Wright the butler encountered him in the smoking room before breaking the news?

Nonetheless, it was not to be much longer before suspicions started to be roused. The Procurator-Fiscal, John Campbell M'Lullich, had been conducting his enquiries from the smoking room of the Royal Hotel in Tighnabruaich, the nearest significant village to Ardlamont though still a journey of some seven miles. M'Lullich had been content enough with Dr Macmillan's take on events, especially given that his Deputy Fiscal, Tom Macnaughton, had a deposition that there was no insurance on Cecil's life. But then M'Lullich received a note on 22 August from Monson advising that he was coming to see him the next day at the Fiscal's office in Inveraray.

M'Lullich was there to meet Monson on the 23rd as he alighted from the paddle-steamer. Monson at once told him that two friends – insurance agents – were following a little behind and wanted to speak with the Fiscal. As Monson walked with M'Lullich to his office, he now informed him that there was indeed insurance on Cecil – a £15,000 policy taken out by the Major without his son's knowledge. It was a statement that took the Fiscal off guard, and would have come as quite a surprise to the Major, too. Realizing that his investigation might be taking on a new air, M'Lullich asked Monson to send over the gun that Cecil had been carrying and its ammunition by the following day's boat. According to M'Lullich, Monson at this time confirmed that Cecil had been using a twenty-bore gun (of a type more likely to be used by a younger or less experienced hunter) on the day of his death, as opposed to the larger twelve-bore gun that the group had also taken with them. The precise distribution of the weapons would become a source of deep contention in the months to come.

By the time the pair arrived at the Fiscal's office, Mr M'Lean and Mr Herbert of the Mutual Life (the same agents as had contacted Macmillan) were there waiting for them. Tot was also in attendance, for it was he who was attempting to cash in the policies. M'Lullich took the insurance agents to a private room out of Tot and Monson's earshot. Within a few minutes he had ascertained that there was in fact £20,000 in insurance, that either Monson or his wife had an interest, and that the Mutual required a certificate confirming that death was accidental.

Troubled by these various discoveries, M'Lullich decided to take the boat to Ardlamont the next day. By the time he left Inveraray around lunchtime, there was still no sign of the gun or the cartridges he had requested from Monson. After he landed at Tighnabruaich, he interviewed Lamont the gamekeeper, who confirmed that Cecil had carried the twenty-bore, with Monson taking his regular twelve-bore. The Fiscal promptly sent Lamont off to collect the items in question. But when he arrived at Ardlamont, Monson is said to have told his gamekeeper that he had 'made a serious mistake' in his evidence and that, in fact, the two men had switched guns. After he had collected the twenty-bore for Cecil, Monson said, he discovered that Scott and Cecil had already set out for the woods. Cecil had taken Monson's twelve-bore and kept it throughout the morning. So it was that Lamont went back to Tighnabruaich with the twelve-bore – but still no cartridges. That Monson should now be revising the details of who was carrying which gun raised all manner of warning flags. Nor were suspicions alleviated when a few weeks later Cecil's jacket that he wore on the morning of the hunt was recovered from his room, its pockets filled with ammunition – eighteen cartridges for the twenty-bore, and just one for the twelve-bore. Tom Macnaughton, the Deputy Fiscal, privately told a reporter friend, Neil Munro: 'I've very grave doubts about the character of that accident.'

On the evening of the 24 August, Monson attempted to meet with the Fiscal at his hotel in Tighnabruaich but M'Lullich refused to entertain a conversation. Monson even suggested later that M'Lullich had made a threat against him, although there were no witnesses to such an exchange. Regardless, a couple of days later the Fiscal received a letter from Monson seemingly attempting to smooth things over and asking how he may assist the investigation. But it was all too little too late by then. Armed with intelligence of the insurance policies and alerted to doubts over which gun Cecil had been carrying, even Dr Macmillan was having serious doubts and decided to attach a supplementary note to his earlier report. He wrote:

> I implicitly accepted the statement of witnesses Monson and Scott that the injuries to Hambrough were due to an accidental shot from his own gun, a short-barrelled 20-bore boy's weapon, charged with amberite [a type of gunpowder that typically left little or no sign of residue]. The apparently entire absence of motive made the bent of my inquiry not so much how could this injury most likely be produced, as how could the deceased have done it accidentally. It now transpires there were no amberite cartridges for this diameter of gun, and that I too hastily came to the conclusion or theory advanced at the end of my former report. Having handled and tried the gun now in the possession of the Procurator-Fiscal, I am convinced the injuries were not caused in the way I thought possible.

He also sent a letter to the Mutual Life: 'Since sending you the report on the above, facts have come to my knowledge which make it certain that the injuries were not caused in the way or with the weapon I then thought them to have been. I therefore now ask that that report be hereby cancelled.'

Events started to move quickly. M'Lullich was satisfied there was sufficient evidence to bring Monson in for formal questioning and so an application was made for an arrest warrant. The Chief Constable of Argyllshire took him into custody on the 29 August and he was transferred to the prison at Inveraray the following day. Meanwhile, the Sheriff made a search of the property at Ardlamont and seized various papers. The decision was also taken to exhume Cecil's body from its resting place in Ventnor. This unenviable task was assigned to the police surgeon, Dr Henry Littlejohn, who straightaway briefed his great collaborator, Joe Bell.

7

An Exact Science

'Detection is, or ought to be, an exact science and should be treated in the same cold and unemotional manner.'

Sherlock Holmes, *The Sign of the Four*

For Bell and Littlejohn, the early months of 1893 had not yielded anything as high profile as the Henry Bury case or the Arran murder trial, but it had nonetheless been an unrelentingly busy year. The cases that crossed Littlejohn's desk included the alleged assault of a former hangman, the death of an infant struck on the head by an ornament thrown by her mother at her father, and the discovery of a child's body found wrapped in brown parcel paper at a farm northwest of Edinburgh. Bell and Littlejohn had also appeared together at the trial of Patrick Griffin for the culpable homicide of Edward Wynn. It was a fairly unedifying case of alcohol-fuelled brawling that resulted in the victim being hit on the head with a hatchet. When a doctor was eventually called, he put Wynn's delirium down to the effects of drink and was not informed that he had been struck with a weapon. But Littlejohn and Bell conducted the post-mortem together and concluded that it was the strike that had caused death. The jury took little time in finding Griffin guilty and the defendant received a merciful sentence of just six months. It was, all told, a regular day at the office for Bell and Littlejohn.

Their workaholic tendencies were fully indulged elsewhere, too. Littlejohn added to his already crippling professional burdens the role of president of the Institute of Public Health. In May, meanwhile, he addressed the House of Commons' Select Committee on death certification. He demanded that a greater level of care be paid to the certification of death, commenting that 'the existing system permitted by law is a farce, so far as the detection of secret crime is concerned in Edinburgh'. As the *Aberdeen Evening News* reported it, his words excited 'visions of slow poisonings and mysterious deaths which can only be held in check by the wholesome knowledge of Littlejohn's skill in diagnosing. But even the active medical officer of health of Edinburgh sometimes fails, and his evidence will be read with uneasy feelings by the citizens.' Littlejohn could not have known how prescient his words would be.

Edinburgh University gave him a brief respite from his responsibilities when in July he was called to receive an honorary law degree in recognition of his extraordinary contributions in the medico-legal field. On rising to his feet to collect the degree, he was greeted with roars and cheers from a crowd eager to recognize a hometown hero.

But for his colleague Joseph Bell, the year had taken a sad turn. The month before, he had lost his beloved son, Benjamin, to peritonitis resulting from complications after a bout of appendicitis. He was just short of his twenty-fourth birthday. Bell maintained outward composure in the immediate aftermath – even at the funeral, where six sergeants from his son's Highland Regiment carried his coffin as pipers played 'Flowers of the Forest'. But the hurt went deep. He wrote letters to friends so full of grief that they refused to ever discuss their contents with others. Nor was it the first time that Bell had faced such sorrow. In 1874, his wife, Edith, had succumbed to puerperal peritonitis just nine years into their apparently idyllic marriage. Bell's hair had, it was said, turned from raven black to snowy white within three days of her death. His response to Benjamin's passing was, as ever, to throw himself into his work. The Ardlamont mystery would ensure that there was no shortage of that.

However, the initial involvement was Littlejohn's alone. At just after 4 p.m. on Monday 11 September, a small crowd gathered around Cecil's graveside to witness his exhumation on the orders of the Home Secretary, Herbert Asquith. Alongside Littlejohn were Macnaughton (the Deputy Fiscal), Dr Macmillan and a Dr Sanders from Edinburgh, who was attending on behalf of Monson. Dr Whithead of Ventnor, representing the Hambroughs, joined them a short while later. The large oak coffin with its silver mountings was raised from the ground and placed on a hearse bound for the mortuary at Ventnor Cemetery, up in the hills above the town.

There the coffin lid and inner metallic shell were lifted. It was immediately obvious that decomposition was advancing, although not quickly enough to prohibit the necessary examination. Cecil's features had swelled but Macmillan was quickly able to confirm his identity. With the public diligently kept clear of proceedings, the corpse was laid out on oil sheets on the grass just outside the mortuary. As Littlejohn noted, 'the cuticle, or outer skin, everywhere separated with facility'. By removing some cloth loosely wrapped around the lower right-hand side of the boy's head, he revealed the fatal wound and made sure that a photographer captured images of it before dissection progressed any further.

The wound itself – caused by the shot which was some inch (according to Dr Macmillan's initial report) or inch-and-a-half (according to Bell's calculations) in diameter – was about three-and-a-half inches in length, triangular in shape, its base (about two-and-a-half inches long) in the direction of the face and its apex located about an inch underneath and slightly in front of the occipital protuberance (the occipital bone being that which forms the base of the back of the skull). A flap of skin about an inch-and-a-half long hung down from its upper edge. The right ear, meanwhile, had been severely mutilated, with about an inch-and-a-half missing from its middle exterior section – blown away by the impact of the shot. There was no evidence of blackening around the wound as might have been expected from gunpowder or scorching. Cecil's hair came away in their fingers as they worked around the wound so it took little effort to remove the entire right side of the scalp. The skull beneath presented a 'localized shattered appearance'. There was also a large hole (around two inches by one) through which the brain was exposed. Closer investigation revealed a significant proportion of the brain to the front of the head was missing. Four small foreign bodies that proved to be shot were removed from the brain matter that remained.

They now moved on to the left side of the head and discovered that it was largely uninjured. The rest of Cecil's body was in a similarly good state, and his major organs were adjudged to have been in fine health prior to death. The stomach was empty and presented no particularly noticeable odour when opened – there was, for instance, no trace of alcohol. The cavities of the heart and the blood vessels were also empty. Littlejohn and Dr Macmillan committed themselves to the opinion that Cecil had died from shock resulting from the gunshot injury to the skull and brain, coupled with a subsequent loss of blood. Moreover, they were nudging towards the idea that there had been foul play: in the words of Macmillan, 'As a result of the post-mortem examination, my opinion was that the wound could not have been caused accidentally.'

Once back in Edinburgh, Littlejohn began to liaise closely with Bell and several other colleagues from the university – chief among them an esteemed surgeon, Dr Patrick Heron Watson, and an anatomist, Dr Macdonald Brown. Having thoroughly surveyed the nature of the victim's injuries, Littlejohn turned his mind to a series of other questions – the type he taught his students to work through in order to establish accident, suicide or murder in cases of mysterious death.

The damage to Cecil's head revealed much but he needed more information. It was not for him to ponder Monson's relationship with Cecil and his father, or to analyse the tutor's financial arrangements, or even to question the motive for taking out life insurance upon the victim. In place of supposition he sought cold, empirical facts through which, he hoped, the truth of the events of 10 August would reveal themselves.

'In ascertaining how an injury has been caused,' he would note, 'there are certain matters familiar to doctors as aids to the determination of the question.' These were the direction of the wound, the direction from which the shot was fired, the position of the weapon with regard to the dead body and the position in which the dead body was found (the latter being 'all important in determining how death occurred'). Answer these questions conclusively and he could be all but sure as to whether there was intent behind Cecil's death. But it would be no easy job given the degradation of the evidence caused by the passage of time and the inadequacies of the initial investigation. He nonetheless threw himself into the task with characteristic energy.

To help with the question of the direction of the shot, he presented Dr Brown with Cecil's skull and a further six bone fragments that had been recovered. The brain had already been removed by sawing one half of the skull cap ('no instrument has ever been devised,' Littlejohn was apt to tell his students, 'which effects the separation of the skullcap better than the ordinary saw'). To facilitate his experiments, Brown prepared a model of the skull that would become a familiar sight at the ensuing trial. Heron Watson, meanwhile, was a veteran of the Crimean War where he gained extensive experience of treating gunshot wounds. Littlejohn plundered his specialist knowledge to help establish the distance and position from which the shot was fired. He too was given the dead man's skull to inspect, along with photographs and the post-mortem report.

As to where Cecil's body had fallen and where his gun had lain in relation to his body, the issue was more vexed. The problem was that, purposefully or not, Monson and Scott had done much to eliminate the relevant evidence. They removed the firearm from the scene before any independent third party could view it and also claimed to have lifted Cecil from the ditch where he fell. But it was only their word that this is really what transpired. Littlejohn was instead forced to form his opinion on the basis of the available eyewitness reports. When he travelled to Ardlamont with Dr Macmillan, he inspected the scene in the company of Whyte and Carmichael, who told him where they had first come across the corpse. He also studied some nearby rowan trees for evidence of pellet marks in a bid to corroborate the location.

Back in Edinburgh, he engaged the services of a gunsmith called James MacNaughton (no relation to the Deputy Fiscal), whom he visited on the 23 September armed with the Hambrough skull. Littlejohn wanted his help in carrying out a series of experiments to determine the different firing patterns of the two guns Monson and Cecil had taken with them, along with the effects of using the various available types of shot (namely, No. 5 and No. 6) and different types of powder (including black powder and amberite). By a careful process of elimination, Littlejohn wanted to be sure exactly which ammunition from which gun had killed Cecil, and from how far away it was fired.

MacNaughton travelled to Ardlamont to make his own inspection of the woods and determined the likely line of fire. He did this by conducting a series of detailed measurements taking into account where the witnesses reported having seen Cecil's body on top of the dyke in relation to the marks on nearby trees that he believed had been caused by the spread of pellets from the fatal shotgun cartridge as it travelled. Afterwards, he designed a series of experiments conducted at his private firing range, which sat on the Water of Leith that runs out of Edinburgh down to the port of Leith. Here he fired into a series of cardboard targets before progressing to heads modelled from cardboard and clay. Littlejohn, Bell and Heron Watson were also in attendance. But however sophisticated the set-up, the doctors realized that firing into cardboard gave results only distantly related to the impact of gunshot on human flesh. It was arranged, therefore, that the three doctors and MacNaughton should meet at the mortuary at Edinburgh, where the gunsmith would fire shots into three specially selected cadavers.

This was forensic science at its most brutally pure. In the 1820s, the notorious grave-robbing antics of William Burke and William Hare – carried out to keep Robert Knox, a Fellow of the Royal Society of Edinburgh, supplied with corpses for his anatomy lectures – forged forever a gruesome link between the city and human anatomical study. Fortunately, by the time that Littlejohn and company were at work, the legal supply of cadavers had been extended. Anatomists had previously been restricted to dissecting the bodies only of orphans and foundlings or else those who were executed, had died in prison or committed suicide. Now, though, it was legal to take the corpses of those who perished in the workhouse as long as their bodies were not claimed within forty-eight hours. Though hardly evidence of a compassionate social response to poverty, it did nonetheless ensure that the illicit exhumations of earlier generations were now unnecessary. It was under these circumstances that the gunsmith and the medics could execute their grim task without compunction, all with a view to securing justice for a man brought down before his time. 'I did not see the results,' MacNaughton recalled of the experiments. 'That was for the doctors to see.'

While Littlejohn was the leading light of Scottish forensics at this time, he was not the only player upon the stage. In August, John Blair, a solicitor with the firm of Davidson & Syme, was hired to conduct Monson's defence. He in turn employed the services of Matthew Hay, who was in many regards Littlejohn's direct counterpart in Aberdeen.

Having studied at the universities of both Glasgow and Edinburgh – as well as on the continent in Strasbourg, Munich and Berlin – Hay became a noted expert in pharmacology and toxicology. He graduated with the gold medal in medicine from Edinburgh in 1881 (the same year as Doyle completed his studies there) and was made chair of forensic medicine at Aberdeen University the following year, when he was just twenty-seven years old. He also served as the city's Medical Officer of Health, gaining a reputation, like Littlejohn, for his farsighted reforms to public health provision. By 1890, he was also working as a police surgeon and medico-legal examiner for the Crown. The Ardlamont mystery thus offered him the perfect public stage on which to play out his respectful professional rivalry with the older, more famous man.

Like Littlejohn, Hay visited Ardlamont to scout out the scene, where John Steven, the factor, served as his guide. He then set about conducting a series of shooting experiments with Tom Speedy, himself an estate factor and also a partner in a firm of Edinburgh shooting agents. In 1884, Speedy had written a book, *Sport in the Highlands and Lowlands of Scotland, with Rod and Gun*, which included a chapter on firearms and how to use them. By his own estimation, 'I have always taken a special interest in the subject of gun accidents.' He made his own survey of Ardlamont prior to beginning work with Hay.

They then began their practical experiments, which were quite as striking and innovative as those conducted by the Littlejohn–Bell side. Hay and Speedy first fired at wooden boards before proceeding to wooden models of the human head, then dog skins and, ultimately, a freshly slaughtered horse. Hay believed that the flesh of a recently deceased horse closely replicated that of human flesh 'because of the skin and underlying tissues being practically alive and showing retraction'. The shots were fired into the base of the animal's head, close to the shoulder, a minute after it had been destroyed. Speedy was just the man for this job. 'In my gamekeeper days,' he explained, 'I had charge of a kennel of dogs. They were fed largely on horse flesh, and it was my duty to slaughter the horses. I have shot a great many horses in my day, probably over five hundred. The method I adopted was to shoot them chiefly on the forehead and sometimes behind the ear.'

The dog skins, meanwhile, were used to study the different effects of various gun powders upon the epidermis. First, a black skin was hung on a board that was fired at from about six inches. In the case of the amberite powder, the shot cut through the hairs on the skin but there was no evidence of scorching. However, aware that the black skin might disguise any subtle discolouration, the experiment was repeated using a white skin. Speedy then went a step further, buying a quantity of human hair to see if it would show signs of singeing from shots fired from a short distance. After discharging his weapon at point-blank range, he next decided to involve his wife in his investigations. The poor woman – accommodating to a fault – let down her hair and allowed her husband to fire a full cartridge of amberite powder through her tresses from a distance of two feet. The powder neither singed the hair nor even left a smell, presumably much to his wife's general relief.

For the time being out of the public gaze, the Crown and the defence were thus busily building their banks of forensic data. Crucially, Hay was arriving at startlingly different conclusions to those of Littlejohn, Bell and their comrades. The scene was set for a mighty courtroom battle, in which not only was the defendant's life at stake but also the reputations of some of the nation's most respected men. Meanwhile, the press was beginning to sniff a story with which they might run and run. It was not long before thoughts turned to the most famous detective in the world. On 1 September 1893, the *Yorkshire Evening Post* had reflected that 'the death of young Mr Hambrough affords exactly the sort of problem which Mr

Sherlock Holmes is wont to solve so prettily. Give him the details –
on paper – and doubtless the eminent detective would pluck out the
heart of the mystery – on paper. But unfortunately the Ardlamont
mystery is fact and not fiction, and in real life detectives are not so
phenomenally acute, nor circumstances so accommodating, as Dr
Conan Doyle loves to paint them.'

Little did the author of those words know that the men who
represented the living embodiment of Holmes were already poised
to enter the fray.

8

The Third Man

'The cunning dog has covered his tracks.'

Sherlock Holmes, 'The Adventure of the Bruce-Partington Plans'

There was much to recommend the Ardlamont affair to a public hungry for a good murder-mystery – not least the tragic victim and a mode of death that fascinated not only for its gruesomeness but also for its rarity. Even Littlejohn, witness to so much of the most serious crime that Scotland saw in the second half of the nineteenth century, could recall just two cases of homicide involving shotguns. Then there was the frisson created by the prestigious bloodlines of both the victim and his alleged killer. That the Hambroughs carried the taint of impecuniosity only served to further spark the popular imagination. Even the setting – a remote estate in one of the most beautiful corners of Scotland – added to the mystique. To newspaper editors, the heady cocktail of tragedy and melodrama made it seem like the story that had everything. But it was also a saga that kept on giving.

One particular twist turned an intriguing case into a full-blown sensation – the disappearance of the man who was presumed to hold the key to the truth, the enigmatic Mr Scott. After it became clear to the Procurator-Fiscal that there were rather more questions surrounding Cecil's death than first believed, all attempts to track down Scott ran into dead end after dead end. The authorities were fatally hindered by the fact that no one seemed to have the slightest idea about his real identity. Mr Scott, who drifted on to the scene at Ardlamont two days before Cecil's death and exited stage left a few hours after it, had apparently disappeared without trace.

So, just who was he? According to Monson, he was an engineer employed to inspect the boilers of the yacht, *Alert*, that Cecil was hoping to buy. Moreover, Monson claimed to know nothing of his background, since it had been Cecil who had hired him. In a statement to the police on 27 August, Monson furnished only these scant details: 'I am informed that Edward Scott started business as an engineer in Glasgow, and that he failed; that he was afterwards working in connection with yachts; and that he was well known in Greenock.' To Mr M'Lean of the Mutual Life, he suggested that the engineer actually came from Stockton-on-Tees.

Nor were the staff at Ardlamont able to shed much more light. James Wright, the butler, noted that there was 'nothing unusual' about him and that he was unable to hazard a guess as to his line of work. 'He might have been anything,' Wright said. Edith Hiron, the governess, was meanwhile unconvinced of his pedigree – 'I should not have called him a gentleman,' she opined – but offered little in the way of solid intelligence.

The last positive sighting of Scott during the investigation into Cecil's death was on the pier at Tighnabruaich on the afternoon of 10 August. Hugh Carmichael, the groom, had taken him there after Dr Macmillan had suggested there was no need for him to stay at Ardlamont. Yet even at the time, Constable M'Calman of the Argyllshire police force was uneasy to see a key witness leave so precipitously. M'Calman happened to be at the pier when Scott arrived and asked him to stay until the enquiry was complete but Scott said he could not wait, instead assuring the policeman that he could be contacted at Glasgow's Central Station Hotel. M'Calman suggested several times that he ought not to go but made no effort to physically restrain him, so that when his steamer docked Scott was able to board it unhindered.

In response to Major Hambrough's questions about the 'third man' who had been present at his son's death, Monson told him that the engineer had returned to Glasgow because he had been too affected by events to remain at Ardlamont. He even suggested that the Major and his wife might call on him on their way back to England, which they duly tried to do on the evening of Monday 14 August. However, none of their interviews with various hotel staff in Glasgow provided further information about Scott or his whereabouts. He most certainly was no longer at the hotel he had left as his forwarding address, if he had ever been there at all.

When the Procurator-Fiscal met with Monson the following week, Monson told him that he did not know Scott's address, had had no communication with him since he had left Ardlamont, and that he knew nothing of him except a few details furnished by Cecil. In his letter to the Fiscal after their frosty meeting at the hotel in Tighnabruaich, Monson also claimed to have made efforts to trace the engineer but so far without success. He had nonetheless instructed his lawyers to persevere with the search, he said.

It was not until the end of August that the police intensified their own efforts to track him down. James Fraser, chief constable of Argyllshire, took on the challenge around 28 or 29 August but, based on the evidence available to him, he confined his search to the relatively localized area of Greenock, Gourock, Glasgow and Paisley. His efforts yielded precious little. The disappearance, naturally, played badly for Monson but it was possible to make a reasonable case for Scott's flight. With Cecil dead, he would surely have presumed there was to be no purchase of the vessel that he was ostensibly there to inspect. Furthermore, he may well have been distressed by events and uncomfortable impinging on his hosts any longer than necessary, especially since Dr Macmillan had given his blessing to the departure. Yet to provide an address for a hotel rather than his permanent residence and then to go to ground, as it seemed he had done, was suspicious to say the least. If there was nothing to hide, the authorities were justifiably left to ponder, then why hide at all. Moreover, any defence would only work if Scott really was an engineer as claimed.

At the beginning of September, it was decided by the local police to seek the assistance of Scotland Yard. Inspector Thomas Greet was put in charge of the investigation in London, where he was assisted by Sergeant Thomas Brockwell. Greet would rise to greater public prominence a couple of years later when, in 1895, he arrested the Marquis of Queensberry in relation to the libelling of Oscar Wilde. With Wilde having taken the aristocrat's son, Alfred Lord Douglas, as his lover, the Marquis left a calling card for Wilde at the Albemarle Club in London in which he notoriously described him as 'posing as a Somdomite [sic]'. Greet was called upon to give evidence to the Old Bailey about the arrest of Queensberry at Carter's Hotel on Albemarle Street, so binding the policeman into the story of the sorry demise of Oscar Wilde.

Although it was this case that brought him most attention, he was already a highly respected officer by the time the Argyllshire police called upon his services. Even Bell, whose attitude to the police was memorably equivocal, acknowledged his abilities. 'I ought to say that I believe there are several very fine police officers in this country,' he said in an interview with the *Pall Mall Gazette*. 'I met Inspector Greet, of London, for instance … and I must say he struck me as being a very smart officer.' Yet for all his abilities, Greet faced a tough task in finding a character as elusive as Scott. Around 2 September, Greet and Brockwell met with the Procurator-Fiscal and his deputy, along with Dr Macmillan, Major Hambrough and Dr Hambleton at the Hotel Metropole, on the corner of Northumberland Avenue and Whitehall Place in London. There they received a description of Scott, a man of thin build but broad shoulders, a pale complexion, steely grey eyes, a long thin face with high cheekbones, dark wavy hair and a moustache (which may or may not have been shaved off by then). Within a few days, the police had their first serious lead. There was a man who went by the name of Edward Sweeney who fitted the description of Scott in its chief respects. Furthermore, there was rumour that he had sometimes adopted the name Scott in his business dealings.

Edward Sweeney, it turned out, was not averse to assuming multiple identities. In his day-to-day business as clerk to the bookmaker Sidney Russell, he was commonly known as Edward Davis (and sometimes 'Long Ted'). He would regularly receive post to that name at 35 Sutherland Street in Pimlico, where he resided with his mother and father. However, when Brockwell went to the house, Sweeney was not there, and none of his associates could – or at least, would – provide any information as to his whereabouts. His brother, George, a hall porter at the Westminster Palace Hotel, was particularly vague. He said that he had last seen his older brother in the middle of September, when Edward was very unwell – he suffered badly with asthma – and planning to go to Bournemouth. He hoped the coastal air would improve his health, George explained. He also speculated that Edward had probably then decided to board a ship to Australia, since he had previously undertaken a similar voyage for the benefit of his asthma. However, there had apparently been no word to confirm whether he was indeed at sea.

The Sweeney family's claims to honesty appeared fragile to say the least. Edward's choice to adopt at least one pseudonym hardly inspired confidence in his probity and it turned out that he was not alone in assuming aliases. As recently as August, George had been introduced to an Eton tailor as George Hunt, for reasons that were never entirely clear. Nor was he keen to make the job of the police any easier than it need be. When they had first called for him at the Westminster Palace Hotel, George refused to expand on the details of a trip he had made to Scotland in August, including whether it had been intended that he should travel with Edward. Nor did he tell them where his mother and father went after leaving their Pimlico address on 12 October. 'The police asked me two days after where he [father] had gone,' George Sweeney would say, 'but I did not know at that time and could not tell them. I was not asked again. Afterwards, I was going home to my father's new address every evening, so that if the police had wanted to find out they could easily have followed me to the new address.'

Yet on one point he was firm with the police – Edward Sweeney alias Edward Davis could in no way be responsible for the death of Cecil Hambrough. 'He was a very gentle, kind, young fellow,' the younger brother insisted. 'I do not believe he could hurt anyone if he tried.' The police, though, remained convinced that they had identified their mystery man even if they could not locate him. His description was circulated to Metropolitan Police stations in September but yielded no results, so a public appeal followed in November. The original description was now supplemented by some additional details: 'suffers from asthma, has a habit of putting his right hand to his side when coughing; in delicate health; dresses well, and generally wears a low, hard felt hat.' But still there were no positive sightings, nor even when a £200 reward for information was offered on 1 December. Officers from Tighnabruaich joined the search in London for fully six weeks but never so much as laid eyes on their suspect. As Sergeant Brockwell would note: 'All the police methods for discovering persons wanted were resorted to, without success.'

The press, meanwhile, engaged in ferocious speculation. There was talk that he was the scion of a noble family, a man of privilege able to call upon Establishment powers to secrete him away until the horrors of Ardlamont receded from the public consciousness. Even more wildly, it was suggested that Mr Scott was in fact a woman whose mastery of disguise had propelled the police on to the ultimate wild goose chase. The truth, though, was rather more mundane. Edward Sweeney, or Edward Davis as many knew him, was indeed Mr Scott of Ardlamont, although it would be months before the facts – which were scant – started to emerge. As of December 1893, with Monson in custody, Scott still missing and preparations for the trial forging ahead, the police remained unable to convert their suspicions about Scott's identity into hard proof. Nonetheless, it came to be accepted by all the major parties involved in the case that Edward Sweeney alias Davis was almost without doubt the man who had gone hunting with Cecil and Monson on the day of the shooting.

Beyond that, Sweeney's life, and particularly his movements in the second half of 1893, were shrouded in doubt and rumour. According to some sources, he had once been employed by the Post Office and had spent time at sea before growing disillusioned with life on the waves. Someone claiming to be a former maritime colleague told a journalist from the *Sun* newspaper in December 1893 that when Sweeney was discharged from the ship upon which he had been working in October 1890, he had alluded to plans for a more lucrative life back on terra firma. 'I never saw Sweeney till May last year,' the journalist's source told him, 'when I accidentally ran against him at Piccadilly Circus. He was then quite "the toff", being well-dressed in a light grey suit, a brown bowler hat, and wearing a diamond cluster ring, a diamond pin, and a heavy gold chain. We recognized each other, and he invited me to drink … He said he was doing well, and had made £600 the year before … He was as cool and determined a card as I ever met, with enough cheek for six, very artful and insinuating, and quiet and inoffensive enough when it suited him, but a demon when roused.' The reliability of such recollections are doubtless questionable, although the story in its fundamentals was feasible.

While Scott's identity remained in doubt, Monson continued to say that he knew virtually nothing of the man and that Hambrough had been the one who had engaged him. Monson, though, was being disingenuous to say the least, since he had certainly done business with Sweeney on a number of occasions in London. In fact, in a private letter to Lord Galway, Monson's own mother claimed that two of her other sons had seen 'this man Scott' in the company of Alfred and Agnes in England. (The senior Mrs Monson, incidentally, seemed to have little time for her daughter-in-law, telling Lord Galway that she had spoken to tradesmen who had previously had dealing with Alfred's household and that they 'have a very low opinion' of Agnes.)

Several months after the trial, in a series of newspaper and book exposés, it would emerge that Monson had, after all, invited Sweeney (alias Davis alias Scott) to Ardlamont, knowing very well his business. His motive was, however, never conclusively proven. There was the suggestion that the invitation was issued in a fit of largesse (perhaps after a particularly fruitful day of betting). Alternatively, a party of Cecil's military colleagues were due to arrive at Ardlamont for the Glorious 12th – the first day of the grouse-shooting season. An on-site bookie would have been a well-received source of entertainment, not to mention a means by which Monson might relieve his guests of a portion of their pay. Or was the reason much baser – was Scott to serve as an accomplice in the murder of Cecil?

The decision to present Sweeney as Scott did little to stem the suspicions that later emerged concerning the shooting. But might there have been some sort of innocent explanation? Sweeney in due course would attempt to suggest there was. He said that Monson had first been introduced to him in May 1893 'as a young swell with plenty of money and a great liking for horse racing and betting ... one from whom I desired and hoped to benefit considerably'. He said he saw Monson perhaps half a dozen times before his trip to Ardlamont on 8 August, when he travelled on the steamer to Kames

Pier from Greenock with him. It was on this leg of the trip that he was introduced to James Donald, the man who expected to sell a yacht to Cecil – it was seemingly a chance meeting, during which Monson referred to his travelling companion simply as a 'person from the estate office'. Donald was supposed to have invited the pair to 'inspect the boilers' – apparently engineer's shorthand for taking a glass of Scotch. It was then, as Sweeney remembered it, that Monson introduced him as Mr Scott. 'Look here, old fellow,' Monson was said to have later commented, 'it will never do for me to introduce you to my wife as Ted Davis the bookmaker, so you mustn't mind if I say you are something else, for I feel sure she would make a fuss about it. Not that she herself would care; but you know some people are funny about the turf, and think anyone connected with it must be a wrong 'un.'

Sweeney was quite sanguine about it: 'It don't matter a jot to me what you call me, so long as you don't make a fool of me. You can call me Juggins or Muggins if you like, but it is no use my trying to be a toff, you know, and it's no use my saying I am a sport, for though I know as much about racing as most men that's about all I know of sport. Can't you say I've come up on business and you have asked me to stay?' So was born Scott the engineer.

Under normal circumstances, this might have been accepted as a highly credible version of events. Gambling was regarded as a real threat to the social fabric of late-Victorian Britain. While predominantly feared as an uncontrollable vice of the working classes (a vice, as one contemporary commentator put it, that played upon the 'ignorance of servants and others of the least intelligent class'), it also had a reputation for laying low the great and the good too. Squire Osbaldeston, for example, was for a while a household name not for his work as a Member of Parliament or even for his excellence at sport (he was a first-class jockey, rower and cricketer) but because he racked up gambling debts in excess of £200,000 (some £2 million in modern money). As a result, he was forced to sell his estates and died in poverty in 1866. Gambling pushed the buttons of the age's social guardians because in virtually no other walk of life were the highest and lowest classes of society brought so close together. The Gaming Act of 1845 even legislated that a wager was an unenforceable legal contract in a bid to free up the courts from the all-too-common sight of eminent figures feuding over gambling debts. By the 1890s the bookmaker was perceived as an illicit figure in society. Bookies such as Sweeney were regarded as particularly heinous, not least for their alleged role in corrupting the 'sport of kings'. It was no stretch of the imagination to think that Agnes Monson might regard him, if she were to know his true vocation, as a 'bad hat' – a swindler. But then if Monson's mother was correct and Agnes knew of Sweeney all along, that story falls apart.

According to Sweeney's account of events, given to a journalist some while after the trial had played itself out, he found the Monsons very hospitable on arriving at Ardlamont, although he remained nervous of the impending sport since he was not comfortable with a gun. Then, on the 10th, events began to overtake him. Recalling the scene in the woods, he said, 'I am not an old soldier or a doctor, and the sight of this fine young gentleman lying dead before me almost took away my sacred senses. I am told I helped lift him up, and if I was asked to, I have no doubt I assisted to the best of my ability; but if my life was staked upon my answer I could not tell you with any minuteness what did or did not happen, or what was or was not said, during the few seconds we were standing by the lifeless body of Cecil Hambrough.'

To be horrified by this close encounter with death was one thing, but why did he then choose to flee the scene? 'Because neither Mr Monson nor myself had anything to fear,' he said. 'Because I had been told by Dr Macmillan I should not be wanted; because it was the most natural and respectful thing to do under the lamentable circumstances, not to intrude myself upon my host and hostess in their awful trouble.' Thus he justified leaving Ardlamont on the afternoon of the 10th 'without concealment or undue haste'. As to why he did not give his home address to M'Calman at Tighnabruaich Pier, but instead that of a hotel in Glasgow, he simply said he was not asked for it and 'because I did not like to give cause for chatter to every busybody by revealing the truth I was so foolishly hiding – namely, my change of name and occupation; and because I did not think it was the right and proper thing to do to Mr and Mrs Monson after their kindness and hospitality to me.'

Having been back in London for a while, Sweeney would recount, he was shocked to read that Monson had fallen under suspicion for Cecil's death. It was news that he said caused his moral courage to fail: 'Charged with murder. Good God! I am no saint. I am a bookmaker but not a murderer – not quite so bad as that.' So, he chose to disappear. By his own account, he packed a few belongings and hit upon a disguise, shaving off his moustache and dressing in old and shabby clothes. He first took a train to Bradford, then on to Halifax – where he assumed the name Mr White – then to Newcastle, back to Halifax and next to Birmingham. He then decided to sail to Ireland from Holyhead but there, he claimed, he spotted a London policeman with whom he was acquainted. Sure that the police were on to him, he decided to turn tail, throwing his bag from the gangplank into the water to cause a distraction while he disappeared into the shadows. From there, if his story is to be believed, he became an itinerant jewellery salesman driving a pony and trap while living hand-to-mouth. In December 1893 he returned to Newcastle before taking a job as a painter in Carlisle. Struck down by a nasty bout of asthma, he then found his way to Bournemouth before finally coming back home to London sometime in the early months of 1894.

This was the story that Scott told to a journalist and it may be true in its entirety or in parts. However, his former landlady at Sutherland Street, Mrs Keen, came forward several years later with a different version. According to her – and on this point, chiming with Sweeney's own account – on 5 September she encountered Mrs Sweeney in the house in Pimlico crying. 'Oh, Mrs Keen,' Sweeney's mother said, 'Ted's gone away, and we shall have to give up the rooms.' They duly did so a few weeks later, although Mrs Keen struggled to believe that her mild-mannered former tenant could be mixed up with the Ardlamont affair. However, the next part of her narrative cast doubt on Sweeney's thrilling account of his flight around the country: 'there is one very interesting fact which the general public does not know and with which very few people have become acquainted,' she revealed. 'It is this – that during all the time the hue and cry was raised after Davis [Sweeney], when frantic efforts were being made to discover his whereabouts, and when not a trace of him could be discovered, he was hiding in the East End of London. He told my husband that he was in the East End all the time, and never left it.'

Whatever the truth, Sweeney's disappearance left Monson in a precarious situation as he prepared to enter the courtroom in December 1893. While Scott could not be produced by the authorities – and if they had been able to, he would surely have been expected to corroborate Monson's account of the fateful morning – the police were all but sure that they knew his real identity. To suggest that Scott and Sweeney might be two separate individuals both connected to Monson, both physically resembling each other to a remarkable degree and both disappearing at the same time but independently was a stretch too far. Monson had surely overplayed his hand by initially denying all but the barest knowledge of Scott. The overwhelming impression was that he had tried to pull the wool over the eyes of those investigating Cecil's death. And why should he do that if the pair did not somehow have a hand in his death?

Equally, why should Scott go into hiding if he was an innocent man? These would be key questions upon which a jury of Monson's contemporaries would adjudicate at his much-anticipated trial, scheduled to start two weeks before Christmas of 1893.

9

A National Sensation

'You slur over work of the utmost finesse and delicacy,
in order to dwell upon sensational details which
may excite, but cannot possibly instruct …'

Sherlock Holmes, 'The Adventure of the Abbey Grange'

From the southernmost tip of Cecil's native Isle of Wight to the
most northerly point of Scotland, there could scarcely have been
anyone in late 1893 who did not have a theory as to what had
happened in the woods at Ardlamont. For some, the fascination
would prove lethal. Take, for example, the curious case of Henry
Card, who lost his life in early September while out walking with
his local pub landlord near Lymington in the New Forest. He had,
it seemed, been attempting to prove how Cecil's injuries might
have been self-inflicted. Taking a gun, he placed it behind his back
with one hand and then pulled the trigger with his other. The
weapon happened to be loaded and the unfortunate Card blew off
the top of his skull by this demonstration. He left a widow and nine
children – yet more victims of the Ardlamont tragedy.

For Monson and those closest to him, the full extent of their
predicament became obvious from the end of August. On the 31st
of the month, Monson was taken before the Sheriff-Substitute of
Argyllshire (in effect, a local judge) and formally charged with

Cecil's murder. Under caution that anything he said may be used in evidence against him, Monson responded, 'I have to say that I am not guilty of the charge brought against me; nor was I with Mr Hambrough, or within sight of him, when the accident happened. Therefore, I cannot explain how it happened. Under the advice of my law agent, I decline to make any further declaration at present. All of which I declare to be the truth.'

He was then returned to jail in Inveraray before a transfer to Greenock Prison a week later. Such was his notoriety by then that great efforts were made to squirrel him from one jail to the other with as little fuss as possible. He was handcuffed to a plain-clothes police officer and taken to the ferry – the same one, *Lord of the Isles*, that had carried Monson and Scott on their journey to Ardlamont a month earlier and which had carried Scott away from the scene on the day of Cecil's death – prior to any other passengers. Once on board, he and his guard holed up in the captain's cabin out of sight, yet still there was a crowd to greet their arrival in Greenock later that day, and again at the jail to which he was conveyed by cab. The tension and excitement among those who hoped to catch a glimpse of the suspected killer hung heavy in the air.

Littlejohn played his part in ratcheting up the sense of drama, giving a brief interview to a journalist as he returned to Edinburgh from the Isle of Wight. What did the doctor make of it all? the pressman wanted to know. While conceding that it was far too early to deliver a fully formed opinion, Littlejohn nonetheless spoke candidly. In his personal estimation, he said, the young victim had not met his death by his own carelessness. Yet almost immediately, he seemed to backtrack, adding that there was a great deal to be said in favour of the idea that the gun may have gone off by accident. Perhaps he felt he had spoken too openly at first, but his second statement seemed strangely at odds with his first. There was nothing to suggest Cecil's gun had gone off because of a malfunction, so surely any accidental firing must to some degree have resulted from the carelessness of he who was holding it? Littlejohn went on to say that he expected the case to be fraught with difficulty in relation to the medical evidence. To anyone prepared to read even a little between the lines, it sounded like Littlejohn was confirming that Cecil's death was anything but an unfortunate tragedy. Within a few weeks, he would not hold back in making that argument but even now his attempts to temper his words were half-hearted at best.

The Monsons, meanwhile, were readying themselves for the trial as best they could. Aware of the large sums they would need to mount a robust defence, they set about using their family connections to bolster their fighting fund. Their first port of call was, naturally enough, Monson's mother, Isabella. But while she was comfortably off in the normal scheme of things, her means were far from limitless. Despite providing him with vital finances to fund his defence, she was not willing to offer her son the blank cheque he wanted. She therefore urged Monson to approach his cousin and her nephew, George Monckton-Arundell, 7th Viscount Galway, along with William Monson, 1st Viscount Oxenbridge (Monson's first cousin once removed). Both were genuinely big-hitters within late Victorian society. Galway, a former Conservative MP for the constituency of Nottinghamshire North, was a noted courtier who had become a viscount in 1876 and went on to variously serve as aide-de-camp to Queen Victoria, Edward VII and George V. Oxenbridge was, by contrast, a high-flying Liberal, who had served as MP for Reigate before entering the House of Lords in 1862. He held an assortment of posts in the governments of William Gladstone and as of 1893 was Master of the Horse, a prestigious – if largely ceremonial – role within the royal household.

At the start of September, Agnes wrote an impassioned note to Lord Galway asking for his help in persuading Isabella to loosen the purse strings. Agnes assured him that Monson was 'perfectly innocent of the charges brought against him' but Galway was nonetheless reticent to commit himself to the cause, telling Agnes that she overestimated the influence he had over Isabella and detailing his reluctance to intervene over the head of his aunt's own legal advisors. Quite what he made of finding himself caught up in such an undignified scandal is uncertain but there was a distinct tone of detachment as he offered Agnes little more than platitudes. 'I need hardly say how shocked and horrified I am at the terrible position in which your husband has been placed,' he wrote, 'and I can assure you that we all feel most acutely for you in this most terrible and trying time and sincerely trust that in a very short time his innocence will be conclusively demonstrated.'

Isabella was herself in regular correspondence with Galway at this time, briefing him on developments and sharing a little of the turmoil that she felt. The sudden drain on her income concerned her deeply, and she wrote to him on 20 September that she had been forced to make a payment of £800 or risk Monson's lawyers walking out on the case. She believed she had no option but to keep finding the money since 'I feel it is a matter of life and death. People shall never say his mother left him undefended so the worst happened ... I feel it is my duty.' In the meantime, Galway made independent efforts to gauge which way the wind was blowing in relation to the case. He called upon his friend, Sir Digby Wentworth Bayard Willoughby, 9th Baron Middleton – a man of significant power and influence in Yorkshire – to sound out attitudes to the Monsons in the county where they had until recently lived. 'My dear George,' Middleton wrote on 10 September, 'I have been trying to pick up what I can since I saw you about your Monson's case, and find that opinions are divided. Of course, some think there is a very strong case against him and others that it looks so fishy that that man Scott has bolted ... I do so feel for the mother and you, and other relations.' The truth was, no one had a clear idea which way the trial was likely to go.

In the middle of September, Major Hambrough decided to leave Glasgow and return to London with his wife amid concerns that events in Scotland were taking their toll on her health. Agnes Monson, on the other hand, resolutely remained on the scene, staying at Ardlamont and at the Western Temperance Hotel in Greenock even as her movements were tracked by an eager press corps. On 18 September, for instance, it was reported by an eyewitness who had seen her on the steamer taking her back to Tighnabruaich from visiting Monson in Greenock, that she was 'bearing her trials with a fine show of pluckiness'. She was alleged to have spent the entire journey walking up and down the deck, chatting with officers and fellow passengers. Happy to discuss her husband's predicament, she told her audience that he was bravely keeping up his spirits. 'No gentleman who knew my husband,' she told one man, 'would believe for a moment that he committed the crimes with which he is charged, because he is utterly incapable of doing such a thing.' She was also said to have remarked that Cecil was notoriously careless with his gun.

Agnes became a figure of intense fascination, not least because she was something of an enigma. Her habit of appearing in public wearing a thick veil that obscured her features created the sense that she was somehow unknowable (much to the chagrin of newspaper editors wanting a sketch or even a photograph of her). With her brunette curls, pale complexion and dark eyes, she was most commonly described as 'prepossessing'. Whenever she was mentioned in the papers, there was an accompanying subtext of sexual allure – Agnes as the loyal beauty to Monson the maybe-murderer.

It was a narrative that served well the purpose of editors intent on hooking their readers into what promised to be a long-running saga full of twists and turns. Nor were the papers, needless to say, shy of engaging in extravagant speculation. Rumour and tittle-tattle were routinely regurgitated, with only the merest nod to journalistic integrity. 'For a day or two past ... local gossip has been busy,' reported the *Aberdeen Weekly Journal* of 19 September 1893, 'with certain relations of a rather peculiar nature supposed to have existed between the late Lieutenant Hambrough and the Monson family.' What could this gossip relate to? It scarcely mattered – the reader was free to let their imagination run riot. Only now did the newspaper feel the need to insert a significant caveat: 'About these alleged relations strange rumours are in circulation, which, however, cannot be traced to any trustworthy source.'

Among other unfounded or unprovable suggestions was the claim that a brother of Monson had been residing in Bedlam – London's notorious psychiatric institution – since the early part of the year suffering from religious mania (there was no mention of the admission of a Monson in the hospital's registers for that year). Another story claimed that Cecil's shooting had been witnessed by a poacher unseen by either Monson or Scott. It was said that this new man had been collecting grouse to sell at market on the Glorious Twelfth and was hidden among brushwood as the three principal players in the drama entered the wood. He had kept his silence for several days, so the report went, fearing bringing trouble upon himself for his poaching activities. A few days later, a follow-up piece told how the police did not believe reports of this pivotal key witness to be credible.

Surely the most impressive climbdown – the sort to give an editor palpitations – belonged to the *Aberdeen Weekly Journal*, which on 15 September published the following general retraction:

> We are informed that there is no foundation for the statement made yesterday by a Dunoon correspondent that Major Hambrough was for some time tenant in the Craighlaw shootings in Wigtownshire. [The newspaper had reported the previous day that 'It was while residing here [near

Wigtownshire] some six years ago that Major Hambrough's groom accidentally shot the nurse while pointing a gun at her in fun, never dreaming that it was loaded.'] In other respects the report sent from Dunoon appears to be entirely wrong. One of the passages it contained was as follows: 'It was about the time of Major Hambrough's bankruptcy that his father willed this money to his grandson, who some time previous had gone in for army tuition under Mr Monson, and out of consideration for the difficulties into which Major Hambrough had been launched through his financial affairs, the old gentleman appointed Monson, in whom he is said to have reposed unfailing confidences, as guardian of the young lad.' Referring to this point Major Hambrough has said to an interviewer: 'Now, my father died in 1862, and Cecil was not born till 1873, so that you see how utterly ridiculous the story is, more especially as at the time of my father's death Mr Monson must have been an infant. It was my grandfather's settlement which created the entail.' As to the reference to bankruptcy, Major Hambrough added: 'That is also untrue. My affairs were in an embarrassed condition, but I never was a bankrupt.' With regard to the statement that Major Hambrough had rented the Wigtownshire shootings [an estate suitable for shooting and hunting] up till the year 1880, the Major said: 'I never was in Scotland until I came here in connection with my son's death, consequently I never rented a shooting estate in Wigtownshire, and there never was a shooting accident. That these statements should go forth under such sad circumstances has naturally caused me much pain and annoyance.'

If the press had stuck only to reporting the solid facts of the case, there would have been more than enough to keep their columns filled

– both dramatic shifts in the main plot and intriguing sideshows. The embarrassed state of the Monsons' finances was particularly fertile ground for subplots. On 29 September, for instance, it was reported that an earlier statement that the couple's outstanding financial obligations to local tradesmen and businesses were to be paid by their friends was not, after all, true. Instead, a number of their creditors clubbed together in order to hire an agent to initiate proceedings at the debt recovery court at Inveraray. A test case was launched against Agnes Monson by a certain Mr Durrant, a ladies' tailor from Glasgow, for payment of £18 18s in respect of monies owed for clothing supplied. In the event, the judge found for Agnes, who successfully argued that being a married woman, she was not personally liable for the debt, but that her husband was instead.

Nor was this the only secondary court action in which the Monsons became entangled. In early December, Agnes's mother, Annie Day, appeared at the Manchester Assizes to defend an action by the Lancashire and Yorkshire Reversionary Interest Company. The case pivoted on whether Mrs Day had lent her signature to a deed for a loan of £600 paid to her son-in-law back in 1890. The deed was purportedly signed by her in the presence of Cecil Hambrough, rendering her liable to repay £54 11s of interest built up on the loan. Agnes travelled from Edinburgh to testify that her mother was lying when she claimed that her signature had been forged. Monson provided a written statement to the same effect. Nonetheless, the jury found in Mrs Day's favour – an implicit acceptance that Monson had faked the signature after all. It was hardly the sort of pre-publicity that a defendant in a murder trial would welcome.

For those following the case from a distance, arguably its most fascinating aspect was the involvement of the types of people rarely to be found embroiled in murder trials. Alfred Monson cut the sort of figure more regularly featured in the society pages than the crime reports. Well-bred and good-looking fellows married to fragrant wives and employed in the education of young gentlemen simply did not go around killing in cold blood. For much of the nineteenth century, the current of academic opinion had favoured the idea that criminality – and especially criminal behaviour of the most brutal kind – was the preserve of the lowest strands of society. The propensity to act contrary to the law was widely viewed as a hereditary condition, passed from generation to generation among the intellectually and morally inferior – a view that its adherents often claimed had found scientific validity in Charles Darwin's theories of evolution and acquired characteristics.

Moreover, it was deemed by many who claimed a scientific bent that criminality manifested itself in physical attributes. In the first half of the century, this idea was encapsulated in the now debunked theory of phrenology. Based on the ideas of an Austrian physician named Franz Joseph Gall, phrenology argued that an individual's mental faculties and moral character could be discerned by studying the shape and size of the cranium (since, so the pseudoscience suggested, the brain is divided into a number of regions each related to a specific faculty, and the cranium reflects the state of development – or under development – in these various regions). Sherlock Holmes himself would flirt with phrenology. In 'The Adventure of the Blue Carbuncle', for example, he deduced the intellect of a man from his sizable hat, noting: 'It is a question of cubic capacity – a man with so large a brain must have something in it.'

Developing the ideas of the phrenologists, Cesare Lombroso – an Italian army doctor – established himself as the virtual inventor of modern criminology as he attempted to determine what he believed were the tell-tale signals of a criminal disposition. To this end, he undertook a vast number of physical examinations of those locked up in prisons and lunatic asylums, along with willing 'ordinary, law-abiding' subjects. In 1876, he published his landmark *Criminal Man*, which claimed to catalogue the 'tells' of criminals of varying type

– the murderer, for instance, was often perceived to have a large, hawk-like nose and a cold stare (surely a worry for the avian Joe Bell). To the modern mind, such wild, sweeping observations are horribly problematic, but to the Victorian psyche intent on imposing order on all aspects of life, they were highly attractive. Some notes Lombroso made on the post-mortem examination of the skull of a convicted criminal are indicative of his approach: 'At the sight of the skull, I seemed to see all of a sudden, lighted up as a vast plain under a flaming sky, the problem of the nature of the criminal – an atavistic being who reproduces his person in the ferocious instincts of primitive humanity and the inferior animals.'

To establish the criminal type by physical examination offered the opportunity, theoretically at least, to identify and eliminate threats to the social order. By claiming to harness science and use it for the betterment of society at large, criminology represented the realization of the highest Victorian ideals. Just as the Western mind justified empire as a means of 'civilizing' the non-European world, so Lombroso and his ilk gave those same Western societies the belief that they could rid themselves of their own uncivilized aspects. It was comforting to think of criminality not as the result of some fundamental social dysfunction – poverty, deprivation, inequality – but as an inherited character trait to be found among the weakest, poorest and least-educated parts of society. A trait that may ultimately perhaps even be bred out of society. As the esteemed medical journal the *Lancet* put it in an article of 1873:

If among any body of the community hereditary trans-
mission of physical and moral attributes is conspicuous,
it is among the population which fill our gaols. Look at its
general physique. Imperfect cranial development, with its
concomitant of feeble cerebration, amounting almost to a
retrogression in the direction of the brutes, is apparent in

(Left) Cecil Hambrough in life: the model of Victorian sophistication and breeding.

(Top right) Steephill Castle, Ventnor – the inheritance that wasn't to be. Cecil was only six months way from achieving the age of majority.

(Below) Ardlamont House, where Cecil eventually ended up instead, provided the backdrop for his undoing.

(Left) The scene of the boating accident of 9 August, the night before the hunting trip.

(Below) The boat used on the splash-fishing outing, showing the part cut out for production in court, which contained the plughole.

(Above) The three men who set out on that infamous hunting excursion on the morning of 10 August 1893: (l–r) Alfred Monson, Cecil Hambrough and Edward Scott. Only two would return.

(Right) The gateway of the field that James Dunn saw the shooting party cross prior to the fateful shot.

(Left) Illustration of the spot where Cecil Hambrough's body was found, showing the ditch and grassy surroundings.

(Bottom) The Royal Hotel, Tighnabruaich, outside of which Monson was arrested on 29 August.

MURDER

WANTED,

On a Sheriff's warrant, for being concerned in the Alleged Murder of WINDSOR DUDLEY CECIL HAMBROUGH, at Ardlamont, Argyllshire, on the 10th August, 1893,

EDWARD SWEENEY

Alias EDWARD DAVIS, alias EDWARD SCOTT,

Known in Racing Circles as

"TED DAVIS" or "LONG TED."

DESCRIPTION.

Age about 30; height about 5 feet 10 inches, thin build, broad shoulders; complexion pale, inclined to be sallow; eyes, full, steel grey, high cheek bones, long thin face, sharp chin, dark wavy hair, brown moustache (may be shaven off); carries his shoulders well back, head slightly forward, suffers from asthma, has a habit of putting his right hand to his side when coughing, in delicate health; dresses well, and generally wears a low hard felt hat.

Is a Bookmaker or Bookmaker's Clerk, and recently resided in Sutherland Street, Pimlico, London.

Information to JAMES FRASER, Chief Constable, Lochgilphead, Argyllshire, Scotland, or at any Police Station.

(Signed)   **JAMES FRASER,**
Chief Constable,
Lochgilphead.

Constabulary Office,
Lochgilphead,
November 6th, 1893.

T. PETTITT & Co., Printers, 23, Frith Street, Soho, London.

In the wake of Cecil's death, the man known as Edward Scott disappeared. A warrant for his arrest was issued as all leads on his whereabouts proved fruitless. Meanwhile, the two men likely to have inspired Arthur Conan Doyle to create Sherlock Holmes were brought in to investigate a mystery worthy of the Great Detective: Joseph Bell, bottom left, and Henry Littlejohn, bottom right.

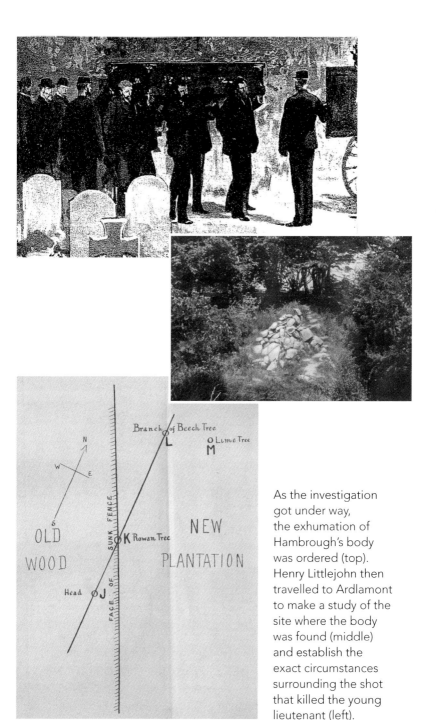

As the investigation got under way, the exhumation of Hambrough's body was ordered (top). Henry Littlejohn then travelled to Ardlamont to make a study of the site where the body was found (middle) and establish the exact circumstances surrounding the shot that killed the young lieutenant (left).

THE ILLUSTRATED POLICE NEWS.
LAW COURTS AND WEEKLY RECORD.

No. 1,537.   (REGISTERED FOR CIRCULATION IN THE UNITED KINGDOM AND ABROAD.)   SATURDAY, DECEMBER 16 1893.   Price One Pe

THE ARDLAMONT SHOOTING CASE

GREENOCK PRISON WHERE MONSON IS CONFINED.

MONSON RESCUING LIEUT: HAMBROUGH.

SCOTT FOR WHOM £200 REWARD IS OFFERED

SPOT WHERE THE BODY OF LIEUT. HAMBROUGH WAS FOUND

ALFRED JOHN MONSON THE PRISONER

COURT-HOUSE, INVERARY.

MRS MONSON'S INTERVIE HER HUSBAND.

(Top) Once news of the death at Ardlamont broke, it became a source of intense press speculation ahead of the most talked-about trial in years.

(Above) Some of the notable figures in the courtroom: (*left to right*) Agnes Monson, the gamekeeper George Lamont and Beresford Loftus Tottenham aka 'Tot'.

(Left) Monson in court.

The key legal players, clockwise: Solicitor-General Alexander Asher, leading the prosecution; John Comrie Thomson, senior defence counsel; the Lord Justice Clerk, Lord Kinsburgh, John Hay Athole Macdonald.

The verdict in the Ardlamont trial proved just as stunning as each of the previous instalments in the case, ensuring it would go down as one of the most remarkable cases in British legal history. It was truly a mystery worthy of Sherlock Holmes.

the mass of its members. Intellectually and morally, they are imbeciles, intelligence being replaced by cunning and the will reduced to its elementary form of desire.

That Monson did not fit the emerging stereotype of the lumbering, intellectually subnormal fiend provided spectators with another intriguing strand to the case. Meanwhile, Arthur Conan Doyle was playing with the notion of the atavistic degenerate blessed with great intellect in his story that first appeared just as Monson was about to stand trial – 'The Final Problem'. In it, Holmes ruminates on the nature of Professor Moriarty, his greatest foe: 'But the man had hereditary tendencies of the most diabolical kind. A criminal strain ran in his blood, which, instead of being modified, was increased and rendered infinitely more dangerous by his extraordinary mental powers.'

Amid this general acceptance that the criminal is born and not made, no wonder a figure such as Monson was so compelling. This son of a vicar and relation of powerful aristocrats who inhabited Parliament and the royal household – could it really be that his bad blood flowed through them, too? There is something delicious in finding out that those who seem to be your betters are in fact as flawed – if not more so – than yourself. The possibility that a scion of the social elite might be a common killer after a quick buck doubtless appealed to the iconoclast in every person who picked up a newspaper and read the latest details of the Ardlamont mystery in that autumn and winter of 1893.

There had been several juicy scandals involving the well-to-do and privileged in the relatively recent past. In 1891, for example, there was the Tranby Croft affair when Edward, Prince of Wales, was compelled to appear at court in a slander trial instigated by his friend, Sir William Gordon-Cumming. The episode began at a house party at Tranby Croft, the Yorkshire home of Arthur Wilson of the wealthy Wilson shipping family. He accused Gordon-Cumming, Edward's close friend, of cheating at baccarat – a serious slur upon his character. The Prince intervened and a deal seemed to have been reached whereby Gordon-Cumming agreed not to play cards again in return for the silence of Wilson and his guests. However, after word of his gaming indiscretions slipped out, Gordon-Cumming decided to sue for slander. He was, rather predictably, unable to prove his case and left with his reputation in tatters. The Prince, meanwhile, found his popularity in the country at large at an all-time low – the great British public gleefully seized their opportunity to, in the words of the *Yorkshire Gazette* of 13 June 1891, 'moralise upon … the iniquities of the higher strata of society'.

Nor was this the first time the Prince of Wales had found himself uncomfortably drawn into a notorious legal case. Back in 1870, he was subpoenaed and forced to deny any 'improper familiarity' with Lady Harriet Mordaunt during divorce proceedings brought by her husband, the Conservative Member of Parliament, Sir Charles Mordaunt. Amid the closing of ranks to protect the Prince, Lady Mordaunt was deemed to be of unfit mind to be able to instruct a solicitor properly – whether fairly or not remains a question much disputed. Sir Charles's petition was duly dismissed and his wife consigned to an asylum, while the Prince's good name was ostensibly preserved – although the whole episode proved a sensation within the many layers of British society.

There was also a royal tie-in to the Cleveland Street scandal of 1889, when assorted eminent members of high society – including, rumour had it, the Prince of Wales's son, Prince Albert Victor – were named as clients by male prostitutes working at a London brothel raided by the police. Albert Victor's name was kept out of the British, although not the international, press, but the affair became notorious for suspicions that powerful figures had effectively shut down the investigation into the brothel and its clientele. Nonetheless, the case once again represented an opportunity for the popular press and its readership to put their supposed social superiors under the microscope. Across the newspapers, homosexuality was characterized as a vice of the upper classes, while the young men who worked as prostitutes were depicted as innocents corrupted by men who ought to have known better.

Such was the public appetite to call the social elite to some kind of account. And while the Ardlamont mystery may have lacked quite so direct an association with the very highest echelons as these other scandals of recent vintage, it did boast the additional frisson of being concerned with that most dramatic and terrible of all crimes. To some extent, though, Monson was cocooned from the worst excesses of the media scrutiny as he dwelt in his cells – firstly at Inveraray, then Greenock and finally in Edinburgh. Indeed, it might even be considered a mercy that his demand to be supplied with an array of daily newspapers was rejected in favour of allowing him just one each day.

Not that Monson could have too many complaints about his pre-trial treatment in the prison system, especially when compared to the traumas experienced by many lower-profile prisoners accused of far less serious misdemeanours. Monson had been transferred from Greenock to Calton Jail in Edinburgh, where he would remain until his trial began the following month. The prison, a bleak castellated edifice built on the rocky inclines of Calton Hill, had earned a fearsome reputation since opening in 1817. It was known for its harsh discipline and squalid conditions, as well as acute overcrowding – unusually, the prison often had a larger population of women than men. Many of the female inmates were charged with relatively minor offences, typically related to drunkenness and prostitution, but lacked the financial wherewithal to pay the fines that would have kept them out of the cells. Often they were brought into the dank belly of the prison along with their unsuspecting children. In the words of Willie Gallacher, the trade-union activist who spent a period in Calton after being charged with sedition in the First World War, 'It was by far the worst prison in Scotland; cold, silent and repellent.'

Monson, however, was destined to see the best of the place. His transfer was conducted in the utmost secrecy, so that he was squirrelled out of Edinburgh's Haymarket Station into an awaiting cab and then into the prison in the company of the Governor – a Mr Napier – plus a warder in plain clothes. He was next led to his cell, a relatively large one that sat at the top of one of the blocks and boasted a table, armchair and fireplace as well as a window high up in the wall to provide natural light. The idea was that he should be kept apart from the mainstream of the prison population as much as possible. In addition, he was assigned another smaller cell with an open iron grating where he could go for fresh air and exercise under the supervision of a warder. Arrangements were also made that he should receive his meals (including a pint of beer) from one of the local hotels, and Agnes was allowed to see him for a full two hours each week. Monson was receiving a level of treatment of which most of the other inmates could only dare dream.

Yet if he was starting to feel something akin to comfortable in his Calton Jail surroundings, the judicial system had other ideas. At the end of October, he was told he was to be charged with a fresh crime – the attempted murder of Cecil, prior to the actual murder for which he was already being held. A month later, just a couple of weeks before his trial was due to start, he was smuggled out of prison and taken to the High Court of Justiciary at ten o'clock on a Saturday night to make his plea in relation to the new charge. Agnes was also in attendance, although no communication between husband and wife was possible. Dressed in a blue serge suit and dark overcoat, he looked remarkably well as he awaited the arrival of Sheriff Blair in the courtroom, using the time to converse with his counsel. When the Sheriff appeared, he read out an indictment accusing Monson and Scott of jointly attempting to murder Cecil Hambrough by means of drowning. Monson, the charge stated, had seen to it that a hole was bored into the side of the boat that he and Cecil had taken out on their fishing trip the night before the shooting. While the boat was in deep water in Ardlamont Bay, it continued, Monson had ensured the removal of the plug from this hole so that Cecil would be thrown into the sea. In a firm voice, Monson pleaded not guilty.

That a charge of attempted murder had been added to the existing charge of murder so late in the day caught Monson off guard. To the press already salivating at the prospect of the dramas to come, it offered a tantalizing new twist, yet more intrigue to rake over and dissect. It also represented something of a legal curiosity – rare was it to try charges of attempted and actual murder of the same victim in a single trial. As it would turn out, bringing together evidence for both charges at once would prove as challenging to the prosecution as the defence. The sense that this was an affair out of the ordinary – a saga more like a work of fiction than a tale from real life – was growing by the day. Again and again, the spectre of Sherlock Holmes was summoned up. As the *Daily Chronicle* neatly summarized it:

> The tragedy in Scotland which has been sprung so suddenly on public attention possesses all the elements of a first-class sensation. As it is already before the Courts we express, of course, no opinion whatever upon the very serious problem which the criminal law has to solve. From the point of view, however, of the expert of what may be called the fiction of criminality – that of Mr Sherlock Holmes, for instance – the case is one of remarkable interest.

With the sage of Baker Street poised to take his final bow (for the time being at least), the stage was set for the most sensational capital case in years – a trial where fact and fiction were destined to crash and collide with exceptional regularity.

10

Two Men in a Boat

'Circumstantial evidence is a very tricky thing. It may seem
to point very straight to one thing, but if you shift your own
point of view a little, you may find it pointing in an equally
uncompromising manner to something entirely different.'

Sherlock Holmes, 'The Boscombe Valley Mystery'

The morning of Tuesday 12 December was snowy, the ground outside the Court of Justiciary cold under foot, the air promising more
storms to come. Yet the weather could not stop a large crowd from
gathering around the public entrance by nine o'clock in the morning,
each person hopeful of claiming their place in the courtroom for the
most eagerly anticipated show in town.

Competition for a seat was intense and several hundred members
of the public passed through the courtroom over the ten days that
the trial lasted. As soon as someone left their place, a new person
was ushered in to fill it, while hundreds more – even thousands,
according to some estimates – made do with merely glancing at the
scene as they passed by a window set behind the judge's chair. The
police would tell of the extraordinary lengths some went to in their
bids to gain admittance. One ruse involved men of 'all sorts and
conditions' appearing at the entrance in legal robes, although their
attempts to pass themselves off as lawyers were often thwarted by the
ragged, decaying state of their costumes.

It was noted that the larger part of the public audience throughout the fortnight was made up of women, a fact that an anonymous female reporter for the *Edinburgh News* – one of over a hundred members of the press in attendance – considered 'proof of the superior patience and perseverance of the so-called weaker sex'. For a brief period, the trial seemed to constitute the focal point of Edinburgh's social whirl. People went to see, of course, but were conscious of being seen, too. 'To the eye of another woman like myself there were some peculiar costumes amongst them,' wrote that Edinburgh correspondent. 'Just imagine a person with red hair wearing a dress of bright blue beneath a cloak of equally vivid red. It was too impressionist for my sensibilities. Then, again, the display of jewellery was something gorgeous. Scarcely a fair arm that leaned upon the front of the gallery or was visible in the seats below that did not scintillate with a mass of such portable property ...'

Yet it was the drama played out daily upon the floor of the courtroom that really captured the imagination. The action of the law courts has been regularly likened over the centuries to that of the theatre, but rarely had the echoes of the stage been more pronounced. As the lady from the *Edinburgh News*, extraordinarily eloquent in relating her impressions of the trial, memorably put it:

> I have never, in any novel or play, seen depicted such an astonishing variety of characters, or been perplexed by a plot so intricate as in the story which has been presented to us during the past fortnight ... But the variety of the characters that appeared in the witness-box was to me in some respects the most interesting phase of the case, including as they did country clowns, polished men of business, scientific and medical experts, officials, pawnbrokers and representatives of certain fascinating phases of London life.

The presiding judge was the Lord Justice Clerk, Lord Kingsburgh (John Hay Athole Macdonald). He was a figure held in generally high regard in the profession, seen as a man of integrity after a long career as both defence counsel and then public prosecutor before his appointment as Lord Justice Clerk five years earlier. He was also known as something of an authority on firearms – a significant attribute given the nature of the case before him. Leading the prosecution, meanwhile, was the Solicitor-General (the second most senior prosecutor in the land), Alexander Asher. He was a lawyer more known for being strong and steady than sparky and spectacular, more composed and dignified than charismatic. But, aware that all eyes were now upon him, he showed remarkable energy as he explicated the prosecution's sprawling and complex evidence, proving himself arguably Scotland's finest legal technician then at work. He was also an imposing physical presence, the *Aberdeen Weekly Journal* noting his 'massive, leonine head, broad of brow and square of jaw' and describing him as 'a man as lucid in resumé as relentless in logic, sitting calmly arranging his papers and making notes'. Against him and leading the defence was the flamboyantly brilliant orator, John Comrie Thomson, who was able to captivate a jury unlike anyone else at the Bar, even if he was perhaps less technically gifted in matters of the law than his opposite number. Comrie Thomson exuded friendly warmth, where Asher sometimes appeared aloof and austere in a way that could unsettle jurors.

Edinburgh had something of a dual personality in the nineteenth century, being at once a great metropolis but with the feel of a village ruled by a small clique of elders. So it was that the Ardlamont case threw up a vast number of interconnections between those professional movers-and-shakers drawn into it. One prominent example was the long-standing friendship that existed between Asher and Lord Kingsburgh. At the start of their careers, both had been members of the Speculative Society, a prestigious public speaking and literary society dominated by Edinburgh University alumni. Kingsburgh was so impressed by Asher's speech-making in those days that he set about persuading him to turn away from his studies to become a solicitor in favour of qualifying to work at the Bar instead. Moreover, in 1859 it was Asher, then working in a solicitor's office, who provided Kingsburgh with his first paid work as an advocate. Both men, though, were unrelentingly professional and there would be not the merest hint of undue favour shown by judge to prosecutor for the duration of the Ardlamont trial.

The formal proceedings got underway on 12 December when Kingsburgh entered the courtroom, bowed to the Bar and took his seat. A hush descended as the macers – responsible for keeping order – lifted the trapdoor from which Monson appeared. Looking well-groomed and dashing – he wore a black melton overcoat with velvet collar, along with kid gloves – Monson nimbly ascended the step up to the dock where he sat between two police officers. A few observers detected a glint of nervousness in his eyes, a certain pallor to his cheeks, a degree of uneasiness in his breathing and agitation in the way he held a roll of papers. He was destined to be a largely silent figure in proceedings, the Scottish rules of evidence precluding him from speaking in his own defence. Nonetheless, over the days that followed he was regularly seen in dialogue with his counsel, sharing the odd joke with his custodians and raising a smile when he deemed the evidence either amusing or risible. He also took copious notes, which he used as the basis for further discussion with his legal team. It was even alleged that he sent a note from the dock to one of the newspaper artists present, a woman called Mary Cameron, asking her to tea in his cell during the afternoon adjournment one day. She discreetly turned down his offer.

Agnes Monson, meanwhile, sat at the back of the court, largely keeping her own counsel and rarely removing the heavy veil from her face. Occasionally, she was accompanied by a gentleman companion, presumed to be one of her husband's brothers. On that first morning, she watched on as several procedural formalities were played out. Among them was the unanswered summoning of 'Edward Sweeney, *alias* Davis, *alias* Scott', who faced the same charges as Monson. When he failed to appear, the unusual step was taken of declaring a sentence of outlawry against him. This effectively stripped Scott of his legal rights while he refused the call of the Scottish court to answer the charges laid against him. That Scott was not now merely a missing suspect but a fully fledged outlaw only added to the sense of melodrama.

Next, Monson was called upon to reconfirm his plea of innocence, and then the jury were sworn in – a band of fifteen men comprising two bakers, two farmers, two grocers, two commercial travellers, a builder, a draper, a provisions merchant, a coal merchant, a plumber, an architect and one man of unspecified profession. In accordance with the Scottish system, there were no opening statements by either side. Instead, the jury was thrust headfirst into a mass of evidence that moved from complicated financial analysis to cutting-edge forensics to eyewitness recollections, often with little clear delineation. There were almost a hundred witnesses called by prosecution and defence combined, along with several hundred items and documents entered into evidence. The effect was at times overwhelming, not only for the jurors but also for the court officials and those watching on. There was a feeling that the advocates were mining all of their vast expertise just to keep on top of this spluttering volcano of evidence. An already complex case of murder was made more unwieldy by the addition of that charge of attempted murder, which ought to have been separated out and heard on its own merits.

The prosecution's case in relation to the attempted murder charge was highly circumstantial. Donald M'Kellar, a boat-hirer from Tighnabruaich, had leased a rowing boat to Cecil some months before his death that had been used throughout the summer without any apparent problem. However, on 9 August, Monson and Scott approached Stewart M'Nicol, a joiner on the estate, to ask him for the loan of his boat, supposedly because M'Kellar's was in a poor state of repair. M'Nicol agreed and his boat was sailed to Ardlamont Bay before lunch. Yet that very afternoon, Monson and Scott were back in the M'Kellar boat, taking two of Monson's children on a jaunt. On their return from this trip, Scott was then observed sitting for a while longer in the boat on the shore.

When Monson (a strong swimmer) and Cecil (a non-swimmer) set out for their splash-fishing trip later that night, they had two boats from which to choose. The apparently unsafe M'Kellar boat or the newly acquired M'Nicol boat. Inexplicably, they went out in the M'Kellar boat and ended up cast into the waters. When the boat was inspected the following day, it was found that a rough plughole (a design feature in some vessels to assist, once back on dry land, draining any water that might be taken on board) had been made in the side of the boat, seemingly with a knife. It was higher up than would normally be expected, at a place where it could easily be obscured from view, by a covering board or some such. The sort of location where the plug might be discreetly removed without a passenger being aware, but still low enough to ensure the vessel started to fill, particularly amid the deluge common in splash-fishing. Had this been what Scott was up to on the beach? Was the story of a collision with a rock just that – a story?

Monson would subsequently claim that Cecil himself made the hole, although there was scant evidence to suggest that he had or that he had even discussed such an intention with any independent witness. Moreover, Monson's claims that the accident had occurred after the boat struck a rock some 200 or 300 yards from the shore was countered by the evidence of numerous sailors and fishermen with years of experience sailing the bay. To a man, they did not recognize the existence of a rock or outcrop capable of causing such damage in that vicinity. In the words of one of the Ardlamont gamekeepers, John Douglas: 'I have fished Ardlamont Bay for twenty-three or twenty-four years, and during all that time I never saw a rock in Ardlamont Bay below low-water mark ... I never saw any rock ... which would be dangerous to a boat.' The Solicitor-General suggested that Monson and Scott between them had ensured that the rough plughole was carved into the boat so that Monson could stage the entire incident, with the intention that the non-swimmer Cecil would perish while Monson either swam to safety or could be rescued by Scott in M'Nicol's newly borrowed vessel.

It was certainly a persuasive case yet hardly any more watertight than the fishing boat in question. There were no witnesses, save Monson and Scott, to the incident itself, no one who could say for sure who had carved the hole in the boat, no one to explain categorically why M'Nicol's boat had been hired and why it had not been used on the expedition. Monson's own statement on the incident gave a rather different slant on things:

> While occupied with the nets, suddenly there was a bump, and the boat tilted, and I fell over the side. At the same time the boat capsized, and for a minute or two I was entangled in the nets. Immediately on getting clear I called out for Hambrough, and then saw him sitting on the rock laughing. The boat had struck the side of this rock and tilted over, which, with the load, and piled up as it was with nets, she would easily do. Hambrough, I knew, could not swim, so I told him to wait while I swam ashore and fetched another boat which was there. The sea was a little rough, and the night was dark. The distance I had to swim would be between 200 and 300 yards. As I was working with the other boat to get her off I observed Scott ... and called out to him to run to the house and fetch a lamp, as I could not find the plug or

the plughole in the boat. The tide, I understood, was then rising, so I deemed it wiser not to wait until Scott returned, and, accordingly, pushed off the boat. I knew that, although the plug might be out, there would be time without danger to row to where Hambrough was and back … I do not know whether the plug was in the boat we first went out in; neither of us looked to see. The plughole in that boat, however, was a homely affair. Hambrough complained that it had no plughole, and that in consequence it was a bother to empty her after he had been out splash-fishing, during which a lot of water gathered, and, accordingly, he himself cut a plughole in the boat … so far from attempting on that evening to take young Hambrough's life, I consider that I saved it.

There was little in Monson's tale that pushed the bounds of credibility. Indeed, several fishermen reported seeing and hearing a furore in the water that night that in its key respects corresponded closely to Monson's account. Even his explanation for why Cecil might have carved out the plughole is convincing. Were Cecil to have not died the following day, would anyone have given much thought to this little episode from the night before? After all, nobody actually came to any real physical harm. Indeed, by the time the three men had made it back to the house and dried off, they were content to share each other's company and started drinking. Surely Cecil would not have joined in had he the slightest suspicion that his companions had meant to do him ill that night. Nor, surely, would he have accepted an invitation to go hunting the next morning if he had even a doubt about their intentions.

This was a strand of reasoning that Comrie Thomson explored very effectively. 'If the Crown theory is correct that an attempt of this kind was made by Monson to murder Hambrough,' he asked the jury, 'could Hambrough have failed to be aware of it? Is it conceivable that this lad should have been taken out into deep water, that he should have seen the plug withdrawn from the boat, that he should have found the boat sinking, and that he should have been allowed, as my learned friend said yesterday, to scramble ashore, without his suspicions being aroused – without his being absolutely certain that a nefarious attempt had been made upon his life? … That is a point which I urge you to keep in your minds. If an attempt was made to drown, it must have been seen and known by the intended victim, who next morning goes out with a gun in his hand, and with the man who made the attempt upon his life with another gun in his hand. Is that consistent with any possible theory? Does it not carry absurdity on the face of it? I say not merely that the Crown have failed to prove this attempt at murder, but that it has been absolutely disproved by the conduct of the parties interested.'

It is not difficult to see why the Crown were tempted to add the charge of attempted murder to the original indictment against Monson and Scott. There was much about the boating accident that was highly suspicious. Moreover, if the jury could be convinced that there was ill intention behind it, then the Crown was very far progressed in making the case that Monson and Scott were engaged in a pre-meditated conspiracy. It would be a short step from there to securing a conviction for the murder of Cecil, as any suggestion by the defence that the victim had succumbed to an accident would be virtually without credibility.

It was, though, an enormous gamble. If the jury did not buy the attempted murder charge, they would naturally be more sceptical of the murder charge, too. Furthermore, with the evidence regarding the boating incident nestling among that relating to the shooting, there was a chance that it would serve only to befuddle the minds of the jurors. In a case that was from the outset wide-ranging and involved, the addition of this subsidiary charge might just prove one step too far for a prosecution striving to carve out a clear case that the jury might easily follow.

It is tempting to ponder whether such thoughts entered the mind of the Solicitor-General as he strived to put forward his case. How much easier to convince on the main charge if less effort were required to make this secondary case. Even the most fervent enemies of Monson would have had to admit that the Crown's argument relied heavily on supposition. One is put in mind of the words of Sherlock Holmes in 'A Scandal in Bohemia', which had appeared in print two years earlier: 'It is a capital mistake to theorize before one has data. Insensibly one begins to twist facts to suit theories, instead of theories to suit facts.' Joe Bell had made a similar point in his interview with the *Pall Mall Gazette*, given as the trial was in progress. 'The fatal mistake which the ordinary policeman makes is this,' he had said, 'that he gets his theory first and then makes the facts fit it'. It could almost have been a coded message to the Crown's lawyers – beware of stretching your case.

Try as he might, the Solicitor-General had little in the way of data upon which to call in this strand of the trial. Which way the jury would jump was anyone's guess.

11

The Smoking Gun

'Data! data! data! I can't make bricks without clay.'
Sherlock Holmes, 'The Adventure of the Copper Beeches'

When separated out from the distraction of the attempted murder allegation, the fundamentals of the prosecution's murder case were straightforward enough. In essence, the narrative went that, after prolonged attempts to manipulate the Hambrough family's finances, Monson hit upon a scheme to kill Cecil and claim a large life insurance payout. The misrepresentation and subsequent disappearance of Scott/Sweeney was, furthermore, evidence of a murderous conspiracy.

Yet for all its seeming simplicity, it was devilishly tricky to prove beyond reasonable doubt. Monson's financial dealings in relation to Cecil and Major Hambrough certainly looked suspicious, and men had been killed for much less than the £20,000. However, without a confession from Monson or Scott, it was difficult to do more than insinuate greed as the motive. Moreover, the defence was convinced they could unpick this argument, and would in due course attempt to do just that. The absence of Scott was also a major setback for the prosecution, even as it cast further shadows on Monson's character and actions. Accepted, nothing looks so guilty as slinking off from the scene of the crime and Monson struggled to escape the taint that went with faking his associate's identity. Nonetheless, without Scott/ Sweeney to interrogate, the Solicitor-General was again left only able to suggest and insinuate. The circumstantial evidence was plentiful but a skilled defence counsel might well tear apart even the most apparently unbreakable web of circumstantial connections.

That was why the forensic evidence was set to be so vital in the case. Prove that Cecil did not die by his own hand, either intentionally or by cruel fate, and the case was all but won for the Crown – for what other suspects were there than Monson and Scott? But should any room for doubt be left, the jury would have no choice but to allow Monson to walk. Understandably, then, there was a certain charge in the air as the courtroom filled ahead of the third day of action, when Henry Littlejohn and Joseph Bell were due to take the stand. After the second day, which had seen a succession of estate staff, local residents and sundry other eyewitnesses give often inconclusive evidence, there was the feeling that this third day was to be pivotal in the proceedings. Although the courtroom was relatively small – no more than seventy or eighty feet across – its extensive panelling, array of frosted circular windows and high ceiling created the subdued lighting and the acoustic conditions that ensured those present were in the mood for some star performances.

Keen historians of the Scottish judicial system had picked up on echoes in the Ardlamont case of a trial that had been heard in the very same building some thirty-nine years earlier – that of Dr William Smith. Its outcome bolstered the idea that much now lay on the shoulders of Littlejohn and Bell as they entered the witness box. Smith had been a respected medical practitioner from the village of St Fergus in Aberdeenshire when, one morning in November 1853, the body of William McDonald, a local young farmer – and friend of Smith – was found lying in a ditch. He had been shot through the head by a bullet from a pistol that was found lying beside him. As was customary, Smith was called as the local doctor to come and certify the death, which he confirmed as having been caused by McDonald himself – either on purpose or by the gun going off accidentally in his pocket. Dr Smith then took personal responsibility for the funeral arrangements. However, it was not long before suspicion began to fall upon the doctor. It turned out that there were three life insurance policies upon McDonald, worth about £1,500 altogether, taken in Smith's name, one of which was due to expire within a week of the death. Moreover, McDonald had left his home the previous evening saying that he was going to meet up with Smith. One witness claimed to have seen a flash and heard a loud bang at half-past seven the same evening, in the direction of Smith's field close to where the body was discovered. There was other circumstantial evidence, too, not least testimony that Smith had several years earlier purchased a pistol very much like the one found by the victim, and had recently bought gunpowder.

However, all the evidence was of the circumstantial variety. Smith denied he had been set to meet McDonald the night before and, indeed, had been seen at various locations around the village that evening on his own (although his alibi was never comprehensively confirmed). He also claimed that the life insurances had been taken out at the behest of the victim's uncle and that Smith had not expected them to pay out anyway, since they were invalid in the case of suicide, which the medical evidence had been insufficient to rule out. Critically for Dr Smith, nor could the authorities say with complete certainty that a murder had even taken place. With his defence conducted eloquently by John Inglis (a future Lord President of the Court) and the judge summing up that there was too little evidence to infer the guilt of the doctor for a murder that might or might not have occurred, Smith walked free after the jury declared the peculiarly Scottish verdict of 'Not proven' (a verdict that acknowledges reasonable doubt while leaving the cloud of suspicion hanging over the defendant). A crowd outside the court hissed its disapproval as the verdict was returned. Fast forward to 1893, and it was now for Littlejohn and Bell to provide the certainty that had eluded the prosecution in the Smith case nearly four decades earlier.

The pressure was palpable on Littlejohn and Bell as they prepared to give their testimony. What thoughts ran in particular through the mind of Bell, the recently bereaved father, as he prepared to give evidence on the death of another poor, unfortunate young man?

The challenge for Littlejohn, the first of the pair to give evidence, was intellectually to remove himself from the growing excitement of the crowded courtroom and focus on presenting his evidence succinctly so as to render it comprehensible to the layman. He would write in an article about expert testimony for the *Edinburgh Medical Journal* a couple of years later:

> An intelligent reporter, indeed, shows his knowledge of his art as much by what he withholds as by what he gives in detailed description. An account of a post-mortem examination may be stated at tedious length, and to an unpractised eye appear from its bulk to be exhaustive and complete. Yet it may be overburdened with details of not the slightest consequence in determining the cause of death or the nature of the case, and the very appearances which alone could settle the question, and which were undoubtedly present, remain unnoticed. The reporter feels himself at sea, and, in his desire to mention everything, allows points of the greatest moment to escape his notice.

They are words closely echoed by Sherlock Holmes in 'The Adventure of the Naval Treaty': 'The principle difficulty lay in the fact of there being too much evidence. What was vital was overlaid and hidden by what was irrelevant.'

As the *Scotsman* reported the next day, he rose above the furore that attended his appearance with consummate professionalism: 'The calling of Dr Littlejohn as the next witness produced a buzz of excitement in Court, and the veteran doctor, without whom no great trial would be complete, stepped into the box, and having taken the oath, poured out a glass of water, and settled down to an examination which lasted well over two hours.'

The courtroom itself had started to take on the look of an eccentric shop of curiosities, a strange array of items having been accepted into evidence. Cluttered around the dock were, for example, the two guns that had been carried during Cecil's last hunting trip (brought into the courtroom covered in black crêpe of the sort then used for mourning dress), as well as the suit of clothes he had been wearing, several packets of cartridges, the side of the boat that had been taken out fishing, three plaster casts of Cecil's head and a goodly portion of a rowan tree that would be vital to contextualizing the evidence the court was about to hear. Littlejohn himself added to the scene by bringing to the witness stand a model skull for the purpose of illustrating the nature of Cecil's injuries. He produced it from his silk hat, where it had been lying along with a pair of white gloves. With his left hand tucked into his pocket, he used his right index finger to point out appropriate details as he began his testimony with a summary of his post-mortem findings – all delivered in the short, sharp sentences so familiar to the students who flooded his lectures.

By close analysis of Cecil's wound, the scene of the shooting and the various experiments subsequently undertaken in partnership with MacNaughton the gunsmith, Littlejohn set out to establish the trajectory of the fatal shot. From there, he would seek to convince the jury that the shot could not possibly have been self-administered but must have been fired by a third party some distance away. However, in order to do so, Littlejohn needed to establish certain facts that were fiercely disputed by the defence.

In terms of the nature of Cecil's wound, everyone was in broad agreement. He had died from a shot that struck the back of the head behind the right ear, part of which had been shot away. The shot was of the No. 5 type fired from the twelve-bore gun that Monson customarily carried. Most of the brain remained intact, save for that part that had been in front of where the skull had been shattered. Only four pellets were found to have entered the brain, out of a total of some 150 to 180 that would have been expected to have filled a gunshot cartridge of the type used. There was little evidence of blackening or scorching around the wound.

As to where Cecil was when he was shot, the prosecution's case relied on the acceptance that he died where he was found – on top of the dyke. This was where all the witnesses present on the day had seen the body and where they had directed the attention of the various expert witnesses as they examined the scene in the weeks after the death. Monson, however, had claimed that he and Scott/Sweeney had moved the body there from the ditch where they said Cecil actually perished. But Littlejohn refused to countenance this version. He explained that, generally speaking, gunshot wounds did not leave much blood, owing to the smashing of the arteries, but one of Cecil's veins had been lacerated so causing a 'profuse haemorrhage'. This was, he went on, why so many witnesses had described seeing the blood slowly oozing from Cecil's head. Littlejohn had examined the turf on the dyke where Cecil had lain and concluded that it perfectly corroborated the suggestion that this was where he was felled. In contrast, there was no evidence in the ditch of profuse bleeding, nor (as other witnesses had noted) any other signs that a body had lain there. Furthermore, there had been no reports that either Monson or Scott/Sweeney had been covered in the blood one might have expected after moving a man with such a wound. Two small pieces of bone were also discovered close to where Cecil had ended up on the dyke, leading Littlejohn to assert: 'If the two pieces of bone …

were found where I was told they were found, and if they belonged to the skull, then the question as to the place where the shot was fired is, in my opinion, settled; the body must have been shot at the place where it was found.'

Having thus striven to establish the spot where Cecil fell, Littlejohn turned his attention to the flight of the shotgun cartridge. In order to establish its trajectory, he had examined trees in the surrounding wood to look for evidence of shot marks. Sure enough, he detected what he described as 'certain wounds' in a rowan tree (the one that, in part, now resided in the courtroom) a short distance away from where Cecil's head had been on the ground. There were similar wounds on two more trees a little way further on, too. 'I am not an expert in shot marks on trees,' Littlejohn conceded, 'but so far as I could make out these wounds appeared to have been produced by pellets … I saw several grooves in the wood, which showed a transverse grooving, and, so far as I could make out, the line of these grooves was exactly in a line with the line of the body. I was informed that two pieces of bone had been found a little way from the head, and these were sent [to] me for examination; I found that there were three distinct metallic fragments driven, so to speak, into the tissue of the bone. I was also informed that a portion of a cartridge was found nearer the rowan tree than the body. Having seen the place where the head was lying, the rowan tree, the pieces of bone, and the wad [a small paper disc used to separate the contents of the cartridge], I formed the opinion that the shot had been fired from behind and slightly to the right side.'

The Ardlamont rowan trees reached a level of fame perhaps unrivalled in arboreal history, since they might serve either to confirm or debunk the prosecution's forensic case. Indeed, their importance was recognized early so that while they were still in situ at Ardlamont, they were given a twenty-four-hour police guard. One night, at around 2 a.m., a policeman emerged from his tent to discover someone grasping the tree that ended up in the Edinburgh courtroom. The identity of this individual and their reasons for their bout of nocturnal tree-hugging were never discovered.

Back in the courtroom, Littlejohn next dealt with the crucial question of how far the shot had travelled before it hit its victim. He directed the jury to the evidence garnered from the various MacNaughton experiments:

> We found that at any distance under three feet the injuries were dissimilar from what we found in the case of the deceased. I therefore would be inclined to place the possible distance between three feet and fifteen feet. In all the experiments we made the wounds at nine feet present the closest similarity to the injuries we found on the deceased's head. Any distance under three feet would be inconsistent with what was found on the skull; the injuries were something frightful under three feet, the head was blown to pieces. We made four experiments on the cadaver, firing to the best of our ability in the direction towards the head which the wounds on Mr Hambrough's head would lead us to expect as to the shot. From these experiments we found that whenever we got beyond four feet the injuries assumed a remarkable similarity to the injuries found on the head of the deceased; at less than four feet we found such a shattering of the head as rendered it quite unlike the comparatively limited shattering in the case of Mr Hambrough.

Nor, he observed, was there either the blackening around the wound from gunpowder or singeing of the hair that he would have expected to see if the shot had been from close range. In other words, unless Cecil had somehow miraculously fired his gun and then thrown himself about nine feet in front of it so that the shot could hit him in the back of the head, someone else pulled the trigger that led to his death. This from the mouth of the most respected forensics expert in the land was bound to carry weight. As a famous judge of the time, Lord Young, would later put it: 'There are four classes of witnesses – liars, damned liars, expert witnesses, and Sir Henry Littlejohn.' And yet, there were some serious caveats surrounding his testimony even before the defence got their teeth into it. Specifically, the doubt over where Cecil had fallen created a real sense of unease. In Littlejohn's own words: 'If it be the case that the body was lying, not on the dyke, but in the ditch, or on the ground on the other side of the ditch, that would undoubtedly neutralize all the deductions that had been drawn from the shot in the trees. My conclusions, I admit, depend very much upon whether it be true that the place pointed out to me as the place where Mr Hambrough fell was really the place where he was shot, and also upon the position of the weapon.' But for all the tension of the occasion, Littlejohn's evidence ended on a light-hearted note. As he went to leave the stand, Comrie Thomson gestured to the skull Littlejohn had not yet retrieved. 'Stay, Dr Littlejohn, stay! You have forgotten your head,' he called out. 'You are very right, sir. I can't afford to lose my head!' replied Littlejohn.

The next two witnesses were Dr Macmillan (the GP local to Ardlamont) and Dr Brown (Littlejohn's Edinburgh colleague), both of whom backed up core details of Littlejohn's testimony. Then came the turn of another Edinburgh alumni, Dr Patrick Heron Watson, who had accompanied Littlejohn and Bell at the MacNaughton experiments. The *Pall Mall Gazette* pithily reminded its readers that Bell was 'the original of Sherlock Holmes' and that, 'Readers of Dr Conan Doyle's stories will remember that there is a Dr Watson, who is the faithful associate of Holmes, and, curiously enough, there was with Dr Joseph Bell to assist in watching the experiments a genuine Dr Watson – Dr Heron Watson.'

In fact, the *Gazette* may have inadvertently stumbled upon a

Holmesian connection that went deeper than they realized. Bell and Watson had a history that stretched far back – all the way to 1865, when the young Bell served as Watson's dresser. While Bell was considered an extremely dextrous surgeon, Heron Watson had a reputation for being even quicker – it was said he could complete an amputation at the hip in under ten seconds. Despite hints of an uneasy relationship in those early years, the two became firm friends and, just as with Littlejohn, Doyle is likely to have encountered Heron Watson regularly during his tenure as Bell's assistant. Moreover, there are striking similarities between the real-life Watson's early biography and that of his fictional counterpart. Both went into the army after completing their medical studies, Heron Watson serving at the front during the Crimean War, where he was awarded several decorations before being invalided home with dysentery in 1856. Holmes's Watson, meanwhile, fought in Afghanistan before his return to London in 1881, having contracted enteric fever and been shot at the Battle of Maiwand. Consider also Heron Watson's obituary in the *British Medical Journal* in 1913, which noted his outstanding character, his calmness and dignity, his self-control and generous kindness: 'withal to those who knew and loved him best,' it concluded, 'at heart, his was an extraordinarily simple nature with intense affections'. The same words could have been used about Holmes's doughty companion. It is far from the realms of the fantastical to think that Doyle had Dr Patrick H. Watson very much in mind as he created the character of Dr John H. Watson. There is the intriguing possibility, then, that on a single day in December 1893, the High Court of Justiciary hosted not only the two men who inspired the creation of Sherlock Holmes, but also entertained the model for his great partner, too.

In his evidence, Heron Watson was if anything less equivocal than Littlejohn had been. He agreed that the shot was likely fired from somewhere between four and eleven feet from Cecil, favouring a

distance of about nine feet given the absence of any singeing and
the nature of the spread of pellets. He also concurred that the victim
likely fell on top of the dyke, rather than having been lifted there,
and that the shot had come from behind him, in a direction slightly
upwards and horizontal. 'The wound, in my opinion,' he stated, 'must
have been the result of a shot fired by the hand of another; it could
not have been fired by Mr Hambrough himself either designedly
or accidentally. My opinion is based upon the situation and the
direction of the wound.' Yet, just like Littlejohn, he had no choice
but to concede that there was margin for error. 'I will grant that to
some extent we have been in the region of conjecture in the evidence
I have led,' he conceded under cross-examination. 'I did not see the
man shot.'

At last it was the turn of Bell, who found himself going before a
jury who had already sat through several hours of complex forensic
analysis and who would also hear evidence on the validity of the life
insurance policies before the day was out. Nonetheless, there was
still an appetite for this cameo by 'the original of Sherlock Holmes'.
Back at the end of September, the *Pall Mall Gazette* had pondered:
'The correspondents who have written re the Ardlamont mystery,
suggesting that now was the time for Sherlock Holmes to show his
prowess are probably not aware that Dr Joseph Bell of Edinburgh, who
has been engaged for the prosecution, is the prototype of the British
Vidocq [the French detective and criminologist who inspired Edgar
Allan Poe and Victor Hugo].' Few in the courtroom in Edinburgh
three months later could have been unaware of his pedigree.

Although, like Littlejohn, he had an air of impressive authority,
Bell nonetheless cut a very different figure. He was just as smartly
attired as his Edinburgh colleague, and blessed with those hawkish
features and piercing eyes that seemed to be able to penetrate into the
very soul of a subject. Yet those who were not familiar with him may
have been rather disconcerted by his slightly jerky gait as he made

his way to the witness stand, and every bit as surprised by the high-pitched timbre of his voice when he began to speak. Yet to Doyle and the thousands of Edinburgh citizens who had encountered him as colleague, teacher or doctor over the years, these were characteristics that had long ago failed to warrant mention. In fact, they were the result of an episode that encapsulated Bell's overwhelming desire to act for the greater good, even at significant personal cost.

In his role as surgeon at the Royal Hospital for Sick Children in the 1860s, Bell had keenly felt the dismay of his young diphtheria patients, particularly when they would cough and choke as they struggled for breath. Intent on finding some practical means to lessen their ordeal, he came up with a technique of sucking out the thick, grey-white coating that characteristically obstructs the back of the throat in diphtheria victims. He even developed a specially adapted pipette for the purpose. It was, however, a treatment with considerable risk attached, given the highly contagious nature of the disease. Late one night in June 1864, Bell was by his own admission feeling very tired and was perhaps less meticulous than usual. This was the occasion, he was convinced, when he himself contracted diphtheria as he made his ward rounds, which in turn led to a bout of post-diptheritic paralysis resulting in his distinctive gait and vocal pitch.

Not that either idiosyncrasy in any way diminished his effectiveness as a witness. Indeed, his manner of answering questions in precise, rapidly delivered staccato sentences, and the way he seemed always ready for the next question thrown at him, made him a favourite with lawyers. In relation to the shot that killed Cecil, he was broadly in concert with the other witnesses heard that day, giving a distance of between four and nine feet between the muzzle of the weapon and victim when the gun went off. Furthermore, he agreed that the shot had come from behind, in a direction almost horizontal but slightly upwards. 'From the information given me,' he said, 'I have formed the opinion that Mr Hambrough died in consequence of a gunshot wound, and I have not been able to make out any way by which the injury could have been done either designedly or accidentally by Mr Hambrough himself ... As the result of my examination of the case, my opinion is that this wound must have been inflicted by a gun in the hand of another than the deceased.'

But just like Littlejohn and Watson before him, under cross-examination Bell was reluctantly made to acknowledge the possibility of alternative explanations – specifically, the theory that the gun had been triggered accidentally as Cecil stumbled on the rough ground. 'I have not visited the scene of the accident,' Bell said. 'If a man carrying a gun makes a bad stumble, and in falling throws the gun away from him behind, there are certainly infinite possibilities as to how he could have shot himself.' But he was determined that the jury should not be left with the impression that this was in any way a likely scenario. 'I have not been able to formulate any idea of how it could be done for myself,' he concluded.

With that, the prosecution's major block of forensic evidence – which it was hoped would remove any doubt that Cecil might have somehow been the architect of his own demise – drew to a close. There were plenty among those who had heard this succession of forensic pioneers who now considered the case all but settled. Even if one accepted that it was theoretically possible for the victim to have had a hand in his own death, here was the most famous forensic expert in the country and an esteemed band of his colleagues telling the court – after their extensive examination of all the available evidence – that Cecil Hambrough had died at the hands of another. Who were the ordinary folk of the jury to doubt their conclusions? Yet by the admission of each of the witnesses, there *was* still an element of doubt. The life-or-death question was, did it amount to reasonable doubt?

12

A Second Opinion

'A clever counsel would tear it all to rags.'

Sherlock Holmes, 'The Adventure of Silver Blaze'

Fifty-four years old, silver-haired and smooth-tongued, John Comrie Thomson, senior counsel for the defence, had a way with juries. It was widely felt that there was not a lawyer then working in Scotland who could best him at pleading out a case. He was persuasive and assertive when he needed to be, yet always showed courtesy to witnesses, even the most hostile ones. But most of all, he had an instinctive feel for what made people tick and an effortless ability to connect with ordinary folk.

He was well aware of the value of his talents, too. Rumour had it that he charged a thousand guineas per trial, which was just short of the Solicitor-General's total annual salary. Conscious that the Monson trial was a perfect showcase, he eagerly gave of his best over its ten-day duration. Central to his aim of dismantling the Crown's forensic case was Matthew Hay, Aberdeen's police surgeon and Littlejohn's potentially upstart rival. Comrie Thomson led him through his evidence with characteristic verve. Nor was it the first time that the two police surgeons had crossed scalpels in the courts. They had been on opposing sides, for example, during the 1889 trial of the Dundee wife-killer William Bury. It was their conflicting interpretations of the medical evidence that prompted the jury to make a plea for mercy on Bury's part despite finding him guilty.

And now Hay enthusiastically set about once again undermining the testimony of Littlejohn, along with that of Bell and Heron Watson. The position of the corpse, the distance and direction of the shot, the validity of the pellet marks on the surrounding trees – all were cast into doubt. Regarding the location where Cecil actually died, he spoke in support of Monson's assertion that the body was moved: 'Assuming that the body had been moved after it fell, I should not be very much surprised that the gardener and others had not observed traces of blood apart from the quantity under the head. Supposing the grass at the place was long and quite wet, and the flow of blood from the head had been gradual, I would not be surprised that blood was not very observable. The bleeding from a gunshot wound is generally slow … There is a track by the south side of the wall across the dyke from the old to the young plantation, and, of course, the grass and brackens in that track are beaten down, so that if Lieutenant Hambrough fell at that place there would be no very obvious mark of pressure on the grass or brackens … Taking the situation into account, I think it quite possible that the deceased could have been shot somewhere about the ditch, and that his body could have afterwards been transferred to the top of the dyke.'

He furthermore dismissed the presence of a bloodstained wad from the cartridge and two pieces of bone about two feet from Cecil's head where he was discovered on top of the dyke as being materially irrelevant. Instead, he argued that both the wad and the bone may have dropped from the head in the process of moving the body, or during a subsequent examination. His acceptance that Cecil's body may have been transferred to the dyke post-mortem was particularly intriguing, since Hay freely acknowledged that his own calculations regarding the flight of the shot were based on the assumption that he fell where he was found by the first witnesses Monson brought to the scene. Hay may have had little choice but to work on this assumption – he had to establish some solid terms of reference, after all – but his doubts about the location of Cecil's body, in stark contrast to Littlejohn and Bell's assuredness, doubtless compromised his evidence. Crucially, he could not, in good conscience, claim his calculations of the shot's flight path as accurate if he was undecided as to where the body had fallen – a fact that the prosecution could have done much more to highlight. Instead, on this point, he was seemingly allowed to cherry pick the arguments that most suited him.

He remained on the front foot throughout his evidence. He was, for instance, curt in his setting aside the pellet marks found in the trees. 'I formed an opinion with reference to the probable age of the pellet marks,' he said, 'that they were at least two or three months old. Certain of the pellet marks on the rowan tree and also on the lime tree showed considerable signs of vital reaction, that is, healing.' In other words, he believed the marks pre-dated Cecil's shooting. He also doubted the ability of the Crown witnesses to establish the true flight of the shot given that there was no way to be certain at what angle the shot entered Cecil's head and what resistance it met from his skull. As Comrie Thomson put it: 'You were told that there were between 200 and 300 pellets in each cartridge, and you are asked to find against this man because the marks of twelve pellets, not discovered, are found in three trees in the neighbourhood! I think it is useless to labour this part of the case further.'

Next came the critical question of the likely distance the shot flew before hitting Cecil – a lesser distance than the nine feet or so posited by the prosecution. Hay was convinced the more likely distance was between a few inches and three or four feet – and probably somewhere around two feet. Whereas the prosecution found the absence of any scorching around Cecil's wound indicative of a shot from further away, Hay argued that the shot had been fired using amberite powder rather than traditional gunpowder (a fact the prosecution did not contest), one of the features of which was the absence of scorching. Furthermore, he argued that what residue there might have been from a short-range amberite shot could have been washed away in the process of cleaning and dressing Cecil's body on the day of the shooting. The relatively smooth nature of the entry wound and the absence of any more than four pellets in Cecil's head was further evidence, he said, that the shot originated very locally. 'In my experiments,' he told the jury, 'it is shown that when you go beyond two feet or thereby the edge of the wound begins to get distinctly ragged on account of the action of the spreading shot.' As for the scarcity of pellets, he simply did not believe there could be so few since pellets characteristically start to disperse as soon as a cartridge leaves a gun, and separate with increasing rapidity beyond a distance of about two or three feet. 'As the result of these experiments,' he went on, 'I conclude that it is quite impossible for a shot to be fired from either the twenty-bore or the twelve-bore gun at a distance of nine feet without the production of numerous pellet marks, whether on a target or on the human head, and whether fired directly at the head or in an oblique direction.'

Bell had earlier attempted to deal with the lack of pellet-scatter evident in Cecil's head, saying that he believed the 'body of the shot went right through the bone *en balle*', i.e. as if it was a compact, single bullet rather than an expanding cartridge, and having struck the bone, 'four pellets appear to have entered the aperture, and the rest to have gone into space'. This assumption further suggested to Bell that the shot came from some considerable distance since if it had struck *en balle* from less than three feet, 'it would have forced the bones from within outwards, shattering them to a greater extent, and probably no bone in the head would have escaped'. Hay was unmoved, however. The absence of pellets was for him indicative of quite the reverse. 'It practically comes to this,' he said, 'that in my opinion the shot which killed the deceased was delivered within arm's length.'

Hay expanded upon his argument, suggesting that the path along the dyke upon which Cecil was said to have been walking was treacherous, with 'projecting pieces of turf, sometimes a stone from the wall beneath, and occasionally holes. Quite close to where I was told the deceased's body was found there was a distinctly large hole, almost a kind of trap to one's foot, in the ground; it was a place where a man might readily have stumbled, especially if he was not watching the ground as he walked along, if his eyes were directed to the search for game, or anything of that sort. The morning of the occurrence was a wet morning, and that would tend to his slipping on the grass if he went off the rough path of the dyke; the ground there slopes up, and the grass would be very wet … After careful examination of the skull and photographs I consider that the injury to the deceased's head was such, in respect of the position of the injury and the line of fire, that it could have been inflicted by a gun held in the deceased's own hand. There are many, almost innumerable, positions permitting of the gun being held in the deceased's own hand when the shot was fired.' He then proceeded to show a number of photographs that he and Dr W. G. W. Saunders, a professor of clinical medicine at Edinburgh, had taken to illustrate the point, for example showing how the gun might have gone off if it got caught in a thicket as Cecil was walking along. 'As a result of the whole examination,' Hay testified, 'and the consideration of this case from a medical point of view, I consider that the death of Lieutenant Hambrough was more likely to be due to an accident from the gun he was carrying than to a shot from the gun of another person.'

There was even time for some heated back-and-forth with the prosecution. The Solicitor-General, for example, cross-examined him on his assertion that the body might have been moved. 'The question is, did you see anything at the bottom of the ditch in any way to indicate that a dead body had been there?' Asher demanded of him.

'I could form no opinion,' Hay replied.

'You are not asked to form an opinion,' Asher fired back. 'Did you see anything tending to indicate that a dead body had been lying in the ditch?'

To which the witness could answer only 'No.' A little later he was pushed still further into a corner, conceding: 'I think the probability is that he was not moved after he fell; that is to say, on the assumption that there was no blood anywhere except under the head [i.e. no blood was found in the ditch].'

These confrontations were given added heat by the fact that the defence had taken the highly unusual step of refusing to allow Hay to undergo a precognition by the prosecution. At trials in Scotland it was the norm that witnesses went through a precognition, during which a witness made a factual statement that, though inadmissible in the trial itself, provided an insight into the evidence they were expecting to give. Thereby both sides could enter the courtroom fully aware of the likely battles they were each to face. The defence justified their position regarding Hay by claiming that they had not requested precognitions of the prosecution's medical experts and that since Hay had professional commitments in Edinburgh at the time he was required by the Crown, they had advised him not to submit to the request. The judge was distinctly unimpressed by the defence's stance. 'It seems to me that nothing could be more prejudicial to either side than that the advisers of one side should direct their witnesses not to be precognosced,' he said. 'I think it is a grievous mistake. I express no ruling of law on the subject at all. There is no doubt about this, that in inquiries by the Crown for criminal prosecution, not only is a witness bound to submit to precognition, but he is bound to submit to precognition upon oath, and may be imprisoned if he refuses to give his evidence, either with or without oath; and I think that the proper course for the witness was to submit to precognition.'

Yet, if the prosecution hoped that this side issue might put Hay on the back foot, there was little evidence that it did. He even found the opportunity to get in a jab or two at Littlejohn and the experiments he conducted with MacNaughton. Referring to the decision to fire shots into cadavers at the mortuary, Hay commented: 'I consider the bodies of persons dead for some time to a certain extent suitable for experiments, but they do not exhibit the exact effect of the shot fired at a living body.' In other words, the prosecutions' grimmest experiments were ultimately futile.

Littlejohn, though, gave as good as he got. Where he had favoured recreating Cecil's last moments with a human corpse, Hay and his team had opted instead for a freshly slaughtered horse. Littlejohn was unconvinced: 'We can make no conclusion from a wound on a horse's head,' he noted. '[T]here is an enormous difference between this and the wound in question … I entirely fail to draw any useful deductions from these photographs of horses' heads.' Nor was he happy with the wooden busts the defence had used to represent the human head, the proportions of which he said were 'most faulty', anatomically incorrect and made of a substance 'very different from the cranium' – Littlejohn's team had used clay-lined pasteboard to represent as closely as possible the condition of matter in the human skull.

Hay's general conclusions were well supported by the follow-up evidence of Dr Saunders of Edinburgh University. One might imagine there were some frosty faculty meetings in the Scottish capital in the weeks and months after the trial finished. Saunders was distinctly Holmesian in parts of his testimony, warning 'how careful one must be in drawing deductions in such a case' and pointing out the 'insufficient data' that blighted many parts of the evidence. What was the jury to make of it all? If they had felt their sympathies moving in one direction after the evidence of Littlejohn, Bell and Heron Watson, they had surely now been thrust back into the no-man's-land of uncertainty. Just as in the Bury case, the diametrically opposed conclusions of such eminent men of medicine could have had no other effect than to leave the jurymen utterly confused as to what to think. It brought to mind the words of Alexander Pope: 'Who shall decide when doctors disagree?'

A very good question indeed.

13

The Element of Doubt

'What you do in this world is a matter of no consequence.
The question is, what can you make people believe
that you have done?'

Sherlock Holmes, *A Study in Scarlet*

Curiously enough, testimony emerged that the defence had, at
least for a time, been in possession of the evidence that could have
conclusively proved Monson's innocence – or perhaps his guilt. Dr
Macmillan was the one who indirectly revealed the fact. 'The day
on which Mr Blair [Monson's solicitor] was at Ardlamont was the
first occasion on which I heard Monson speak about killing a rabbit
on the day of the accident. On that occasion Mr Blair and Monson
went to the wood; I was a little behind them, and overtook them
when they reached the spot where the rabbit was found.' If this was,
in fact, the same rabbit that Monson had shot, a post-mortem on the
unfortunate creature would likely have confirmed with what type of
shot it was killed and, thus, which gun Monson had been carrying
that day. If it was killed with a cartridge from the twenty-bore gun, it
would have confirmed Monson's story that Cecil was in possession
of the twelve-bore gun that killed him. If, on the other hand, it had
been killed with ammunition from the twelve-bore, things would
have looked very dark for Monson. That the carcass of the rabbit

was never entered into evidence is certainly suggestive, although hardly conclusive.

Comrie Thomson, meanwhile, ploughed the furrow of the 'accidental death' argument for all he was worth. He was aided in that enterprise by two witnesses who provided some particularly entertaining evidence. First came Tom Speedy, the estate factor and shooting agent, who gave the court the benefit of his anecdotal evidence (as well as supporting Hay's assertion that the fatal shot probably came from around two feet). 'According to my experience,' he said, 'accidents with guns happen in the most inconceivable ways. I remember the case of a gentleman who was out shooting a year or two ago, and who met with an accident. He felt himself falling and flung the gun from him.' When the Solicitor-General asked if he had been present at the event itself, Speedy confirmed that he hadn't been but that he collected 'the facts about such accidents and take an interest in them'. 'Accidents happen in the most unexplainable ways,' he went on, 'and the shot, when the gun goes off accidentally, enters the body, to my knowledge, in the most unaccountable manner by the crown of the head, the back of the neck, or the sole of the foot. The last-mentioned case was one which came under my own personal knowledge. An Edinburgh gentleman let his gun fall, both barrels went off and one of the shots went through the sole of his foot horizontally. There was another man, whom I knew, who shot himself in the palm of his hand and the shot went up his arm.' Somewhat ruefully, he added, 'I did not see him just when it happened.' The judge, meanwhile, had heard enough, his frustration clear as he stepped into proceedings: 'I do not see how these illustrations can possibly be of the least use.'

Next to the stand was the remarkable figure of George Tillard. A retired colonel of the Madras Staff Corps, he explained that his former brother-officer, one Colonel Kilgour, had persuaded him that it was his duty to come forward in the Ardlamont investigation. His moment arrived late in the trial, coming only on the afternoon of the ninth day, but it proved something of a sensation to those who heard it. 'I was twenty-eight years in India,' he explained. 'I had a gun accident in March 1871. I was just starting out for snipe shooting, and was carrying a small double-barrelled covert gun. It was at half-cock. I turned round to call my servant, who was loitering behind. As I turned round my foot slipped on some rocks I was walking over, and I fell backwards. I have no recollection of what happened after that for some minutes. My last sensation was feeling myself going backward. On coming to myself I found my servant standing at the same place where he was before, and called for him to assist me. I got back to my tent about five minutes afterwards, and found both barrels of the gun had gone off. The gunshot blew away a portion of my ear, and dug a trench in behind the ear in a horizontal direction. The shot scraped the periosteum of the skull. It was a glancing shot through the flap of the ear, furrowing the flesh and scraping the bone, but no part of the shot entered the skull. The shot came from the front. That was my idea. The doctor said so. The direction of the shot was as nearly as possible horizontal. I cannot say how I was carrying my gun.' With the light fading on the trial, Colonel Tillard had thrown a late curveball with the potential to alter the entire direction of the trial. Here was a man with no axe to grind and of unimpeachable pedigree, presenting himself as living proof that an individual could inflict upon themselves injuries remarkably similar to those endured by Cecil, and to do so entirely accidentally.

It all ensured that the closing statements of Asher and Comrie Thomson were more important than ever. The pressure was on each side to tie together the vast array of evidence that had been set before the court and build around it the narrative that would decide the case one way or the other. The Solicitor-General was the first to go. Over six hours, Asher gave a bravura performance – many regarded it as the finest address to a jury that he ever gave. He explicated the financial evidence, unpicking what he claimed was the devious manner in which Monson came to insure the life of his young charge. As for the suggestion that Monson knew that the policies would be invalid should Cecil die before his twenty-first birthday, he was dismissive. Why, he demanded, would Monson have got Cecil to author letters of assignation if he did not believe they would have any legal value? Similarly, why did he allow Tot to seek a payout from them if he knew that there was no such entitlement? As he convincingly put it: 'Mr Monson manifestly thought he was armed with the necessary means of securing the total amount of both of the policies, in the event of anything afterwards happening to Cecil Hambrough.'

As well as making his own case as strongly as he could, Asher sought to head off the defence wherever possible. Monson said he and Scott had moved the body, yet there was absolutely no evidence to support the claim. The defence would claim the ground was dangerous underfoot, ripe for an accident to occur. Yet the land surveyor, James Brand, engaged to survey the scene of death, found that the ground where Cecil likely walked was almost level. Then there was the question of who was carrying which gun. Monson did nothing to disabuse Dr Macmillan of his belief on the day of the shooting that Cecil had been carrying the twenty-bore. Yet when the Procurator-Fiscal began to show reservations about Monson's version of events, Monson was at pains to suggest he had carried the twenty-bore and Cecil the twelve-bore. And why were the guns taken straight from the scene of the accident and unloaded, even before anybody else had been told what had occurred? Then there was Cecil's jacket, worn the morning of the hunt and stuffed with ammunition for the twenty-bore. What was one to make of that?

The Solicitor-General also made much of the appearance and then disappearance of Scott. 'Why has a person who was present on the scene absolutely disappeared from all human ken?' he asked. 'What are likely to have been the circumstances in which he was participating when at Ardlamont as deduced or inferred from the fact of his disappearance? I am not now dealing with any doubtful question as to his identity. I am dealing with a matter as to which there is no dispute. One of the men who was there has fled and hidden himself. Why has he done that?' Furthermore, he demanded, what was Monson's motive for stating to the police that Scott was an engineer with connections in Greenock? 'For what purpose was that statement made?' he asked. 'Was it for the purpose of giving truthful information, or deceiving and misleading the authorities?'

Conscious of potential weaknesses in the individual links of the case, Asher was desperate that the jury consider the mass of evidence in the round – the suggestions of Monson's bad character, his shady financial dealings, the incriminating insurance policies, the forensic evidence that pointed to a third-party shooter and the disappearance of Monson's putative (and highly mysterious) partner in crime. Succeed in that plea, and the day would surely be his.

He ended his address with the following words: 'I shall not detain you, gentlemen, by reviewing all the facts, all the various heads under which I have grouped the points on which I have thought it my duty to speak. But, gentlemen, whilst I have repeated them one by one – compelled to do so by the circumstances of the case – I say again to you that you must take them not only singly, but in the lump. You must take the features of this case as they occur, and make up your minds, I repeat, severally and separately. But when you have done that my wish is that you should place them side by side, look at them in their relationship to one another, and consider whether they do not establish the grave and serious chain to which I have referred – whether the circumstances do not infallibly and inevitably lead to one result, connecting the prisoner with the crimes with which he is charged. If you can find serious, intelligible, and honest ground that will influence you in coming to the conclusion that these facts are quite consistent with the innocence of the prisoner, by all means acquit him. But, gentlemen, if on the consideration of these you come to the conclusion that they are reasonably consistent with one, and only one, result, then your duty to the public, your duty to the oath which you have taken, is to find the prisoner guilty of the crime with which he is charged.'

If Comrie Thomson was surprised by the aplomb with which Asher delivered his argument, he was nonetheless up for the fight. Crucially, he realized that his job was not to prove beyond doubt Monson's innocence but simply to show that the prosecution had failed to prove his guilt. He picked away at every hole he could find in the opposition's case. Why, he asked the jury, would Monson kill a man who was worth far more to him alive? The Monsons, he argued, were reliant upon the money bestowed upon them by Tot, which he only supplied in the hope that the relationship with Cecil could be cultivated to the point of life-altering profitability. Cecil, he suggested, would be at the peak of his earning potential for Monson and Tot only when he gained the age of majority. By killing Cecil, he insisted, Monson was killing 'a man upon whose life his income and subsistence depended'. No Cecil, no oof.

As for the insurance policies, he maintained that negotiations for the future of the Steephill estate on the Isle of Wight had still been up for grabs. The insurance on Cecil, he said, was a crucial step towards satisfying Eagle Insurance that the Cecil–Monson–Tot consortium could take over the mortgage. Comrie Thomson went as far as to suggest that 'nothing was more natural than that Monson should proceed to effect insurances the moment the 1st of August arrived, because he knew that that had been the difficulty in the way of the competing scheme, and that if he went to Eagle Insurance with good policies of insurance in his hand, and said, "Here are the policies – this young man has consented that his life should be insured – here they are," he would have been certain to get the contract.' This was perhaps a liberal reading of how warmly Eagle Insurance felt to the

Cecil grouping but to a jury rendered somewhat punch-drunk by the complexity of the financial evidence, it must surely have seemed at least a credible interpretation of affairs. Moreover, Comrie Thomson insisted, Monson knew that he could not claim upon those same insurance policies in the event of Cecil's death before his next birthday in 1894. 'Where the motive to take the life of a man ... comes in, I confess myself entirely unable to see,' Comrie Thomson opined. 'Their one interest, the one thing that was essential to the carrying out of this arrangement, was that the young man should live.'

So what of Tot's attempt to cash-in the policies? Comrie Thomson was well aware that Tot was hardly the kind of witness likely to win the hearts of a jury, yet he actively played upon Tot's shady image. 'I rather think Tottenham produced the impression upon you of being rather a queer fish,' he acknowledged. 'I do not think he is the kind of man that you and I – quiet-going Scottish folk – are in the habit of meeting, or even I do not know that any of us desire to make his more intimate acquaintance. But he told us quite distinctly, after a little hesitation and pressing, when asked why he made a claim when Monson knew, as he said, that the policy was worthless, because it was not a good assignation, he told us, what I have no doubt you believe to be absolute truth, that he was "trying it on" with the insurance company. "I was bluffing them," he said; and observe, it is well known that insurance companies – there being such great competition in the business – very often pay claims in order to save their credit, in order to keep them popular, which they know are not strictly and legally due by them.'

He then explored the doubts pertaining to the forensic evidence. On the possibility that the body had been moved, he asserted: 'Now, then ... if you think it is proved that he was moved, the whole foundation of the Crown case crumbles to pieces, because they have no data for which there is any justification on which their measurements and evidence as to direction shall depend.' He also once more went over the disparity among the expert witnesses as to the distance at which the shot was fired, and claimed that Monson had mentioned to two witnesses on the day of the shooting that he had been carrying the twenty-bore gun and Cecil the twelve-bore (although by his own admission, this evidence only emerged through indirect statements). As to the cartridges found in Cecil's jacket pocket, he implied Monson had put them there for convenience when preparing the package of clothes, guns and ammunition requested by the Procurator-Fiscal at the end of August. Not unreasonably, he pointed out that if the pockets had been stuffed with nineteen cartridges on the day of the shooting, surely Steven or Dr Macmillan would have noticed them when attending to the body.

There was even time for an *ad hominem* assault on Littlejohn, whom he characterized as the 'only witness in the case who seems not to be open to entertaining any view but that which involves the guilt of the prisoner ... I claim as witnesses in my favour both Dr Heron Watson and Dr Bell, and I will tell you why. Because they say that in the conclusions they arrived at, I do not doubt with perfect accuracy, they were in the region of conjecture, and that there were infinite possibilities by which Hambrough's life might have been lost besides that which involves guilt on the part of the accused. I claim these two gentlemen, from the Crown list. It is all I need. If you are in the region of conjecture you cannot convict. If there is a reasonable possibility you must give effect to it. Both of these men say that they are in the region of conjecture, and that the possibilities are infinite. And I add to these Professor Hay, whose evidence you heard given under great physical weakness, he having risen from his bed, to which he had been confined by a severe attack of influenza.'

Once again, Comrie Thomson was not averse to stretching his interpretation of testimony in the interests of his client. It was true that Littlejohn certainly believed in Monson's guilt but he was no more aggressive in asserting the fact than his colleagues, nor any less willing to accept that his evidence relied on accepting that the body fell where it was first seen by the estate staff. By sowing the idea that the prosecution's experts were somehow split among themselves (they clearly weren't), Comrie Thomson hoped not only to diminish the impact of their combined testimony but to undermine the authority of each individually.

As for the Scott problem, he employed skilled sleight of hand. Firstly, he sought to suggest that Monson had been in no way disingenuous in his representation of the supposed yacht engineer. 'The statement was made,' Comrie Thomson said, 'and it has not been contradicted by anybody, that Scott came in order to act for Hambrough in connection with the boilers of the yacht.' This statement was, of course, disputed by many – it was instead the case that those voicing their doubts could not prove their misgivings in the absence of the man himself. Comrie Thomson was thus free to brazenly explain away the mystery man's disappearance:

> After the accident Scott's position is this, that his occupation is gone, that the man who hired him is dead. There is to be no yacht now, because there is no owner of the yacht. He is very much shocked at what has happened, necessarily – I am assuming, of course, that it was an accident – but there is no reason for his remaining. He does not, however, go away at once. He waits till the afternoon before he leaves, and takes the fifth boat which left Tighnabruaich that day. He remains in the neighbourhood with those who are concerned with the moving and the dressing of the body. He remains to the sad and silent luncheon that they partook of in the middle of the day.

But Comrie Thomson was wily enough to know that Scott was a problematic figure. What if he really was the bookies' clerk, as had been suggested? It was a question he couldn't avoid. So, he set out to paint Edward Sweeney – the man who might be Scott – as 'one of the gentlest, most amiable, and quietest of men'. 'A bookmaker he was, but he was a sick bookmaker, a dying bookmaker,' he said, conjuring up an image of Dickens-esque pathos. 'And Sidney Russell [Sweeney's bookmaker employer] and his brother both concurred in telling you that he was the last man that would be party to a cruel act – he would not harm a fly; and yet the suggestion is, the most preposterous I ever listened to, that, for some mysterious reason, Monson invites this mild, amiable man to come down and be an eyewitness to an attempt to murder, and then takes him along with him to be an eyewitness to an act of murder, and does not take means to detain him so that he may give evidence in his favour. Is not that a thing perfectly absurd on the face of it? If Monson was to drown this man, or shoot him, why does he bring Scott? He does not want any assistance; wants no third party to throw him out of the boat; wants no third party to shoot him. He brings down this man, the suggestion is, that he might aid and abet him. What earthly help could be got from him? Did he not bring down a man who could have deponed here, if there was foul play, "I saw it."' Whether the individual jurymen believed Scott to be an engineer or a turf accountant, Comrie Thomson had done his best to tackle their various presumptions. 'Gentlemen,' he told them, 'it is probably the greatest calamity that could befall my client that Scott is not here. I do not pretend to know what he would have said, but according to my information, according to the instructions by which I am guided – I go no further than that, but I am justified in going so far as that – I think it is the greatest calamity that ever befell mortal man that Scott has not been able to enter this witness box.'

No motive, no forensic case, nor anything in the least bit suggestive in the disappearance of Scott – the defence counsel had finished its attempts to dismantle the case against Monson. 'In most cases of crime,' he argued, 'the fact that a crime has been committed is easily demonstrated. If a house is broken into and goods are removed, you know that there has been a crime – housebreaking. If a man is found shattered, as with the blows of a sledgehammer, you know that he has been murdered. But in the present case the question you have to determine is, has there been a crime at all?'

Only three men truly knew what happened out in those woods, he said – one being dead, one silenced by the judicial system, and the third not to be got. The Crown, then, was forced to rely upon indirect or circumstantial evidence. It was on this point that Comrie Thomson was perhaps at his eloquent best: 'Now, gentlemen, it has often been said that, in a certain sense, you can never get better evidence than circumstantial evidence, because facts do not lie, as human beings sometimes do. But it is essential that you should realize exactly what is meant by circumstantial evidence, and what is necessary before circumstantial evidence can be taken as valuable at all, or as equivalent in value to direct evidence. In the first place, gentlemen, observe this – and I have suspected it is sometimes overlooked – that it is an essential part of the value of circumstantial evidence that each circumstance should be distinctly proved. Circumstantial evidence does not mean a lot of suspicious circumstances. That is not it at all. You must have each circumstance which is founded upon, those which are to be pieced together into one whole, and from which the conclusion is to be derived, clearly demonstrated by evidence. It will not do to say, "That is rather suspicious," unless it is proved, proved in the usual way, proved by direct evidence. Then, gentlemen, having got your full proof of each circumstance, it is necessary that the effect of each shall not be misapprehended, or misapplied, or misjudged. And it is only when you have got each circumstance established by evidence, and when you are satisfied not only of its full authentication, but also that the inferences drawn from it have been justifiable and true inferences, that you are in a position to determine when that body of evidence so established and so applied is sufficient to exclude every theory except that of guilt.'

Comrie Thomson then adopted a risky tactic: he referred to the fact that Monson had taken his son with him when he showed Dr Macmillan the scene of the shooting just a few hours after it had occurred. 'Can you conceive,' the defence counsel pondered, 'that, if that man had within recent hours been guilty of murdering his friend who had been living with him, and had been attached to him for years past, he would take probably the purest and the simplest being within his reach to show him the place at which that horrible crime had been committed by his own father? We know that there is almost no limit to the depths of human depravity; but the notion that a murderer, when his hand was still red with the blood of the victim, would take his little boy by the hand to show him the spot where he had committed the crime is, I think, absolutely incredible.' It takes a brave lawyer to declare the charges laid against his client to be so monstrous as to be unbelievable. But that was just what Comrie Thomson urged the jury to conclude. They might, though, have decided that the allegation was actually proof of Monson's monstrousness.

Comrie Thomson then revisited his core theme one final time: 'Have I not demonstrated that there is ample room for entertaining serious doubt?' he asked. 'Gentlemen, we are all liable to make mistakes. I pray you make no mistake in this terribly serious matter. The result of your verdict is final, irreparable. What would any of you think if some day, it may be soon, this mystery is entirely unravelled, and it is demonstrated that that man was innocent, while your verdict has sent him to his death? He will not go unpunished if he is guilty. There is One in Whose hands he is. Who is Infallible and Omniscient. "I will repay, vengeance is mine, saith the Lord."'

And so the defence rested.

14

The Jury Returns

'… we balance probabilities and choose the most likely.
It is the scientific use of the imagination …'

Sherlock Holmes, *The Hound of the Baskervilles*

The judge, Lord Kingsburgh – an old school friend of Joseph Bell's, as it happened – presented his summing-up to the jury on the afternoon of Friday 22 December. It had been, he told them, a 'long and anxious trial' and there was no doubt he was relieved it was coming to an end. Of all the cases in which he had served as judge since being appointed to the bench in 1888, this was the one that placed most strain upon him. At its midway point he took the highly unusual step of addressing the general public. 'Before the trial resumes,' he had announced at the start of the fifth day, 'I wish to say that since the trial began I have received several letters, some signed and some anonymous, with reference to this case. I do not read such letters, and I wish it to be publicly known that the writing of such letters to a judge in this court, when trying a case, is not only reprehensible, but might subject the person doing it to severe punishment for contempt of court.' It would later be revealed that among the piles of unwanted mail was a postcard sent from Liverpool to the effect that if Monson was acquitted, the missive's author would take it upon himself to shoot him. It was signed

'Scott'. There was no pretending that this was like other cases.

Yet, despite the intense pressure under which he found himself, Kingsburgh laid out his thoughts on the case in a typically lucid and sober manner. To many ears, however, he showed a distinct leaning towards the defence. This was perhaps no surprise. Although he had served in the two most senior prosecuting roles in the Scottish judicial system (Solicitor-General and Lord Advocate) and had even led the prosecution at the Eugene Chantrelle trial, the early and larger part of his career was spent as a defence counsel. As Kingsburgh would note in his memoirs: 'Down to the last year when I was free to take up the defence, before I became Lord Advocate, I never had a client convicted of murder, except the one who was insane, and was proved to be insane after the trial. In all my other cases there was either an acquittal or a verdict of culpable homicide. But this was too much of a success to last out one's time. On two occasions in my last year or eighteen months of defence, I was called on to act for first one pair of poachers, and then another pair, for the murder of gamekeepers. There was not a vestige of a defence, and the whole four died on the gallows. The spell of success was broken, and very shortly after my career on the left side of the table came to an end.' It was clearly a badge of pride that he had so consistently ensured verdicts of innocence for his clients, and was suggestive of a feeling that defender was somehow a nobler role than prosecutor. Was it possible that he harboured at least a slight unconscious prejudice?

His summing-up was certainly generous to Monson's team in several respects. Early on, he characterized the case as 'one purely of circumstantial evidence. It is not a case in which there is any direct evidence.' Although their evidence may have been disputed, it is unlikely that Littlejohn, Bell or Heron Watson agreed with him on that point. While acknowledging an unavoidable element of conjecture, they were to a man convinced that their experiments and analysis provided just the direct evidence the judge was now discounting. Nor would they have appreciated the way Kingsburgh questioned the credibility of what he called 'the theoretical evidence of the case – that is to say, the evidence of persons of skill, drawing inferences from their skill for the purpose of aiding you in your decision'. While recognizing the importance of the evidence of 'gun-makers, the evidence of persons skilled in the use and carrying of guns, the evidence of doctors skilled in wounds and their effects', Kingsburgh stated that it was a misfortune of the prosecution that their investigations were only able to start several weeks after the incident itself. This was absolutely not the fault of the prisoner, he said, and 'in so far as the case of the prosecution is weakened by their being of late date, so far the prosecution has to suffer in the consideration of that evidence'. It was a bitter blow for the prosecution to have the forensic strand of its attack called into question at such a fundamental level.

Nor can the Crown have been much keener on Kingsburgh's treatment of their argument for motive – the insurance policies. After a generally balanced summary of the evidence on this particular aspect, Kingsburgh suddenly launched another torpedo in the prosecution's direction: 'If it is clear and certain that a crime has been committed, it is not an essential part of the public prosecutor's case to prove that there was motive for the crime. If he can prove the case without any motive, he is entitled to a verdict. But, then, another thing. Where the evidence is circumstantial only, and the guilt of a prisoner is only inferential and is not proved as a matter of fact by the evidence of witnesses who saw the crime, then the question of motive becomes of vital importance. If there is motive clearly and distinctly proved, then it is of enormous importance to the prosecution. If motive is displaced, or even made reasonably doubtful, it is enormously in favour of the prisoner.'

As for the mystery surrounding Scott, Kingsburgh again expressed little sympathy for Asher's arguments. 'The Solicitor-General made a strong point of his allegation that this man Scott came there as a party to a plot for murder,' he said. 'Can you come to any conclusion in your own minds why he should be there as a co-conspirator for any such purpose? In regard to either of the crimes charged in the indictment, the drowning attempt or the successful shooting, I must say I have a difficulty in seeing what he was there for ... It has not been shown that this man Scott had any connection with the affairs of Hambrough and Monson; and, so far as I can see, if the drowning or the shooting was to be carried out, there was no need for the presence of this stranger at all. Therefore, if there was no interest on the part of this third party, it must have been as a hired assassin to assist that he was there, if the Crown's theory be correct; but for this view, too, there is no basis that I can see. No doubt his presence there is mysterious in many ways, but, gentlemen, it is for the Crown to solve that mystery. If there be anything to make the matter one involving a criminal charge, it is for the Crown to solve the mystery. It will not do for the Crown just to point into the dark and say, "Unless you, the prisoner, throw light into that darkness, you must be held to have been engaged in a crime."'

He was similarly, and perhaps most justifiably, dismissive of the attempted murder charge, noting that it had not seemingly entered the minds of the authorities to add this charge to the indictment until the end of October – over two-and-a-half months after the attack had supposedly taken place. 'In point of fact, Cecil Hambrough and Mr Monson got into the water that night,' he began. 'In point of fact, Cecil Hambrough and Monson got to shore; and in point of fact, it is plain it never entered Cecil's mind that anything of the kind suggested had been done for the purpose of murdering him.' Case closed on that charge at least, one might think.

He even urged against taking Monson's bad character (in his memoirs he actually referred to the defendant's 'evil character') as evidence of his guilt on any of the charges. 'It is always a very dreadful thing to find out that people are liars, and possibly consistent liars,' he said. 'It gives one a very bad impression of their general character, and one cannot trust such people after making such discoveries in the ordinary transactions of life, and to a certain extent it shows a serious moral breakdown. There are some people to whom it has become so natural to state what is untrue that, without any object at all – as was apparent in this case; on various occasions statements were made in matters of business by the prisoner and by his wife which were not true, without any conceivable object. I would caution you not to deduce too much from that. It is a long way from being dishonest to being murderers ...'

Finally, he left the jurymen in no doubt as to the onerous nature of the task that had been thrust upon them: 'Now, gentlemen, you must consider how this case is to be disposed of. You have got a path to go on in this case in which you must see your way. You must neither walk through darkness at any point of it, nor leap over anything that you meet in it. It must be a straight path, and a path on which you have light. If you have light which takes you to the end of that path, so that you can give a verdict for the prosecution, then you must do it manfully, and you must not allow yourselves to be stopped, though Pity, with uplifted hands, stand pleading and entreating that you shall not go on. On the other hand, if there is any darkness or dimness on that path which you cannot clear away, you cannot go on to the end. If there is any obstruction on that path you have to stop there. The prisoner is entitled to that. And, lastly, if you yourselves do not see your way along that path without passing through darkness or dimness or other obstruction, you must not allow yourselves to be urged forward along that path blindly by any demon pushing you from behind, telling you that the prisoner is a bad man, a liar, and a cheat, and that, therefore, you should send him to his doom. You must keep yourselves free from that.'

At seven minutes to four, the jury was sent out to consider its verdict. Perhaps buoyed by the tone of the judge's address, Monson seems to have been in remarkably jovial spirits as he awaited news of his fate. He even started cracking jokes with a couple of nearby journalists. 'Why am I like a railway engine?' he asked. Then, looking down at the hard, wooden bench upon which he had been sitting throughout the trial: 'Because I have a tender behind.' But what of the thoughts running through the mind of Agnes, his stalwart throughout the ordeal? She had cut a lonely figure for much of the proceedings, sitting veiled, alone or with a single companion, keeping her counsel day after day at the back of the courtroom. During the trial, she stayed in rooms in Edinburgh that she could scant afford and it was said that in her private moments she solaced her melancholy by playing the banjo. Indeed, a note in her handwriting had been passed around parts of the court showing an order with a Glasgow music-seller for popular hits including 'The Future Mrs 'Awkins' and 'The Man that Broke the Bank at Monte Carlo'. It is tempting to imagine her husband humming along to the latter's opening line: 'And I've now such lots of money, I'm a gent.'

The public, meanwhile, were champing at the bit. It was indicative of the clamour surrounding the trial that on average over 150,000 words of newspaper coverage was sent by telegraph from Edinburgh's General Post Office on each day of proceedings. Bookmakers even offered odds on the verdict – in the last few days of the trial, you could get 9–4 on an acquittal. The anticipation was palpable when the jury returned some seventy-three minutes after the judge had sent them out. 'Gentlemen, what is your verdict?' asked the clerk of the court. The foreman of the jury rose to his feet: 'My Lord, the verdict of the jury is one of not proven on both charges.'

A strange, muffled murmur went around the court and then a ripple of applause that was soon stifled. Beyond, though, the response was less restrained. Within thirty seconds of the news breaking, the large crowd that had gathered on the square outside the courtroom gave a resounding cheer. Quite what they were celebrating was unclear. Surely Monson had not been elevated to the status of popular hero in the mould of a Robin Hood or even a Dick Turpin? Whether or not he had been responsible for the death of Cecil Hambrough, the trial had hardly shown Monson in a good light. Nor was the verdict itself particularly satisfying, leaving, as it did, lingering suspicion and unanswered questions. This was, after all, what Sir Walter Scott had memorably described as 'the bastard verdict'. Perhaps it was simply relief that the tension was over, or appreciation for a drama well performed, that prompted the crowd's spontaneous applause.

Monson, meanwhile, stood up in the dock on hearing the news, his smile eventually breaking into something like contained laughter. His solicitor, Mr Blair, and his junior counsel, John Wilson, came over to shake his hand. Notably, Comrie Thomson did not, instead leaving the court straightaway without so much as a glance towards his client. The freed man was then conducted downstairs from the dock, and was shortly afterwards spotted in deep conversation with the Chief Constable and his officials. They were likely discussing how best to smuggle Monson past the mass of people congregated outside. In the end, Monson simply turned up his collar, swapped his felt hat for a cap and was taken out of a side exit towards a waiting cab. It was not a ruse that fooled all of those in the crowd, and before long the police were required to hold back a throng who had rushed across the square to catch a glimpse of the man who was just then the most famous person in Edinburgh. By the time Monson got into the cab and the horses had got going, he was surrounded by a large group cheering his emancipation. A short while later, he arrived at an address in a quiet corner of the city's West End where Agnes had been staying during the trial.

The next day he wrote a letter to Comrie Thomson. A curious note, it read as follows:

Dear Mr Thompson [*sic*],
I feel anxious to express my gratitude to you for the able
and powerful speech which you addressed to the jury on
my behalf yesterday. I regret very much that I am unable to
thank you personally before leaving Edinburgh, because I feel
that I cannot properly convey my thanks in writing ... I fully
appreciate that the close of your address was so impressively
pathetic that the jury were visibly affected to such an extent
that the case for the Crown was so shaken as to render it
impossible for the jury to find a verdict of Guilty.
I am leaving for Scarboro' but expect to be in Edinburgh again
soon, when I hope I may have the opportunity of thanking
you in person. I remain, yours truly,
A. J. Monson

Nowhere does Monson talk of the injustice of the charges against
him, instead congratulating Comrie Thomson for spiking the
prosecution so that the jury had no choice but to reject a guilty
verdict. If Comrie Thomson's hasty retreat from the courtroom was
indicative of a certain disquiet in his relationship with Monson, the
passage of time evidently did not soften his feelings. Several years
later at a dinner party, he was heard to say: 'I don't know whether
Monson killed Hambrough, but he nearly killed me.'

Nonetheless, most of the press was in agreement that the jury had
arrived at the only acceptable verdict given the evidence put before
them. The *Daily News* neatly summarised the consensus opinion:
'It was the verdict which most persons expected, and it was exactly
the right verdict. The charges against the prisoner were rendered
plausible by the evidence, but they were not proved.' The *Spectator*
reached the same conclusion and used a long editorial to warn of the
press and the public's proclivity towards prejudging:

The Ardlamont trial is a sharp object-lesson in the difference between violent presumption and solid evidence. We do not suppose Mr Monson's closest friends would deny that when his trial began there was a violent presumption that he had been concerned in the death ... Everyone expected that the facts would be proved by the Crown, and that being proved the Court of Session would have no hesitation in convicting and sentencing the accused ... Nevertheless, the jury found a verdict of 'Not proven', and we do not believe that any competent person who has read the Lord Justice Clerk's summing-up of the evidence can doubt that the verdict was correct. The testimony was all presumption, and not evidence. The facts were all correct, but there was nothing whatever except his presence on the ground to connect them with the accused ... The case for the prosecution consisted in fact of more or less probable guesses, upon which the jury could hardly decide; and accordingly they brought in the verdict which means just that, – namely, 'Not proven'. Had they been trying the case in England, they must have acquitted the accused, and in returning the verdict they did, they went to the very verge of justice ... beliefs, accorded without solid evidence, constantly deflect the course of affairs, and sometimes work the irreparable kind of mischief which, but for an able Judge and a patient jury, popular presumption would have worked in the case of the man accused of the Ardlamont murder. We use the word 'mischief' with no intention of implying complete belief in Monson's innocence. We have no such certainty any more than the jury had, but the point is not our certainty or the jury's, but the evidence against the accused, and except the fact that he was on the spot when the death occurred, there was practically none.

The *Glasgow Herald*, meanwhile, took a different line, celebrating the trial for the window it opened on to the condition of the social hierarchy:

> Greater romances have been revealed in the Law Courts than that story which must perhaps for ever be known as the Ardlamont tragedy. It has none of the piquancy of 'fashionable vice' in the worst sense of the phrase. Yet what a revelation of the shifts that impecuniosity is put to we have in this marvellous story of financial agents and bookmakers, pawn tickets, insurances and mortgages, which has been told in Edinburgh this past fortnight! ... It is proverbial, of course, that the one-half of the world does not know how the other half lives; but one wonders how many Major Hambroughs there are, getting through a respectable fortune in a few years, and then living almost entirely on wretched and precarious pittances doled out by their sons' tutors. Does Monson stand alone, or are there many other 'scions of the aristocracy' who can live for years in comfort, if not luxury, on what Mr Comrie Thomson's 'quiet living' Scotch folks would regard as nothing a year plus pawn tickets.

Although the members of the jury had agreed not to discuss the case with the newspapers, it was not long before several broke rank to give their take on events. As the *Edinburgh Evening News* put it, 'they are so imbued with a sense of its importance and their own share in its decision that a little persuasion has induced a few of them to unburden their minds of some of their impressions'. According to one, although there had been general admiration for the closing speech of the Solicitor-General, the summing up of the judge left them little room to return any verdict other than 'not proven'. Another claimed that initially there were one or two jurors keen to find Monson guilty but, after a short discussion, 'not proven' was agreed to unanimously. In fact, it was claimed, the jurymen were ready to return much sooner than they did, but delayed as they considered there ought to be a decent interval. In a revelation dripping with pathos, it was also revealed that a child of one of the jurymen had died on the evening of the trial's penultimate day.

The fate of Monson became an ongoing subject of debate in both private and public forums. During the trial, for example, a miner called Alexander Mair got on a train at Glasgow Central station with his wife and struck up a conversation with two men in his compartment as to the probable fate of the defendant. Before long there was an altercation which developed into a fight, during which Mair was stabbed in the forehead. Fortunately, he survived. More peaceably, a vicar at an Aberdeen church chose to ruminate on the case on the Sunday after the verdict. He based his sermon around the words found in the book of Isaiah 3:11: 'Woe unto the wicked, for the reward of his hands shall be over him.' While denying that he had necessarily made up his mind as to Monson's guilt, the vicar did say that the trial had revealed 'much of the life of godlessness, wickedness, scheming, shift, falsehood, and deception'. It had, he said, 'given an insight into the state of society in some of its circles where they would expect better things'.

During what was his first weekend of freedom since the summer, Monson offered up his own thoughts on the affair. 'Yes,' he said, 'I am feeling pretty well on the whole; but of course I am dreadfully pulled down – the period of suspense has been so long, it is over four months now since I was first placed under arrest.' On being asked about the result, he was reported to have smiled. 'Of course, in one sense, I am very well pleased,' he said, adding that 'in another I am disappointed. I am glad that the verdict was not a conviction, as I need hardly tell you; but I think, on the other hand, that after the very strong charge of the judge, it should have been a complete acquittal, and not merely a verdict of "Not Proven". Considering, too, that the jury were, as I am told, absolutely unanimous, I feel this all the more strongly. It is quite certain that in England after such a decided summing-up as that of Lord Kingsburgh, no jury would have returned any other verdict than "not guilty", and thenceforth I feel that to this extent I am a sufferer by different procedure adopted in Scotland.' He did, however, concede that the prosecution case was 'undoubtedly a strong one'. 'The Crown had had so long to make their preparation,' he explained, 'that their evidence, such as it was, was very complete ... but I must say there appeared to me less desire to ascertain the actual truth in the matter than to make the facts fit in with their own preconceived theory.'

These last words echoed both Bell's observation (made to the *Pall Mall Gazette*) that the police tended to make a 'fatal mistake' in getting 'his theory first and then [making] the facts fit it' and Sherlock Holmes's admonition against theorizing 'in advance of the facts'. But perhaps there was also something disconcerting about the language Monson used. His words sounded less like the impassioned outpourings of an innocent man exonerated of the most ghastly charges, but more like the cool appraisal of a legal commentator analysing the ebb and flow of the judicial proceedings. To some, there was the immutable suspicion that this was a man who had just spectacularly gamed the system. Others, meanwhile, maintained he was merely the victim of circumstantial evidence and unjust innuendo.

15

For a Sheep as a Lamb

'For once you have fallen low. Let us see
in the future how high you can rise.'

Sherlock Holmes, 'The Adventure of the Three Students'

What does a person do when he is allowed to walk free from court but with his name destined to bear the taint of suspicion for evermore? That was the quandary that faced Monson as the euphoria of dodging a capital sentence subsided.

It was quickly obvious that he could put away hope of fading into the shadows – assuming that he wanted to, anyway. As a new year rolled along and the weeks turned into months since the curtain fell on Edinburgh's hottest show of 1893, there was still an appetite for Ardlamont stories no matter how superficial their link to the case. For instance, in January 1894, the *Sketch*, a new journal for the 'cultivated people who in their leisure moments look for light reading and amusing pictures', published an interview with Helen Mathers – a popular novelist of the time. She also happened to be Cecil Hambrough's aunt, and coincidentally had worked with Doyle the previous year on *The Fate of Fenella*, a collaborative serial novel by twenty-four authors. Despite a general unwillingness to discuss her nephew's demise, she did reveal an uncanny feeling she'd had the night before his death, when she was staying in Brighton. She described how she had woken in a state of depression and full of fear, telling her hostess that she was sure that something dreadful had happened – a claim, she explained, that was met by general derision. As she took the train later that day, she was full of foreboding in regard to her son, Phil. When she arrived home, she discovered her husband carrying a telegram in his hand, which he at first refused to share with her. 'It's Phil,' she said, pleadingly. At that point, he handed it to her and she read the news: 'Cecil is killed – gun accident.'

This was the sort of melodramatic fluff lapped up by those not yet ready to give up on the Ardlamont saga. Nor did Monson prove much good at keeping his name out of legal proceedings. Little over a month after his acquittal, bankruptcy proceedings began against the Leicester Industrial Assurance and Building Company, a business of which he was nominally a director even if he seems to have had little active involvement in its running. In its advertisements, the company had boasted it possessed the 'experience of wise men who are entitled to public faith and trust'. Given the nature of his newfound fame, it goes without saying that Monson hardly qualified as their poster boy.

For a while, it seems that Monson had entertained the idea of running away from all the adverse attention – a tactic he had employed so regularly throughout his life. Back in October 1893, while his fate remained in the balance, he had written to his cousin, Lord Galway:

I am as you are probably aware placed in a position of extreme difficulty. My mother refused to afford any assistance [this was, of course, not actually true – rather, she had not given him as much as he had wanted] unless she was backed up by other members of the family – your name was mentioned coupled with Lord Oxenbridge. My request simply amounts to this, that if I had a sum of £500 placed at my disposal I would at once leave the country and start life

> elsewhere but although pressed and advised by her solicitors
> my mother refused to accede to the request unless she was
> supported by others.

This money was not apparently forthcoming, so his plans were forced to change. In the immediate aftermath of the trial, he and Agnes returned to the north of England. For a few weeks the couple found relative happiness, staying in a house not far from York that boasted a view of the Minster. As Agnes would tell it, Monson was in good spirits as his health and energies revived. Before long, though, his restless spirit returned. He grew tired of having no money and decided to seek his fortune anew in London. Having survived the ordeal of having his name dragged through the courts and his reputation picked apart by the newspapers, he was now eager to turn some profit from his torment.

In short order, he signed a deal with Charles Morritt, who worked variously as impresario, mentalist, hypnotist and magician – indeed, he is credited with having created several of Harry Houdini's spectacular tricks, including the 'Vanishing Elephant'. Monson signed a year-long, twelve-performances-per-week contract for a princely £500 per month. The show was to comprise a first half of ventriloquism and conjuring acts, with Monson making his appearance in the second half to lecture upon his experiences. The show was scheduled to open in January 1894 at Prince's Hall in London's Piccadilly, before travelling around the provinces for a year. However, for some reason Monson got cold feet and just two hours before curtain-up on the first night – at least, according to Morritt's account – Monson withdrew.

He did, however, see through his contractual obligations to the publisher Marlo & Company, writing *The Ardlamont Mystery Solved*, which was released early in 1894. Running to just under a hundred pages, it was a remarkably dull affair, mainly regurgitating the evidence that the defence had offered in court just a few weeks earlier and which had been so assiduously reported by the newspapers. Anyone expecting dramatic revelations was to be sorely disappointed. In terms of original insight, Monson gave little beyond his general annoyance at the Scottish judicial system. He remained convinced, at least in public, that an English coroner would have undertaken a proper initial investigation into Cecil's death, which would have precluded the chance of Monson being arrested on trumped-up charges weeks after the event. It was an ambitious argument. An English coroner discovering a man dead from a shot to the back of the head, fired while in the company of another man theoretically set to benefit from his death, would surely have reached a similar conclusion to the Scottish authorities – that there was a case to answer.

The most intriguing part of the book was the section that purported to be Scott's diary, covering the period from 7 August until Christmas Day 1893. This was published, it should be remembered, at a time when Scott/Sweeney was still missing as far as the world at large was concerned. Elements of the Canadian press, for example, were reporting quite erroneously that the mystery man was likely then residing in their country. One newspaper also bizarrely asserted that he was 'well known in London music halls as an expert shot, whose business is trick shooting with saloon firearms'. The diary that Monson published as Scott's account of events was truly a curiosity. If Monson intended it to sound authentic, he failed dismally. It was, for one thing, written in a retrospective voice and full of unsubtle attempts to prove how neither Scott nor Monson could have been involved in the death. On the morning of the shooting, for instance, Scott 'chaffed Hambrough about the way he carried his gun – everyone noticed this', and on 18 August, after apparently leaving Glasgow for London, Scott ruminated: 'Don't like the notion of appearing to have run away.'

There was also a distinct element of the picaresque to the narrative. On 16 August, Scott reportedly had a drink with a policeman, who was of course unaware of his identity. 'I am always pretty chummy with "the force",' Scott revealed. 'They're not bad chaps in their way, but it takes a lot of intellectual dynamite to make a hole in a policeman's helmet, and let a new idea in.' On 12 September, he decided to don a disguise as the wanted posters sprang up around him: 'Now, as the police were looking for a man in a jacket and a bowler, it was highly improbable that they would arrest a man in a frock coat and a chimney-pot.' The diary then proceeded to describe Scott's imagined travels, first to Birmingham and then Manchester, where he overheard a man in a café saying that Hambrough had committed suicide to escape Scott's clutches and was 'only one of many victims'. 'I could not stand it any longer,' the diarist exclaimed, 'but, seizing a box of draughts that were on the table before me, I hurled it at the speaker's head. He dodged, but the corner of the box caught his cheek, making an ugly gash, and finished by dropping on a table and upsetting a tray full of cups of hot coffee that had just been placed there by the waitress.' Coffee spilled over a table full of men who tried to beat Scott up before the proprietor stepped in to save him.

Next, it was to Leeds, then Liverpool and back to London, where Scott slept rough and was woken from his slumbers one night by a copper on the Embankment: 'You'd have been a dead 'un if I hadn't woken you up,' the oblivious bobby is supposed to have said, even as Scott feared the end of the road. As for the period of the trial, the diary claimed Scott was in court for its duration, ready to show himself if the interests of justice demanded it. However, believing that the result was never in doubt and that Monson was destined to walk free, he decided instead to remain a mere spectre at the feast. The final entry, written on 25 December, comprised but three words: 'A Merry Christmas.'

There can hardly have been anyone unable to see through the diary's artifice, yet Monson maintained its legitimacy, claiming he had received it through the post. 'I have hesitated whether or not I should publish this remarkable diary,' he wrote. However, he explained, he 'considered it my duty to do [so] – I feel that I have no alternative but to lay it before the public, leaving them to form their own judgements, without any comments from me'. *The Ardlamont Mystery Solved* was, quite rightly, a commercial flop.

For anyone who hung on to the belief that 'Scott's diary' was a genuine artefact, Scott/Sweeney himself stepped back into the light three months later to confirm it was none of his doing and entirely fictitious. Sweeney effectively handed himself into the offices of the *Pall Mall Gazette* on 5 April, whereupon the public-spirited editorial staff persuaded him to turn himself over to the police. They even provided him with legal representation, not to mention the platform from which to deliver his take on events. The paper made much of its role in securing his 'surrender', although in truth Scotland Yard no longer had a warrant out for him and nor was the Procurator-Fiscal searching for him.

The *Gazette* ran daily pieces over the course of a week under the headline: 'The Truth Out at Last: by Scott (the Missing Man)'. 'I make no claim to literary powers,' Scott/Sweeney began, 'but will do my best to show by my statement how by one mistake (I mean my harmless adoption of a name other than that by which I was commonly known on the turf for reasons which I will explain) I woke up to find myself involved in a mystery, charged with murder, hunted like a dog, declared an outlaw, and doomed to suffer more than by my poor ability I can ever hope to make my readers appreciate.' Fleet Street rivals were largely underwhelmed, and not merely because they had missed out on a scoop. The *Sketch* memorably voiced its thoughts in verse:

In vain is 'Scott' paraded round
By journalists undaunted;
When wanted, he could not be found,
When found, he isn't wanted.

In May 1894, Scott/Sweeney made his way to Edinburgh, where he formally petitioned the courts for the recall of his sentence of outlawry. The Crown offered no opposition and the motion was accepted in a matter of just a few minutes.

While Monson and Scott/Sweeney remained figures of public interest, there was limited appetite to embrace them as celebrities. Nor was their cause helped by their insistence on peddling their essentially quite dull version of what happened at Ardlamont. It would, of course, have been folly for them to do otherwise – it was the narrative that had saved Monson from the noose and which also effectively ended the pursuit of Scott/Sweeney. But it did not make for the sorts of headlines that the nation's editors had enjoyed printing when their fates were up in the air and conjecture was the order of the day.

Monson's tentative forays into the entertainment business were also held back by his involvement in yet another trial in early 1894. Although it lacked the obvious explosiveness of December's proceedings, it nonetheless had significant legal implications. Indeed, it is fair to say that this second trial impacted the practice of law far more than his murder trial. And this time, it was Monson who instigated proceedings. In January 1894, he began an action against Madame Tussauds, the famous waxworks museum. Monson accused Tussauds of having libelled him. It was an ambitious writ but, if proven, might have netted him a tidy sum in compensation.

As with all things Monson-related, it was a far from straightforward story. The saga began two weeks after the murder trial ended when Madame Tussauds, on Marylebone Road in London, began exhibiting a figure of Monson along with an encased landscape entitled 'The Scene of the Tragedy'. All might have been well were it not for the positioning of the exhibit – just by the entrance to 'The Chamber of Horrors', preserved for effigies of murderers, conmen and other infamous figures from history. Moreover, the waxworks who shared the room with Monson included such publicly reviled characters as Napoleon, Mrs Maybrick (convicted of murdering her husband with arsenic in 1889) and Richard Pigott, who killed himself after being revealed as a forger. On 22 January, Monson appealed for an injunction to remove his likeness on the grounds of libel. The court initially agreed with him but the ruling was overturned on appeal a few days later, not least because there was a significant question as to whether Monson had originally given his consent to the display. Madame Tussauds argued that they had bought certain mementos included in the exhibit from Tot, who had claimed he was acting as Monson's agent. Yet another plot began to thicken around the pair.

According to Monson's version of events, he had been staying at Tot's house in London when Tot began negotiations with Tussauds. It was agreed that Monson would sit for a modelling session and would also supply the gun he had been carrying and the suit he was wearing at the time of the shooting. The Procurator-Fiscal being still in possession of the weapon, Tot bought a stand-in for £34 10s from Charing Cross Road and presented it to the waxworks along with Monson's brown knickerbocker suit. In return, he received a £50 down payment, with a further £50 to come once Monson had completed his sitting. However, a couple of days later Tot returned the cheque, saying that Monson would not cooperate and was furious that such a deal had been struck without his consultation. As ever with Monson and Tot, it is difficult to discern with precision where truth lies but Tot would later claim that Monson was initially keen to strike a deal but soon felt he was being undersold at negotiations where he was not present.

However, John Tussaud – owner of the museum – was just as put out since he had undertaken the negotiations in good faith. Monson must be made to comply, he insisted. Meanwhile, Tot suggested to Monson an approach to Louis Tussaud's waxworks in Birmingham, with the intention of arranging a new deal but at an inflated price – somewhere in the region of £200 this time. Louis Tussaud was the brother of John Tussaud, but he had struck out on his own so the two museums were separate legal entities. He, too, however, had chosen to display Monson near a turnstile for his 'Chamber of Horrors', although Monson's waxwork was this time among a fairly respectable crowd that included members of the royal family, the Pope and the Archbishop of Canterbury. Despite Tot's efforts, no deal was reached.

It was at this point that Monson lost patience and adopted a new strategy. His privacy had been breached and his name besmirched, he would claim as he sought an injunction forcing Tussaud to remove the display. It would be a year of legal to-ing and fro-ing before the full libel trial began at the law courts on the Strand in London on 28 January 1895. The case was heard in front of a special jury and lasted three days. In court, Monson expressly denied an allegation that he hoped to make a thousand pounds from the action. This was, he suggested, a case about protecting his rights.

While Monson's lawyers portrayed him as a man publicly wronged yet again, Tot made a sensational appearance as a defence witness. He was accompanied by a jail warder, since he was by then serving a sentence of three-month's hard labour, having been convicted in December 1894 of theft. It was symptomatic of the rapid decline in his friendship with Monson over the twelve months following the Ardlamont acquittal. Monson had accused Tot of dispensing of some £700 worth of furniture that the moneylender had been holding in trust for him in Leeds under the pseudonym of John Kempton. Tot argued instead that he had been swindled by Monson and so felt entitled to sell the property in lieu of monies owed. Alas for him, the court did not agree and found him guilty of larceny as a bailee.

Now, just a few weeks later, the pair faced-off once more and Tot was not about to hold back. He claimed that the negotiations with John Tussaud had gone awry because Monson felt that the £100 fee was far too low. Nonetheless, it had been Monson who suggested buying a gun to replace the original artefact held by the Procurator-Fiscal – evidence, it was claimed, that he did not object to the display per se, but only to the amount of money he was getting for it. Moreover, he had accompanied Tot on his way to the waxworks when Tot had sought a renegotiation of the financial terms. Monson, Tot said, was meant to stay in a hotel around the corner while the talks were ongoing but when Tot went to find him – having been unable to squeeze any more cash from Tussaud – he discovered him already gone. Tot thus concluded the deal on the original terms.

When Monson learned what had transpired, he was deeply unhappy but Tot reminded Monson that he owed him a significant sum of money (by his own admission, Monson was not paying Tot any rent at this time) and there the matter seemed to have been laid to rest. Tot also took his chance in the witness box to announce his intention, once free, to prosecute Monson on charges of perjury and theft relating to the larceny trial.

All in all, Monson's conduct as described by Tot did not seem like that of a man whose primary concern was either his privacy or his good name. Moreover, the counsel for Tussauds rejected the idea that Monson had been defamed at all, arguing that any public figure could be pictorially represented without risk of libel. Furthermore, the inclusion of the twenty-bore gun was said to be proof that the museum was casting no aspersions, given that it had been the twelve-bore that was responsible for Hambrough's death. The waxworks were merely showing that Monson was connected to a murder trial, not suggesting that he was the murderer.

In his summing-up, the judge suggested the question was less whether Monson was being cast as the murderer full-stop, but instead whether he was being depicted as 'a notorious person connected with a tragedy (which was still a mystery) in a way discreditable to him'. The judge then outlined to the jury the dual purpose of a libel action – to vindicate character and determine the extent of damages. The jury was sent to consider its verdict, taking only about fifteen minutes to find for Monson. In doing so they established a legal precedent, that of 'libel by innuendo', that has informed the drafting of libel laws ever since. In essence, the Monson case acknowledged two principles – that a waxwork effigy may be libellous and that even an apparently innocuous statement or representation may be considered libellous if it suggests a defamatory meaning to those with special knowledge. In this case, the waxwork of Monson did not explicitly suggest Monson's guilt, but its siting close to the Chamber of Horrors implied as much. As to the extent of damage his reputation had suffered, the jury put it at just a farthing (a quarter of a penny). To add insult to injury, Monson was also made responsible for paying his own costs. The *Scotsman* wryly noted: 'There is a Portuguese coin called a *maravedi*, a shovelful of which are said to be a penny. A *maravedi* would have been a more accurate estimate of the solatium due in this case; but a farthing is near enough for practical purposes.'

Monson's attempts to extract some profit from the tumult in which he found himself after Cecil's death were, like so many of his get-rich schemes over the years, ill-conceived and poorly executed. It would take a man more agreeable and empathetic to persuade a sceptical public that he was worthy of their sympathy, let alone their money. Or perhaps he needed to play his hand entirely differently, acting up to his dastardly image rather than attempting to portray himself still as the wronged innocent. He may have avoided the prison cell, but the shackles of suspicion and innuendo were harder to escape.

There was, nonetheless, one curious incident that found its way into the papers and hinted at a different side to the man. It occurred in late August 1894, at Mablethorpe, a seaside town on the Lincolnshire coast. A party of bathers were paddling in the sea when they discovered that the tide had rapidly come in. When they returned to their bathing machine (a contraption that allowed modest bathers to change from daywear to swimming costume and back again away from prying eyes), they discovered its floor was under water. Nor could the attached horse budge it, since the wheels had become embedded in the sand. As the wind got up and the sea came in further, a crowd gathered on the shore as the machine began to rock. In the words of the *Huddersfield Chronicle*:

> The onlookers ... although fully realizing the danger, seemed powerless to render assistance, until a young gentleman said to be Mr A. J. Monson, dressed in flannels, came hurrying up to the scene. Without a moment's hesitation he pluckily plunged into the sea and soon reached the bathing machine. One child was conveyed from the machine to one of the horses, and two others were rescued in a similar manner. Next the rescuer conveyed two scantily attired young ladies safely to shore, but not without considerable effort, as at one moment struck by a large wave his burden appeared too much for him. He again returned to the machine, and released another lady from her perilous position. There then only remained one occupant of the machine, an elderly lady. A huge wave now lifted the machine and threw the lady into the water. She struggled until she succeeded in grasping the collar of the bathing van horse, and was conveyed on shore.

Monson was thus elevated – in Mablethorpe at least – from villain to hero. It was not, however, a status he would enjoy for long.

16

The One that Got Away

'There's a cold-blooded scoundrel!'

Sherlock Holmes, 'A Case of Identity'

While Monson attempted to rebuild his life after the murder trial, Littlejohn and Bell were left to lick their wounds. The verdict had come as a bitter blow and it rankled long after it was delivered. Naturally, it was not the first time that the two doctors had found themselves on the 'losing side' in a legal case, nor would it be the last. After all, even the great Sherlock Holmes was allowed a few setbacks along the way – and he was not at the disadvantage of having to operate in the real world. In one such case, 'The Adventure of the Yellow Face' – published in 1893 and set in Norbury to the southwest of London – Holmes embarked on a series of deductions that proved to be quite wrong. After the story's denouement, he urged Watson, 'if it should ever strike you that I am getting a little over-confident in my powers … kindly whisper "Norbury" in my ear, and I shall be infinitely obliged to you.' One might imagine that Ardlamont was Bell and Littlejohn's Norbury.

It is clear from Bell's interview published in the *Pall Mall Gazette* on 28 December 1893 that the pair had been confident of Monson's conviction. Although published after the verdict was delivered, the interview had taken place while the trial was still ongoing. The piece concluded:

> Then the conversation fell into a private chat about the Ardlamont murder, concerning which I was pledged to secrecy. But I do not think the embargo extended to the doctor's mention that he and his colleagues in the Crown case, Dr Littlejohn and Dr Heron Watson, contemplate a further move which will excite the deepest ... but on second reflection this may have been a confidential communication.

It is an intriguing couple of sentences. In due course, Bell would confide in his author friend Jessie Saxby: 'Just see what the wretch from the *Pall Mall* has inveigled me into confessing ... However, I did not give the devil any secrets.' Still, there is much that is hinted at. Firstly, there is the use of the word 'murder' – a bold assertion given that the defence had argued that no crime had been committed and that the jurymen had been unable to decide for certain. Then there was Bell's desire to keep talk of the case off the record. Why should that have been? If it was simply a case of professional integrity and a desire not to undermine due process, why then engage with a journalist in the first place? Was Bell privy to some information that he wished discreetly to filter out to the press? Something that was perhaps not among the Crown's evidence? For if it were, there would have been no need for him to be so cautious. And what of the 'further move' that Bell, Littlejohn and Heron Watson were contemplating? One that would excite the deepest ... what? Suspicion? Excitement? Scandal? Alas, we will never know for certain the contents of this private conversation. In fact, we cannot even be sure whether the 'further move' was enacted during the trial. If it was, it is difficult to identify exactly *what* it was, since the combined evidence of the Edinburgh trio was played by the book. If, on the other hand, they did not unleash this mystery move, what on earth had Bell been referring to?

Although neither Bell nor Littlejohn went on the public record to express their disgruntlement at the verdict, they were less reticent in private. Both were adamant that the judge had been unduly lenient towards Monson in the summing-up. Indeed, the post-trial opinion pieces in the newspapers, along with interviews from members of the jury, confirmed their fears that the judge's contribution had been decisive. The doctors were convinced that he had been overcome by the pressures of the trial. The complexity of the case combined with the intense scrutiny he was under had combined to warp his judgement, they believed. And they may have had a point. Many years later, in 1915, Lord Kingsburgh had this to say of the events of December 1893:

… It fell to me to preside at the trial of Alfred John Monson for murder, the longest and the most protracted inquiry since I joined the profession. I went through nine days of anxiety, such as I have never experienced before or since. The case was one which so bristled with points, that one had to watch its course from moment to moment, and to take scrupulous care lest the jury should be misled by feelings roused by the disclosure of the evil character of the accused. So dominant was the anxiety, that morning after morning I awoke long before my usual time, and lay in dull perspiration, turning things over and over, endeavouring to weigh them and determine their weight in the balance. Never before had I gone through an experience the least like it, and I am well pleased that I have never had a similar experience since. It was all the more trying because I felt quite unable to form a determined opinion in my own mind. The way never seemed to me clear. In the end I was able to feel that I had done my best to put the case in a fair light before the jury, and can freely say that the verdict they returned was that which in all the circumstances was the safe one. I have more than once been comforted by the assurance of judges, including some of other parts of the United Kingdom, that in their opinion the jury were led to the proper conclusion. This trial was, in my judgement, the most severe strain I have ever undergone, and not one or two nights of quiet repose were sufficient to restore mind and body.

By his own admission, the judge had been in turmoil throughout. Sleep-deprived, anxious and unable to get on top of his own thoughts, these were hardly the ideal circumstances in which he would have wished to make his closing address. It was unsurprising then that he should press home those elements of uncertainty in the case that mirrored the uncertainty in his own mind. Perhaps in good faith he had no choice but to do so. Yet, writing some twenty-two years later, he seemed to have had no doubt as to the true nature of the defendant – Monson was, he said, an 'evil character'. While working to the letter of the law, did Kingsburgh ill-serve justice? That was certainly the view of Bell, Littlejohn and Heron Watson – as they were rumoured to keenly remind a good many of their acquaintances.

Others, though, were more eager to accept the verdict as the least bad option. In January 1894, the *Edinburgh Evening News* covered two shooting incidents that it claimed both had parallels to the Ardlamont case. The first, reported on 8 January, took place in the village of Fintry in Stirlingshire. A party of six shooters and thirty beaters were hunting on the Culcreuch estate when one of the men crossed a dyke with both barrels of his gun cocked. When the butt of the gun struck an unknown object, it went off and the shot glanced off the side of the head of another member of the party, taking away a good part of the scalp. The next incident, which took place in Yeovil in Somerset towards the end of the month, was described by the coroner as 'alike in almost every particular to the Ardlamont mystery'. One Dr F. H. Hudson gave evidence in relation to the death of a seventy-one-year-old man, Mr Rossiter:

> On Tuesday morning I was called to see the body, which was lying in a room at the farmhouse. I found a lacerated wound behind the right ear, with the brain protruding. On examining the head I found every bone shattered and loose, but there was no external wound except that behind the right ear. The hole in the skull admitted three fingers. There was no singeing of the hair, but there was a slight blackening of the lower part of the wound. Death must have occurred instantly. I think that the wound could not intentionally have been self inflicted, taking into consideration the situation in which [the] deceased was and the position of the wound and its direction. I am of [the] opinion that the accident occurred in the following manner: The deceased was coming out of the granary with the measure of barley in his left hand, the gun being held by the barrel in the right hand. Possibly Mr Rossiter was coming down the steps sideways, as one often did. This would bring the position of the wound in a direct line with the door of the granary. He was probably not more than one step down, and slipping, the trigger hitched in some projection.

The jury returned a verdict of accidental death. The similarities between the three cases were doubtless striking and they contributed to the feeling that maybe, just maybe, Cecil's death had been accidental after all. But it was far from enough to convince Littlejohn and Bell, who not only maintained utter faith in the validity of their own forensic investigations but also had the wealth of circumstantial evidence to draw upon, too. They had long ago concluded that if it looked and felt that much like a murder, then surely it was just that.

Although the lives of Littlejohn and Bell were as hectic as ever in 1894 in terms of their professional and public duties, their courtroom experiences were decidedly more muted than the previous year. Bell hinted to various of his friends that the police were inviting his cooperation in still more criminal investigations, but, as was the pattern prior the Ardlamont case, his investigative work barely garnered a mention in the press. He also indulged more time upon himself and his family, perhaps partly as a delayed reaction to the loss of his son the previous summer. As well as paying regular visits to his grown-up daughters, Joan and Cecil (short for Cecilia), he also bought Mauricewood, a grand Victorian mansion complete with rounded turret and set in some three-and-a quarter acres of wooded grounds at Milton Bridge, Midlothian. A little under ten miles from the centre of Edinburgh, Bell enjoyed giving his horses a workout on his way to and from work each day, so that his grandchildren came to give him the nickname 'Gigs'. He also enjoyed an active social life at this time – buoyed by his Holmes-linked celebrity – and he counted among his friends such eminent figures as Robert Louis Stevenson and the actress Ellen Terry.

As for Littlejohn, he was confronted by a series of major public health issues, not least an outbreak of smallpox that claimed one of his own staff. In the courts, there was nothing remotely to match the fireworks of Monson's trial but there were nonetheless several cases of interest. He was involved, for instance, in the tragic affair of Donald MacDonald, who was accused of slitting his sister's throat and who himself was found drowned in Glasgow's docks before the matter could come to trial. Then there was the curious incident of a justice of the peace charged with stealing six small Wedgwood plates and three pieces of Spode crockery from a local cottage sale. With the defendant claiming 'insane impulse', Littlejohn caused some consternation by diagnosing him with kleptomania – a psychological compulsion to steal. Several commentators feared the floodgates opening so that every common thief might claim their crimes resulted from an unavoidable urge beyond their control. The judge was nonetheless sympathetic to Littlejohn's argument and landed the JP with a fine rather than prison.

Meanwhile, the trial of a sixteen-year-old boy called Alan Fergusson allowed for a reunion of several of the Ardlamont mystery's key players – Littlejohn, Comrie Thomson and Lord Kingsburgh. The defendant happened to be the son of Sir James Fergusson, a former Postmaster General (a senior cabinet position). It caused something of a stir, then, when the boy was arrested for two episodes of 'wilful fire-raising' at his exclusive school, Trinity College in Glenalmond, Perthshire. After examining the young Fergusson, Littlejohn concluded that he was suffering from 'arrested and imperfect development of the intellectual powers', a view that was not enough to save Fergusson from prison but which saw him receive a relatively merciful sentence of only twelve months.

In November 1894, Littlejohn was called upon to adjudge the mental state of another defendant, James Connor, who was accused of wilfully and maliciously placing a chair on a railway line, so endangering the lives of all those on board a train. Connor – who had already pleaded guilty when Littlejohn testified that he was 'a little stupid' – received thirty days with hard labour, but it was for the efforts of one of the investigating officers that the story was most interesting. One Constable Gerrie of the local police force had, on visiting the crime scene, noticed footprints created by boots recently patched on the sole. With a rigour that would surely have delighted Sherlock Holmes, Gerrie noted the pattern of the repair and then made a tour of the various farmhouses in the local district to inspect the boots of the labourers working there. Sure enough, before long he had collared his man.

For all that Littlejohn and Bell had plenty to occupy their time and thoughts in the post-Monson period, their sense of burning injustice would not dissipate. The manner in which their evidence had been, to all intents and purposes, passed over – and with the encouragement of such prestigious counterparts as Dr Hay – left them exasperated. It was perhaps the unavoidable cost of working on the cutting edge, engaging in scientific analysis far ahead of its time. In 1933, Robert Churchill – Scotland Yard's leading firearms expert for some half a century – carried out a review of the trial transcript. 'It is more thrilling than anything Edgar Wallace ever wrote,' he commented enthusiastically, referencing the man who for a while was the world's bestselling author. Churchill then continued: 'The evidence is one-hundred per cent for conviction, so the jury were either blind or kind.' It is likely that Littlejohn and Bell considered the jury blind and the judge too kind.

To add to their disquiet, at some point they came into possession of evidence that was not heard during the trial but which, if it had been, would surely have delivered a different result. We know of it only indirectly, via a reference that Arthur Conan Doyle made in a letter to his mother, Mary, dated 23 January 1894. It was sent from Davos in Switzerland, where Doyle had spent a good deal of time in late 1893 and early 1894 in the hope that the alpine air might improve the health of his sickly wife, Louisa (known as Touie). In a postscript to the letter written as he was completing one of his non-Holmesian works, *The Stark Munro Letters*, Doyle wrote: 'Have had pleasant letters from Barrie [J. M. Barrie, author of *Peter Pan*], Stevenson [Robert Louis Stevenson, author of *Treasure Island* and *The Strange Case of Dr Jekyll and Mr Hyde*] and Dr Joe Bell – the latter still convinced that Monson did the murder. Scott's brother was told by Scott that he saw Monson kill Hambrough, but was prevented by Scots law from saying so.'

Tucked away in Doyle's copious correspondence, here is perhaps definitive proof of Alfred Monson's guilt. So, what is to be made of the extraordinary claim? Unfortunately, it is impossible to know when Bell came into this intelligence. He and Littlejohn both gave evidence on the third day of the trial, with Littlejohn also briefly recalled on day six. Scott/Sweeney's brother, George Sweeney, testified on the seventh day. It is certainly possible that their paths crossed as each awaited their moment in court. Yet, of course, George Sweeney had committed to giving a very different version of events under oath, claiming no knowledge of his brother's whereabouts and insisting that he could no way be involved in Cecil's demise. This was the strategy he hoped would see his brother saved from the gallows for ever. There was good reason, then, not to start contradicting himself with new and perhaps unprovable revelations of Monson's guilt, even if he knew them to be true. But would he have then gossiped with fellow witnesses in the manner suggested by Doyle's letter? It seems unlikely, but a humble hotel porter put into an extraordinarily stressful situation in a strange city ... well, one might imagine his jaw might be loosened under certain circumstances.

Was Sweeney's revelation perhaps related to the 'further move' Bell had discussed with the journalist from the *Pall Mall Gazette*? Might the Edinburgh doctors have had it in mind to twist the arm of Sweeney so that he could deliver the death blow to Monson's defence? Imagine their disappointment as Sweeney's actual testimony merely contributed to the feelings of confusion and contradiction that prevailed over the trial. And if Sweeney revealed his inside knowledge to them after the trial, how frustrated they must have felt to know that Scott had held the key to the whole mystery all along. Quite what was meant by the assertion that Scott/Sweeney was 'prevented by Scots law' from denouncing Monson is unclear, though. There is certainly no legal barrier to exposing a murderer, and Scott/Sweeney had the opportunity to speak freely at the outset. But once he had gone to ground and then been subject to a sentence of outlawry, he would surely have feared being charged with murder if he attempted to engage with the authorities. Just like Monson, as a defendant he would not have had the right to speak up at his own trial, so was this perhaps the legal impediment he envisaged? Regardless, by the time Bell was disclosing this new evidence to Doyle, the game was already up. The law would not allow a retrial. Sweeney, Bell and Littlejohn could say whatever they liked to whomever was willing to listen, but Monson would never have to face them in a courtroom again.

Nor, agonisingly, would he disappear from view. Again and again, Monson found his way into the newspapers, a recurring reminder to Littlejohn and Bell that they had been unable to deliver him to justice. After popping up all over the place in 1894 – lecturing, writing his book, suing Madame Tussauds – he came into view again in May 1895. Back in league with the showman Charles Morritt, Monson accepted a challenge to be publicly hypnotised and then to answer a series of questions from the audience. (In fact, Morritt and Monson were spotted enjoying a drink together at a pub in the middle of Edinburgh in the afternoon before their purported 'grudge match'.) On the evening of the performance, Monson was quickly 'put under' to a crescendo of boos and hisses, along with a faint mingling of applause. Then the interrogation began, with Morritt reading questions from cards that had been circulated around the audience. The first question was, inevitably: 'Did you murder Cecil Hambrough?' Monson replied in the negative. The next question: 'Do you know who killed him?' 'I don't know,' came the response.

It was a most puzzling response, coming from a man who had maintained from the outset that Cecil had died by his own hand.

17

A Dog with a Bad Name

'… the sword of justice is still there to avenge.'

Sherlock Holmes, 'The Adventure of the Resident Patient'

As 1894 turned into 1895, there was a sense that the Ardlamont trial had been an extraordinary 'moment' punctuating the lives of Bell and Littlejohn and, indirectly, Doyle and Sherlock Holmes, too. The court hearings in Edinburgh at the end of 1893 had thrown the first two into the spotlight just as Doyle was orchestrating the latter's departure from the public stage. Two years on and life had returned to a normality of sorts. Bell and Littlejohn maintained their hectic schedules – Bell, for instance, intimated to his friends that his professional involvement with the police actually grew in this period, while he and his team at the Royal Hospital for Sick Children dealt with no less than 1,222 surgical cases in 1895 alone – but the public microscope had now moved its focus on to other subjects of interest. Doyle, meanwhile, undertook a successful tour of the United States, where he informed journalists and fans that there was little prospect of resurrecting his great detective. He was having far too much fun introducing, for example, his Brigadier Gerard character to the world. And there was no shortage of rival authors bringing their own fictional detectives to the reading public, often under the banner of 'the new Sherlock Holmes'. Bell, moreover, seems to have become tired with his literary association – never more focused upon than during the Ardlamont trial – describing the Holmes stories to a correspondent as a 'cataract of drivel' that brought 'a heap of rubbish [falling] on my head'. It was indicative that his experiences of fame had not all been pleasing. Nonetheless, while Ardlamont had placed Littlejohn, Bell and Doyle in the eye of a perfect storm, its memory, for them, was now starting to fade a little.

For Monson, though, the prospect of carving out an 'ordinary' life was as distant as ever. As his efforts to capitalize on his notoriety failed, he struggled to impose much order upon his world. 'There is an ancient proverb,' he would comment in 1898, '"give a dog a bad name and you may as well hang him," an adage which applies with a more appreciable effect to a human being'. In his own estimation, despite being acquitted of Cecil's murder, the nature of the charge made it impossible for him to embark on what might have been considered a normal, respectable life. The verdict of the jury in 1893 may have granted him a second chance, but how to seize it with any effectiveness evaded him.

After his unfulfilling stint in London in the early part of 1894, Monson again relocated to Yorkshire. Ever willing to surrender to his sense of entitlement, he was of the mind that his wealthy relatives, and his mother in particular, ought to be dipping into their pockets to support him and his family. 'Under the circumstances,' he said, 'surely it was their duty to render some such assistance. At least one has, I think, a right to expect persons endowed with titles and wealth and honourable distinction to set examples of charity towards a member of their family who was in such dire necessity as I was.' His aim was to tap the extended family for a few pounds per week – enough to cover board and lodgings – but such support was not forthcoming. His mother – who had, it should be remembered, bankrolled his defence – referred him to her solicitors. They in turn offered him £100 plus travel expenses on condition that he, his wife and children settled abroad.

Before long, the Monsons had worked through their funds yet again. Alfred decided to move back to London once more, where he fancied his chances were greater of making a living of sorts. For a year or so, he just about managed to eke out an existence – including by his exploits with Morritt – but the family endured severe hardship. The strain told upon Agnes, who at one stage took to her bed for a period of ten weeks, until her mother, Annie Day, nursed her back to health and relocated her daughter and the children to Doncaster.

Then, in December 1894, Monson's name took another battering when Major Hambrough sued the Mutual Life Insurance Company of New York for the recovery of £20,000 for the insurances Monson had taken out on Cecil. The case minutely examined Monson's conduct as he made no less than ten attempts to have Cecil insured between December 1890 and August 1893, with the special jury concluding after three days of evidence that the Mutual policies were obtained using false and fraudulent claims. Major Hambrough thus could make no claim on the monies, nor Agnes Monson who had also tentatively begun action against the insurance company. In a coruscating judgment, Cecil was characterized as putty in Monson's hands. Lord Esher, the Master of the Rolls (the second most senior judge in England and Wales), noted: 'A greater mass of impudent falsehoods has never been told. The statements were infamous lies, and upon them these policies were issued. Monson was clearly acting for Cecil throughout; the boy was under his influence, and had been, so to speak, mesmerized into signing the false statements in the proposal which his tyrant had written for him.' Yet despite this damning indictment, Monson would not face charges for fraud. By this time, there was little will to put him through another criminal trial in relation to his dealings with the Hambroughs. What was to be gained anyway? The insurance company had proved its case and could leave the episode behind without incurring any further costs. The Major had nothing to gain financially and lacked the resources to pursue additional legal avenues even if he had wanted to take things further. The matter was now dealt with as far as the courts were concerned.

Meanwhile, Monson simmered resentment at his mother-in-law's role in separating him from his wife. Before long, he hit upon a plan to wrest her back. Having managed to secure something in the region of £200 from his long-suffering relatives, he announced to Agnes his wish to move the family to Montreal in Canada. By September 1895, he had a second-class stateroom booked on a ship sailing out of Liverpool. Agnes and the children were all set to go with him, but at the last minute something changed. Seemingly, Agnes rejected the accommodation as unsuitable for such a long voyage and so their emigration was aborted. Instead, they all took a ferry to the Isle of Man.

Here, Monson fell back into his old ways with consummate ease. He unburdened them of the Monson name, instead restyling as the Wyvills (Wyvill being his maternal grandmother's maiden name). He then set about concocting a credible backstory for the family, which involved them having spent a long period of time in Canada. It was because of this, Monson would suggest, that he could not provide the bank references necessary to rent a large house that had caught his eye. In the end, the landlord took him on good faith and Monson signed a ten-year lease on a spectacular mansion called Ballabrooie, in the island's capital, Douglas. He then engaged a local carpenter to craft bespoke furniture to fill the new home – on credit, naturally. The carpenter was content that a man who could move into a property such as Ballabrooie was to be trusted. The Monsons had soon ingratiated themselves into Manx polite society, enjoying all the trappings that went with it.

But by the end of 1895, Monson had accumulated a large overdraft on his account with the local bank. Then, Ballabrooie caught fire, seemingly the result of a gas explosion. The *Isle of Man Times* reported that, several weeks earlier, the tenant had complained of a gassy smell in the house but that plumbers brought in to investigate had not been able to find any leakage. It was also noted that Mr Wyvill had suffered a bruised and swollen arm when a section of exploding brickwork struck him. Despite the best efforts of the local fire brigade, not to mention the Bishop of Sodor and Man who was taking tea nearby, the building burnt to the ground. Monson had, of course, taken out insurance on the contents, and soon made a claim for £500. The insurance company, however, disputed the claim. Rumour had it that silver and other valuables for which Monson was claiming were discovered secreted around the property.

Monson could not afford to let the matter rest and so began legal proceedings against the insurers. This proved to be his undoing, for one of the island's most prominent lawyers happened to have been present in London for the Madame Tussauds hearings. He already harboured suspicions as to Mr Wyvill's true identity but now he became convinced that Wyvill and Monson were one and the same man. He duly contacted the police with his suspicions. When a number of books were recovered from Ballabrooie bearing Monson's name, the game was up. Before long, the Leeds police arrived on the scene and arrested him in relation to Tottenham's perjury accusations – having seemingly been unable to track him down in the year or more since Tot had first made his accusations. The allegations centred on a letter that Tot had claimed Monson had sent him and which was read out at Tot's larceny trial. Monson had said that parts of the letter, which dealt with the supposed negotiations to buy Ardlamont, had been forged by Tot. However, at Monson's perjury trial in January 1896, a handwriting expert gave testimony that the letter was produced by a single hand – the defendant's. Nonetheless, the case was dismissed when the judge ruled that the evidence concerning the letter had not materially affected the jury's verdict in the original larceny case. Once again, Monson walked free but with a new stain on his character.

His 'new start' thus over in just a few months, Monson returned to London and worked variously as a tout, moneylender and even a hair-restorer salesman. In his own words, he was forced 'to beg, borrow, or steal, and obtain the necessities of life as chance came in my way'. His main ruse involved scouring the wills held at Somerset House in London in a hunt for young men expected to inherit large sums. He would then track down these gentlemen with proposals to realize advances on the monies destined to come their way. Acting as the go-between to unscrupulous moneylenders – most notably a man named Victor Honour, who also went by the unlikely names of John Milton and William Shakespeare – Monson engineered often fraudulent advances, taking a share of the total sum as his reward. So, for instance, he took on the case of the Earl of Rosslyn, whom he had heard needed £300 in a hurry. Alas for Rosslyn, he had already mortgaged his properties to the hilt and so had little chance of agreeing credit with a reputable bank. Monson thus introduced him to Honour and a loan was agreed on punitive terms for the aristocrat. Moreover, Rosslyn was strong-armed into buying a perfumery business that Honour held in his name (Honor Frères) and which the Lord had no interest in taking on. Monson earned a quick £15 for thus shackling Rosslyn with a new bundle of unwanted debt, while Rosslyn was soon forced to declare himself a bankrupt. He joined a long roll call of eminent young gents who lost their fortunes at the hands of Monson and Honour.

As well as indebting young men impatient to get their hands on the family wealth, Monson and Honour employed a secondary tactic of blackmail. If they could persuade any of their gullible marks to commit a legal faux pas in the course of their financial dealings – for instance, faking a parent's signature – they would seize the opportunity to put the squeeze on the victim's parents, who as often as not agreed to pay up in order to avoid a scandal. It was all in all a tidy business. Monson claimed he had up to a dozen approaches a day for help. 'Amongst the vendors or borrowers I have acted for either directly or indirectly,' he claimed, 'are enumerated one prince, two marquises, three earls, four baronets, about eight sons of peers (one of whom was an eldest son who sold his reversions to everything he was entitled, and he will thus succeed to an empty title on the death of his father, a judge). I can also number amongst my clientele several magistrates, county gentlemen, clergymen, etc.'

Meanwhile, Monson's marriage to Agnes had gone into terminal decline. Forced into ever less salubrious dwellings, Agnes struggled to provide for herself and her children on the meagre and intermittent handouts that Monson gave her. This despite Monson regularly being seen dining out and playing the gent around town. Although the couple had two more children in the period after the trial, there was little love left between them and the relationship was soon over in all but name. Almost exclusively reliant on the support of her mother, in November 1897 Agnes took her husband to court on grounds of desertion. He failed to attend the hearing in Leeds where she gave brief testimony dressed all in black, save for a white sailor hat and signature thick veil. The court ruled that Monson should pay her 40s per week plus costs.

Somewhat predictably, this money was not forthcoming. In August the following year, Agnes's mother sued Monson for £465 11s to cover the cost of board and lodgings for Agnes and her children. Again, there was no representation from Monson. Agnes was the only witness as she told how Mrs May had kept them since 1893 – evidence that convinced the jury to find in the plaintiff's favour. Still no money arrived. Instead, in November 1898 Agnes faced the indignity of appealing to the board of guardians in Bridlington for poor relief. She was awarded 1s 5d for each child per week, but more importantly she had the board's backing to compel her mother-in-law to contribute financially to their upkeep, too. Mrs Monson, though, fought the move with all her might.

By that time, Monson had faced a legal reckoning of sorts. In August 1898 he appeared at the Old Bailey on charges of conspiracy to obtain a life policy by false pretences. Alongside him in the dock were Victor Honour and another 'financial agent', Robert Ives Metcalfe. The case centred on Percival Norgate – twenty-eight years old and, like Monson, a rector's son. The prosecution alleged that in order to procure a life insurance policy for Norgate from the Norwich Union Life Insurance Society, Monson and his confederates had substituted him with an associate, Stanley Hobson, to undergo the medical that they knew Norgate, a man of long-term delicate health, would likely fail. Furthermore, it was shown that they had persuaded Norgate to forge his mother's signature on various bills of exchange, which were then used to extort money from his parents in return for silence regarding the young man's misdemeanour. Despite Monson's lawyer pleading that his client had 'struggled hard against prejudice to lead an honest life', the jury took just fifteen minutes to convict. Both Monson and Honour were sentenced to five years' hard labour, with Metcalfe receiving eighteen months. It was not, the judge said, likely that this was an isolated case. Monson reportedly flushed on hearing his punishment.

His reaction was in stark contrast to that of Bell, Littlejohn and Heron Watson, all of whom delighted in what they considered a long-overdue victory for justice. Of course, it could not make up for the disappointment of losing the Ardlamont case, but at least, in the word of the *Scotsman*, 'these specimens of the worst type of social pest have been safely locked up for some time to come'. The London correspondent of the *Scottish Law Review* wryly noted that the English law had brought to justice he whom the Scots law had let go free. Moreover, the result confirmed in the public mind that

Monson was a man routinely drawn to insurance frauds and willing to sacrifice the lives of innocents on the altar of his own avarice. Where Monson had been given the benefit of the doubt in 1893, he had surely exhausted that privilege now. For a while, he and Honour seemed to have their names linked to every episode of theft or financial skulduggery imaginable. In January 1899, for instance, the *Manchester Courier* reported that 'Monson, of Ardlamont fame, who is now undergoing a term of imprisonment in connection with moneylending fraud, together with Victor Honour, is connected with the scheme which resulted in the robbery of jewels from the Dowager Duchess of Sutherland, at the Gare du Nord, Paris, in October'. No charges were ever brought.

While serving his sentence, Monson boldly attempted to recast himself as a kind of moral crusader. Having been set adrift by his family, he suggested, he had been given no choice but to make a living any way he could. But now he was out of the moneylending business, he was quick to condemn it. 'There is one – and to my mind only one – step necessary to stop the evils attendant on moneylending,' he proclaimed, 'and that is to establish a court where a borrower can take his case to be investigated in the event of his disputing the claim of the moneylender, such court to be closed to reporters and the enquiry to be conducted in privacy, such court having power to adjudicate on the amount to be paid … One hears people say that such and such a person is a respectable moneylender. I say I don't believe it. There is no such person. It is an impossible condition. The business is immoral, and, consequently, the persons implicated are bound to become to a certain extent demoralized'.

Few, though, had much time for his critique. As the *To-Day* magazine put it: 'He was a clever man, and carried his coolness and unscrupulousness to a point where most criminals would have broken down'. The *Bridlington Free Press* for its part took the opportunity to paint Monson as an example of wider social ills. He was, they said,

The most perfect type of the swell mobsman the present century has seen. Monson's life has been that of a large, and, I am afraid, increasing class of young men whose birthright is their curse. Too highly born to work, educated in a manner that proved utterly useless for a business career, even had he desired to work, brought up amid surroundings that rendered a life of ease almost indispensable and fostered tastes that he could never expect to be able to honestly gratify. Monson received a terrible shock when he reached the age of manhood ... Monson was one of the most dangerous scoundrels in Europe ... his career points with terrible emphasis to a ghastly flaw in the social system of the day, which alone has rendered such a personality possible.

And so Monson found himself locked away in London's Holloway Prison, his remarkable record of outpacing the justice system at last at an end. More than that, he had also definitively exhausted the love of Agnes. She, who had stood loyally behind him during his darkest days and accepted the brickbats of public condemnation, was lost to him. As Dr Watson himself was once moved to observe: 'Evil indeed is the man who has not one woman to mourn him.' Yet any thoughts that Monson might be crushed by his demise and disgrace were premature. Instead, his infamous streak of impudence was as evident as ever. When a visiting magistrate encountered him in his cell, he asked, 'Have you any complaints to make?' 'No,' Monson replied. 'Is there anything you want?' enquired the justice. Monson's answer: 'Only a latch-key.'

Monson's 1898 conviction proved something else – even the rolling by of the years had not diminished the facility of the Ardlamont affair to excite and stimulate public feeling. In the same way, the five years since Sherlock Holmes's legendary episode at the Reichenbach Falls had done little to lessen passion for the Great Detective – if anything, the hunger for more of his adventures was growing by the day, a hunger that would soon demand sating. Meanwhile, the two unassuming figures – Littlejohn and Bell – who provided the common thread between the most sensational murder trial and the most beloved fictional creation of the age went on with business as usual.

18

The Veiled Lover?

'Poor girl! The ways of fate are indeed hard to understand.'

Sherlock Holmes, 'The Adventure of the Veiled Lodger'

It is not impossible that Alfred Monson was, as he claimed, innocent of the murder of Cecil Hambrough. Accidental deaths involving shotguns were, after all, far more common than homicides. Maybe Cecil – a little hazy from the previous night's misadventure on the water, not to mention the drinks that flowed freely afterwards – lost his footing in the woods at Ardlamont, catching his gun on a bush or tree stump and inadvertently setting it off. As the prosecution and the newspapers showed, such freakish occurrences happened more than one might think.

And yet. Such a view of the events of 10 August 1893 demand the setting aside of a vast bank of suspicious circumstances. We are forced to accept as just coincidence that Monson had only days earlier secured life insurance upon the victim, that only the night before the non-swimmer Cecil had been thrown from a boat in which a hole had been purposefully gorged, that one of his hunting companions was masquerading behind an assumed identity and subsequently went to ground for entirely innocent reasons, that Cecil was carrying a gun that was normally in the possession of Alfred Monson, and that the shot which killed him should have hit him in the head from behind. Away from the strictures of a judicial system that demands the prosecution prove its case beyond doubt, it is difficult rationally to avoid the conclusion that Cecil died at his tutor's hand. Furthermore, there is other suggestive evidence of which the jury was unaware – beyond even Bell's revelation that, according to George Sweeney, Edward Sweeney had witnessed the slaying.

From the outset, the problem faced by those who suspected Monson's involvement was how to explain various anomalous aspects of the case. With the forensics disputed – although experts as eminent as Robert Churchill in due course suggested it should not have been – the prosecution had to establish an inviolable motive. They hit, naturally enough, upon financial gain – specifically, £20,000 of life insurance. Yet several lingering questions undermined the assertion. Why would a man apparently skilled in insurance fraud take out a policy on his victim that was legally invalid? If murder was always the intention, why not wait until Cecil turned twenty-one and the insurance could be legitimately activated? Moreover, why kill him anyway if there was the prospect of greater profit in keeping him alive?

To take the last of those questions first, the truth was that no one seemed quite sure just how valuable an asset Cecil's life might prove to be. The press had spoken of clauses in his grandfather's will that would see him inherit something approaching a quarter of a million pounds on reaching his majority, although this would never have been the case in reality – there was never such an explicit guarantee. Then, during the course of the trial, a value was put on Steephill and his father's other property in Middlesex that was confidently in the region of six figures. Yet this was also a misrepresentation of the wealth that Cecil might have expected to come into anytime soon. In fact, he would have been entitled to nothing automatically on turning twenty-one. Only when his father died – and the Major was just forty-four at the time of Cecil's death – would he inherit the right to the family estates. On his next birthday, Cecil might have sought to limit the succession on Steephill with his father's permission – that is to say, they could have removed the legal provisions to pass the property on to the next generation – and then they could have sold the estate as a freehold. Equally, Cecil could have taken a mortgage on his prospective inheritance, although any responsible mortgager would have demanded a sizable life insurance against his predeceasing his father. Neither strategy was straightforward or a guarantee of riches.

All of which is to say that Cecil was not the easy meal-ticket he might once have seemed to Monson. In October 1893, Mr Kime, a solicitor who had acted for several members of the Hambrough family over a period of years, went public to say that the Hambrough estates had been considerably overvalued. In Kime's opinion, on coming of age Cecil would have been in little better financial position than he was as a minor. He believed that if Cecil had mortgaged his prospective interest he would have raised a sum amounting only to a few years' purchase of his birthright – especially since the solicitor did not believe the boy to qualify medically as a first-class risk. On the other hand, if father and son chose to cut off the entail and sell the estates as freeholds, the obviously forced nature of such a sale would ensure they received a price much lower than the paper value. They would then need to settle the various debts accrued by both father and son, leaving little in the pot for their futures or, indeed, to pay commission to Monson and Tot. Kime went so far as to suggest that any attempt by Cecil to raise money on turning twenty-one would likely prove ruinous. Once it became clear that the Cecil–Monson–Tot axis was not going to be able to remortgage Steephill – and whatever the defence suggested at trial, it was obvious by the early summer of 1893 that that particular opportunity was dead and buried once the Eagle Insurance Company had expressed their preference for a proposed deal with the Major – Cecil was suddenly a much less attractive financial prospect. Furthermore, Monson likely realized that any new scheme would probably need the cooperation of Cecil's father, which was by then in very short supply.

Under such circumstances, it is easy to see why Monson might have been tempted by a quick cash-in via an insurance claim on Cecil's life. Except that the policy was not valid while Cecil remained a minor. Monson, Tot and several other witnesses testified that they clearly understood this at the time the policy was taken, and so could not have possibly killed in the expectation of gaining financially from it. This, though, was an argument flawed at many levels. Firstly, if they knew it to be invalid, why go to the effort of purchasing the policy and then having Cecil go through the motions of reassigning it unless they thought that such actions might suffice in the eyes of the law? Even more pertinently, why put in a claim on that insurance if they knew there was no entitlement?

The answer, surely, is there in the evidence of Tottenham. Asked why he had made the claim on Mrs Monson's behalf, having been told by her husband that the assignment was no good, he replied: 'I thought I might possibly get the money paid by "bluffing" the insurance office.' This was the basis upon which Monson and Tot had based their careers – trying it on. Often enough, it had worked. There was a long line of, on the one hand, unpaid creditors and, on the other, indebted clients to prove that. And what was there to lose? The doctor had signed off the death as an accident and Cecil was safely in the ground at Ventnor. Given all that followed, it is easy to forget that the story might have been very different if only the perturbed Procurator-Fiscal had not ordered an exhumation. Even if the insurance company baulked at paying, the worse that Monson might have expected is an undignified retreat from the claim. Once Cecil's funeral was complete, he would surely have calculated that the chance of being accused of killing him as very low. We know from Monson's previous brushes with the law that he did not fear the finger of suspicion. As long as there was insufficient evidence to actually ensnare him, he could brush off accusations and insinuations quite happily. Build trust, defraud, move on – that had long been the Monson way.

Next, the apparently perplexing question of why Monson would ever have inveigled a character as flaky as Scott/Sweeney into proceedings at all? Sweeney, a man much less physically imposing than Cecil, was an odd choice of henchman. All the evidence suggests he was just what he seemed to be – a bookie's clerk operating on the fringes of society. Not a thug and certainly not a murderer. The idea that he was at Ardlamont to assist Monson in killing Cecil lacks credibility. So why was he there? Most probably, Monson invited him ostensibly to serve as a bookie with a view to sharing the profits. Cecil's army friends were due on the estate ahead of the Glorious Twelfth, and military men with money in their pockets and a little free time offered rich pickings. Sweeney would surely have jumped at the invitation. But what of taking on the identity of Scott the engineer? According to Sweeney, it was not a persona he assumed but one that was thrust upon him by Monson, on the grounds that the presence of a man of such an undistinguished profession might raise eyebrows. If we take this at face value, Sweeney was thus coerced into playing a role.

But for what purpose? If Monson intended to kill Cecil, he must have known that suspicion would fall immediately upon him if Cecil were to die while alone in his company. But if there might be a third-party witness to testify that there had been an accident … Sweeney, a youngish man of poorish health and lacking social graces, was just the sort of chap that Monson would feel confident of being able to manipulate. Imagine Sweeney's dilemma as he stood over the body of Cecil Hambrough. There he is, up from London to make a little oof, swanning around pretending he is someone he isn't. Monson tells him that Hambrough has shot himself. What should Sweeney do? Go along with it? He may not have seen the fatal shot fired, in which case maybe he convinces himself that Monson is telling the truth. But what if he has seen a murder? Who is to believe him? Over Monson, a man of manners and breeding? Best just to go along with things and then get away from there as quickly as possible.

For his part, Monson has his alibi. Sweeney can back him up with the doctor and then go on his merry way. And should the bookie go rogue and implicate him, it will be easy enough to unmask him. To say, 'Here is a fellow who is not at all whom he claims to be. Here must be the real killer.' Out among the rowan trees that morning, Sweeney is doubtless already fearing for his neck. And so Monson's scheme plays out beautifully. Dr Macmillan is persuaded that Cecil's death is but a terrible accident, and assures the men that there will be no need for a more formal enquiry. Sweeney leaves the scene just after lunch, a little earlier than Monson hopes. He is heard to exclaim his disappointment that Scott is going so soon. No need to arouse suspicions by being too hasty, surely. But no matter, the job has been done. All is on track.

Even Scott/Sweeney's subsequent disappearance didn't hamper Monson's cause. It merely added to the sense of confusion that Monson has been careful to cultivate. At the time of going to trial, nothing of substance was known for sure about Scott. Even as his retreat raised suspicions against Monson, it was all but impossible for the prosecution to make much of it. Again, Monson's accusers were left to make insinuations but unable to deliver hard proof. Moreover, Monson's actions in removing and cleaning the guns, suggesting that he and Cecil had swapped guns, and claiming that Cecil's body had been moved from where it fell all helped to create the uncertainty upon which his defence would rely. Even the life insurance evidence, which had seemed the prosecution's trump card, became so blurred over the question of who knew what about its validity that it ended up playing into the hands of Monson and his team. It is possible to see Monson as a bank robber who lets off a smoke bomb that allows him calmly to go about his business amid the pandemonium he has initiated. If Monson was the murderer that Bell and Littlejohn believed him to be, his conduct was a masterclass in obfuscation. After a career of fairly crude get-rich-quick schemes, it seems possible that Monson had brought to bear a hitherto well disguised level of criminal sophistication. This was an exhibition of misdirection more astounding than anything Charles Morritt might have devised. Or perhaps he had simply got lucky, circumstances conspiring to veil the truth in uncertainty and contradiction. Monson could not claim to have committed the perfect crime but he did, nonetheless, walk away from the affair with his freedom intact.

But what if the prosecution had it wrong as to why Monson killed Cecil? Suppose that financial gain was not the motive – or at least, not the main motive. Could this have been instead a *crime passionnel*? While the defence stretched their case to suggest that Cecil was worth more to Monson alive than dead, the timing was nonetheless curious. In less than a year, Cecil could have legally reassigned the life insurance policies, ensuring the matter of getting a payout on his death was a much simpler one. True, Monson was always in need of a quick buck but if the killing was an insurance job, it had the hallmarks of being over hasty. But what if the insurance was only ever meant to be a secondary benefit to Cecil's death, on the off-chance that Tot could chivvy through the claim? Or what if the insurance was always supposed to serve as a diversion – suggestive of a motive that might be discredited when the policy was exposed as invalid. More smoke and mirrors.

Agnes Monson is an enigmatic figure in the story of Cecil Hambrough's death. She is the veiled beauty who might occasionally show herself for a moment before retreating back into the shadows. She was, we may assume, a free spirit in her youth – the fearless risk-taker prepared to take off around the world in pursuit of love. She was devoted, too, standing by her man even as their hopes of a happy and settled life faded. No matter what trouble her husband found himself in, what new depths he plumbed, what indignity she faced, she remained constant. Where he went, she followed. Whether she turned a blind eye to his criminal schemes or became actively embroiled in them, we cannot know for sure. She did, though, allow her name to be used by him as required in his financial dealings. And even as her husband faced public denunciation, she was there, striding across the deck of the *Lord of the Isles*, proclaiming his innocence to all who would listen – just as she would be present at the back of the court for the duration of his trial.

Yet if she expected her devotion to be repaid even in small part, she was to be savagely disappointed. Virtually as soon as the trial ended, the Monsons were living separate lives – she trying to raise a large family as he embarked on money-making schemes that were either madcap or dodgy, and often both. The little money that came his way generally went out again to support his gentleman's lifestyle, rather than his family. Eventually she was compelled to turn to the courts in a last, desperate bid to make him face up to his responsibilities. Even then, the judgments in her favour went unheeded. Had Monson simply grown tired of his wife? Had the trauma of the Ardlamont affair extinguished the feelings they once had for each other? Or was he perhaps harbouring a longer-term resentment? On 20 June 1898, Monson petitioned his wife for divorce. In the petition, he alleged that on 24 July 1891 Agnes had committed adultery with an unknown person at Riseley Hall. Furthermore, in October and November 1891 she had 'committed adultery with one Cecil Hambrough at the Hotel Metropole, Whitehall in the County of London'.

The divorce was never formalized, probably because Monson started his five-year sentence for fraud before it could be completed. The petition did, however, cast a new light on the events of 1893.

But was his claim true? By 1898 relations were so poor between husband and wife that he was doubtless happy to throw enough mud at her in the hope that some might stick. If she was intent on taking him through the courts for maintenance, he might at least take what remained of her reputation. He may even have thought that there may be some money to be had by reigniting memories of the events at Ardlamont. But for all that, his claim is not without some credibility.

From her various cameo appearances, a picture begins to build. Agnes herself told a journalist in 1898 that by the time the Monsons were living at Riseley Hall, the family home had become 'unbearable' and that she had relied upon Cecil to protect her from 'brutal violence'. Then there was the evidence given at the trial by Alexandra Shand, the family's nursemaid. In an incidental aside, she described seeing Cecil and Agnes walking together along the cliffs below Ardlamont Point, while her husband and the man Shand knew as Scott were out boating. How often did the pair go for walks together, and how might their relations have developed during those periods in each other's company. In the parlour rooms of Victorian Britain, it took less than a walk along the romantic Scottish coastline to set tongues wagging. Meanwhile, the *Aberdeen Weekly Journal* in September 1893 alluded to local gossip concerning 'certain relations of a rather peculiar nature' that were 'supposed to have existed between the late Lieutenant Hambrough and the Monson family'. As was surely intended by the journalist responsible, the mind boggles and the suspicion of untoward sexual relations is unavoidable. After all, Cecil was young and handsome, and Agnes beguiling. It is not beyond the bounds of possibility that they may have found sanctuary in one another, especially if, as Agnes implied, her marriage was already in the doldrums.

Cecil and the Monsons were also known to visit the Hotel Metropole on occasion. Having opened in 1885 at the corner of Northumberland Avenue and Whitehall Place in London, the

Metropole quickly established itself as a favourite with the capital's smart set. Boasting 'every possible convenience and comfort', it was said to regularly host parties for the Prince of Wales and it is even thought to have been featured in a Sherlock Holmes story, as the 'select London hotel' where Francis H. Moulton stayed in 'The Adventure of the Noble Bachelor'. In January 1893, an irate Major Hambrough had tracked Cecil down there, where he found him in the company of Alfred and Agnes.

During Monson's trial there was also an extraordinary exchange between the opposing lawyers and John Campbell Shairp, the Sheriff-Substitute of Argyllshire. On 30 August 1893 – the day of Monson's arrest – Shairp supervised a search of Ardlamont House for any relevant papers, which in the event included letters, pawn tickets and Monson's diary. 'When the search was being made that day, did you see Mrs Monson?' Shairp was asked.

'I did,' he replied.

'Did you ask her about any documents?'

At this point, Comrie Thomson for the defence objected, and the judge expressed his doubts as to it being a 'competent question'. The witness then continued his testimony: 'I saw a small bundle of documents in a sliding drawer in the wardrobe in Mrs Monson's room. I glanced at them, but did not take possession of them. There were two letters, but I cannot say what their contents were. I cannot explain why I did not take possession of the letters without saying what Mrs Monson said to me.'

The judge then interjected, 'In consequence of what she said you did not think it necessary to take possession of them?'

Shairp: 'I did not.'

Comrie Thomson then objected to any further questioning as to the contents of the letters on the grounds that they had not been entered into evidence – they could not have been, since Agnes had squirrelled them away.

There is no way of knowing what was in these letters, nor is it clear why the witness could not reveal what Agnes had said to him to persuade him to leave them as they were. However, it does not take a huge leap of imagination to think that she may have implied that the correspondence was of such a sensitive and personal nature – love letters, say – that she must be allowed to retain them. Faced with an alluring damsel in distress, how could a noble sheriff-substitute deny her. It was the sort of evidence-gathering failure that would have driven Holmes, Littlejohn and Bell to despair. But were these missives perhaps evidence of the affair between his student and his wife that Monson suspected?

As to Cecil's fate, it probably mattered less whether he was indeed Agnes's lover than whether Monson truly believed him to be so. Alternatively, if Monson considered that Cecil and Agnes had a developing bond, might he have feared her telling Cecil something about the schemes Monson and Tot had been plotting for so long? Cecil's correspondence with his father revealed an innocent's faith in Monson's good intentions. But should Agnes warn him that their plans were not as virtuous as he believed, Monson's house of cards risked toppling.

We might then speculate that by early August 1893, Monson had concluded Cecil was expendable: he offered no guarantee of a financial bonanza anymore and he also posed an existential threat to Monson's marriage. Monson could perhaps just about stomach the thought of a flirtation, perhaps even a fully formed liaison, between Agnes and Cecil while Cecil might still deliver a financial windfall. But with that hope dissipated, did two years' worth of suspicions of infidelity at last boil over? Furthermore, if Agnes's loyalty extended to warning Cecil against Monson and Tot, there may be legal repercussions, too. Major Hambrough was convinced that Monson was fraudulently after his family's rightful wealth and, if Cecil provided any corroborating evidence, Monson could be in danger.

In short, Cecil had become a problem that needed removing. Throw in a last-minute life insurance policy and his elimination might even bring monetary reward. Those few days in the relative solitude of Ardlamont before Cecil's friends arrived on 11 August provided the ideal window of opportunity to enact a plan.

This is, of course, merely hypothesis. To paraphrase the words of Heron Watson, I will grant that we are in the region of conjecture. Nonetheless, by entertaining the idea – as perhaps the prosecution ought to have done – that Cecil's death was motivated by more than a hoped-for insurance scam, it is possible to explain some of the apparent oddities in the evidence against Monson. Indeed, the *Sketch* raised the spectre of adultery while the trial was still ongoing:

> Of course, there have been cynics who, adopting the maxim of '*Cherchez la femme*', have suggested that it is a case of a crime coming from jealousy, well or ill-founded; and others, more cruel still, who pretend that there ought to have been a third name in the 'indication'; but, however strong the rumours may be, nothing has been published of a character to justify these suggestions and, therefore, they may be put aside. Notwithstanding this, they lend an air of romance to the many mysterious circumstances that surround this striking case.

It would be another five years before Monson gave public voice to his suspicions that Agnes and Cecil had been lovers. As Sherlock Holmes noted in 'The Adventure of the Noble Bachelor' – published just over a year before Cecil's death – 'Jealousy is a strange transformer of characters.'

19

Aftermath

'Is it possible that you succeeded in climbing out
of that awful abyss?'

Dr Watson, 'The Adventure of the Empty House'

Although some emerged from the experience better than others,
the Ardlamont affair imprinted itself upon the lives of all those who
played a prominent part within it. Even for those who could count
the most extraordinary achievements in their careers, involvement
with the case would forever feature in broad-brush summaries of
their lives. For the less fortunate (and less deserving), those few
months at the end of 1893 would define their entire lives.

His 1898 trial for fraud was for many confirmation that Monson
had got away with murder five years earlier. At the very least, it
condemned his character forever in the eyes of but a small few. In
the generally measured words of the *Scotsman*: 'It is inevitable that
public opinion at least should be influenced in forming a view of
the man's character and conduct by the revelations made before the
High Court of Justiciary, and other appearances in Court which
Monson has since made. Whatever may not have been proved,
it was proved to the hilt that Alfred John Monson was absolutely
without scruple or conscience, and was capable of going to any
depth of baseness for gain.'

Yet despite the wretched state of his reputation, Monson was remarkably not without his defenders. In 1909, the prestigious literary journal the *Academy* reviewed a recently published transcript of his trial, which came with an introductory essay by John W. More. The *Academy's* review included a coruscating attack upon the system that had called Monson to account: 'the verdict in the Monson case was a disgrace to Scotland, a disgrace to Scottish justice and fair play, and a disgrace to humanity ... let this article serve as a tardy reparation offered to the memory of one of the most piteous victims of man's inhumanity to man who ever turned a face brave, undaunted and debonair to the pack of howling dogs that hounded him down.'

It is widely believed that the author of the piece was none other than Lord Alfred Douglas – better known as Bosie, poet and then editor of the magazine, not to mention the lover of Oscar Wilde, whose father, the Marquess of Queensberry, was so instrumental in Wilde's downfall. Whether Bosie truly believed in Monson's innocence or simply distrusted the British systems of justice that had brought low his former paramour, we will never know. It is difficult to see what claim Monson could have had upon his sympathy, though. Could Monson really claim to have been 'hounded', let alone portray himself as a victim of 'man's inhumanity'?

Having been moved to Parkhurst Prison on the Isle of Wight to serve his sentence, Monson was released early on licence (either in 1901 or 1902) and was last heard of back in Africa. In 1902, he wrote to Lord Galway from the Cape Colony, where he had assumed a new identity and was after money so that he might set up business as a horse breeder. What became of him afterwards is anybody's guess, although it is difficult to imagine he saw out whatever remained of his life living quietly or entirely honestly. Agnes, meanwhile, struggled on with life in England. At the census of 1901, she was living in Leeds as Agnes Wyvill, and a decade later went by the same name in Brighton. She died in September 1941 in Bournemouth, having resumed use of the tainted Monson name.

As for Cecil's parents, they never recovered from the nightmarish events in which they found themselves caught up. Marion Hambrough died in 1900, with the Major following eight years later. Having failed to recover his former properties, he left an estate valued at less than £100. Every year on the anniversary of Cecil's death, the Hambroughs placed a notice in the major newspapers that echoed the words of the defence counsel at Monson's trial: 'In loving memory of our dear son, Windsor Dudley Cecil Hambrough, found shot dead in a wood at Ardlamont, Argyllshire, August 10, 1893, in his twenty-first year. "Vengeance is mine; I will repay, saith the Lord."'

And what of Tot and Sweeney? The former was last heard of in 1901, when he made an appearance in the London bankruptcy courts, explaining his losses as in part the result of financial advances he had made to the Hambroughs and the Monsons. It would be fair to say that few wept for his predicament. Sweeney, meanwhile, quickly faded from public view after briefly trying to milk his notoriety – teaming up, as Monson had done, with the showman Mr Morritt in 1894. He appeared in 'a bewildering illusion' at Piccadilly's 'theatre of varieties', the London Pavilion, entitled *The Missing Man*. Strapped into a chair, he was lifted into the air as stage lights flickered around him before the chair tumbled back to earth, *sans* Sweeney. It was perhaps sobering for the young man that he succeeded Arthur Orton in the role. Orton, better known as the Tichborne Claimant, was a butcher's son from the East End of London who in the 1870s had received a fourteen-year sentence after he returned from years in Australia claiming to be the legitimate heir to the Tichborne baronetcy. Weighing in at some twenty stone, Orton's was quite a form to disappear but audiences soon tired of the novelty of seeing (and, indeed, not seeing) him. A similar fate quickly befell Sweeney, who was last spotted in 1895 testifying at a trial in which a solicitor from Lincoln's Inn Fields was attempting to sue Morritt for twenty-five guineas for unpaid fees in relation to introducing Morritt and the former outlaw in the first place.

For the head of Monson's defence team, John Comrie Thomson, the Ardlamont case proved the last great criminal trial of his life. He died suddenly in August 1898 having slipped and fallen on deck while on a cruise. He was attended in his final days by none other than Joseph Bell. Comrie Thomson's opposite number, Alexander Asher, also never featured in such a high-profile courtroom shoot-out again, resigning his position as Solicitor-General in 1894. According to *The Times*, his decision was 'largely owing to the very inadequate remuneration then paid' for holding the post. One suspects the Monson trial did little to persuade him that the job was worth the trouble. A Liberal Member of Parliament for the Elgin Burghs since 1881, Asher fell ill when leaving an evening session at the House of Commons in July 1905 and died the following month.

The judge, Lord Kingsburgh, outlived both the prosecution and defence counsels, only passing away in 1919, but his career never entirely escaped the shadow of 1893. As the *Dundee Evening Telegraph* noted in a tribute to him:

> With a record of twenty-seven years' service as Lord Justice Clerk it fell to the lot of the late Lord Kingsburgh – Sir John Hay Athole Macdonald – to play a prominent part in a larger proportion of the famous Scottish trials of the last half century than any other judge at the Scottish bar ... Of all the late Lord Justice Clerk's cases, however, the extended trial in what was, and still is, the Ardlamont mystery, was undoubtedly the outstanding case. No trial in the annals of the Scottish Law Courts has created greater interest at the time or has been more talked of since.

As for the Edinburgh University triumvirate – Littlejohn, Bell and Heron Watson – the irksome nature of the trial's denouement never entirely diminished. Nonetheless, their failure to ensure a guilty verdict did little to diminish the esteem in which they were held. If Sherlock Holmes was, as Dr Watson famously once described him, 'a brain without a heart, as deficient in human sympathy as he was preeminent in intelligence', Littlejohn, Bell and Heron Watson overflowed with compassion just as much as they delighted in intellectualism. While the Monson verdict was a crushing blow and an affront to their shared faith in rationalism, the affair as a whole highlighted the overriding humanity that had informed their careers over many decades. The jury's verdict hurt because they cared so much – not about simply solving the case but about securing justice for Cecil and his family. Even as the Ardlamont case must count as a professional defeat, they each emerged perhaps even greater in stature than when they had embarked upon their investigations into the events at Ardlamont.

Heron Watson would go on to serve as surgeon to both Queen Victoria and then Edward VII, received a knighthood in 1903 and was elected for a second stint as president of the Royal College of Surgeons of Edinburgh in 1905. He died just before Christmas of 1907, a few weeks short of his seventy-sixth birthday. Littlejohn had to wait only until 1895 for his knighthood, then two years later was appointed Edinburgh University's first chair of medical jurisprudence – a position he ceded to his son, Harvey, in 1906. It was not until 1908 that Henry Littlejohn resigned as the city's medical officer for health, a full forty years after assuming the role. In 1907 one of his former students, Dr William Smith, went some way to isolating the unique position he held in Scottish society, saying, 'Littlejohn has the brain of a lawyer as well as that of a doctor, his work has been midway between the two professions, he is a master of both.' However, following his death in 1914, barely a soul suggested his influence upon the work of Arthur Conan Doyle, with only the *Liverpool Daily Post* heading its obituary: 'The Original Sherlock Holmes'.

That was a title far more regularly bestowed upon Joseph Bell. Bell slowly began to lessen his workload in the years after Ardlamont, allowing himself a little spare time to indulge his many passions, which included the natural world, long walks and, latterly, motoring (in 1907 he became one of Edinburgh's first car owners). Despite having relatively little to do with Doyle after the turn of the century, in 1900 he assisted the now world-famous author and public figure in his bid for a seat in parliament. Doyle was standing as the Liberal Unionist candidate in the Edinburgh Central constituency when he was publicly attacked as a 'papist'. Bell, incensed by such baiting, leapt to his defence and accompanied him on the campaign trail. Appearing alongside him at the Edinburgh Literary Institute, he urged a lively crowd to vote for 'my former dresser', adding, 'if Conan Doyle does half as well in Parliament as he did in the Royal Edinburgh Infirmary, he will make an unforgettable impression on English politics'. Alas, his intervention was not enough to swing the election in Doyle's favour.

Bell was still seeing patients until just a few months before his death in 1911. The *Edinburgh Academy Chronicle* declared that his passing had left 'his native city appreciably smaller', while *The Times* found space to acknowledge his role not only as a medical man but as an expert witness, too. He was, his obituary said, ideal for the job, being 'cool, collected, accurate, and concise … there were few cases, whether criminal or civil, in which his expert knowledge was not called for either by the Crown or the opposite side.' Doyle in turn revealed, 'I always thought what a fine brain like his could have done in detecting crime.'

Yet the fame of none of these figures came close to that enjoyed by Sherlock Holmes – news of whose death as revealed at the moment when Monson faced trial for Cecil Hambrough's murder proved much exaggerated. Doyle was offered such riches to resurrect him that he did just that in 1901, when he published the most famous Holmes story of them all, *The Hound of the Baskervilles*. In 1903, there followed a short story – 'The Adventure of the Empty House' – in which Holmes's apparent death at the Reichenbach Falls was explained away. A further twenty-nine short stories and a novel were to come before Doyle at last finished with the character in 1927. Speaking a year later, and just two before his own death, Doyle reflected: 'I've written a good deal more about him than I ever intended to do but my hand has been forced by kind friends who continually wanted to know more, and so it is that this monstrous growth has come out of what was really a comparatively small seed.'

The author never truly comprehended the hold his detective had upon the reading public. In part, Holmes's allure was that he tapped into a fundamental desire within us, a wish to confront – perhaps even revel in – man's darkest instincts and then to master them. That is, too, what was occurring in Edinburgh's High Court of Justiciary in December 1893, even as Holmes was plunging over his Swiss waterfall. Bell and Littlejohn – Holmes made living flesh – sought to make sense of unexplained, brutal death by imposing cool, calm reason upon it. In *A Study in Scarlet*, Holmes reflected: 'There's the scarlet thread of murder running through the colourless skein of life, and our duty is to unravel it, and isolate it, and expose every inch of it.' Littlejohn and Bell, his spiritual forefathers, would surely have said amen to that.

Bibliography

Researching this book has been a joyous labour of love that has
taken me down many interesting roads and the odd cul-de-sac.
It would be impractical to detail every source I have used along
the way but the major ones are listed here.

I have delved into several archives and special collections, and
found their respective staffs unstintingly helpful. Among the most
important were the National Records of Scotland (notably pre-trial
reports, refs AD14/93/1/23, AD14/93/1/24/89, AD14/93/1/28,
AD14/93/1/30 and AD14/93/1/31), the Royal College of
Surgeons (various correspondence and documentation related
to Bell and Littlejohn, refs GD16/2/1/1/1, GD16/2/1/5/1,
GD16/2/3/1, GB 779 GD23/1/2/4, GB 779 GD23/1/3/2/1
and GB779 GD23/2/1/5), Edinburgh University Library's Special
Collections Division (particularly Littlejohn's lecture notes, refs
EUA IN1/ACU/F1/1), Nottingham University's Manuscripts
and Special Collections (notably Monson family correspondence
refs GA 2 E 1068, 1069, 1070, 1077, 1078, 1079, 1080, 1081,
1082, 1083, 1089 and 1563) and the Wellcome Library (especially
John Dixon Comrie's notes taken at Littlejohn's lectures in 1897,
ref. MS3305). I am also indebted to the National Archives, the
University of Aberdeen's Special Collections Centre, and the
archives of Linley Sambourne House, Rugby School and the
University of Oxford.

Between August 1893 and April 1894 especially, the Ardlamont
affair was a regular fixture in national and local newspapers. Those
I referred to most were the *Aberdeen Evening News*, the *Aberdeen
Weekly Journal*, the *Dundee Courier*, the *Edinburgh Evening News*,

the *Graphic*, the *Illustrated Police News*, the *Pall Mall Gazette*, the *Scotsman*, the *Sketch*, *The Times*, *Tit-Bits* and *To-Day*.

Alborn, Timothy, *Regulated Lives: Life Insurance and British Society, 1800–1914*, University of Toronto Press (2009)

Baggoley, Martin, *Scottish Murders*, The History Press (2013)

Bain, M., Bentley, A. and Squires, T., 'Sir Henry Duncan Littlejohn – a Dynamic Figure in Forensic Medicine and Public Health in the Nineteenth Century', *Proceedings of the Royal College of Physicians of Edinburgh*, Vol. 29, No. 3 (1999)

Bell, Suzanne, *Crime and Circumstance: Investigating the History of Forensic Science*, Praeger Publishers Inc. (2008)

Booth, Martin, *The Doctor, The Detective and Arthur Conan Doyle*, Hodder & Stoughton (1997)

Bray, Peter, *Steephill*, Ventnor Local History Society (1991)

Bray, R. M. and Boxall, W. P. G., 'Hambrough Versus the Mutual Life Insurance Company of New York', *Journal of the Institute of Actuaries*, Vol. 31, No. 6 (1895)

Burnaby, Evelyn, *Memories of Famous Trials*, Sisley's Ltd (1907)

Burney, Ian A., *Bodies of Evidence: Medicine and the Politics of the English Inquest, 1830–1926*, Johns Hopkins University Press (2000)

Carr, John Dickson, *The Life of Sir Arthur Conan Doyle*, Harper and Brothers Publishers (1949)

Clark, Michael and Crawford, Catherine (eds), *Legal Medicine in History*, Cambridge University Press (1994)

Costello, Peter, *The Real World of Sherlock Holmes: The True Crimes Investigated by Arthur Conan Doyle*, Robinson Publishing (1991)

Crowther, M. Anne and White, Brenda, *On Soul and Conscience: The Medical Expert and Crime*, Aberdeen University Press (1988)

Davie, Neil, *Tracing the Criminal: The Rise of Scientific Criminology in Britain, 1860–1918*, The Bardwell Press (2006)

Denby, Elaine, *Grand Hotels: Reality and Illusion*, Reaktion Books (1998)

Doyle, Arthur Conan (ed. Howard Haycraft), *The Boys' Sherlock Holmes*, Harper & Row (1961)

Doyle, Arthur Conan, *The Penguin Complete Sherlock Holmes*, Penguin Books (1981)

Flanders, Judith, *The Invention of Murder: How the Victorians Revelled in Death and Detection and Created Modern Crime*, HarperPress (2011)

Green, Richard Lancelyn, *The Uncollected Sherlock Holmes*, Penguin Books (1983)

Guthrie, Douglas, 'Medicine and Detection', *Medicine Illustrated*, III, No. 5 (1949)

House, Jack, *Murder Not Proven?*, Penguin Books (1989)

Hyde, H. Montgomery, *Their Good Names: A Collection of Libel and Slander Cases*, Hamilton (1970)

Jaeger, Jens, 'Police and Forensic Photography' in *The Oxford Companion to the Photograph* (ed. Robin Lenman), Oxford University Press (2005)

Kemp, Dawn and Mackaill, Alan, *Conan Doyle and Joseph Bell: The Real Sherlock Holmes*, Royal College of Surgeons (2007)

Laxton, Paul and Rodger, Richard, *Insanitary City: Henry Littlejohn and the Condition of Edinburgh*, Carnegie Publishing Ltd (2013)

Lellenberg, Jon L. and Lofts, W. O. G., 'John H(eron) Watson, M.D.', *The Baker Street Journal*, Vol. 30, No. 2 (1980)

Lellenberg, Jon, Stashower, Daniel and Foley, Charles, *Arthur Conan Doyle: A Life in Letters*, HarperPress (2007)

Lewis, John Benjamin and Bombaugh, Charles Carroll, *Stratagems and Conspiracies to Defraud Life Insurance Companies: An Authentic Record of Remarkable Cases*, J. H. McClellan (1896)

Liebow, Ely M., *Dr. Joe Bell: Model for Sherlock Holmes*, Bowling Green University Press (1982)

Littlejohn, H. D. 'On the Practice of Medical Jurisprudence', *Edinburgh Medical Journal*, Vol. 21, No. 1 (1875)

Littlejohn, H. D., obituary, *The British Medical Journal*, Vol. 2, No. 2806 (1914)

Lycett, Andrew, *Conan Doyle: The Man Who Created Sherlock*, Weidenfeld & Nicolson (2007)

Macdonald, Sir J. H. A., *Life Jottings of an Old Edinburgh Citizen*, T. N. Foulis (1915)

Macintyre, Iain and MacLaren, Iain (eds), *Surgeons' Lives: Royal College of Surgeons of Edinburgh: An Anthology of College Fellows Over 500 Years*, Royal College of Surgeons of Edinburgh (2005)

Marsh, John B., *Steephill Castle*, Dangerfield Printing Company (1907)

Monson, Alfred John, *The Ardlamont Mystery Solved*, Marlo & Co. (1894)

More, John W., *Trial of A. J. Monson*, William Hodge & Company (1908)

Munting, Roger, *An Economic and Social History of Gambling in Britain and the USA*, Manchester University Press (1996)

O'Brien, James, *The Scientific Sherlock Holmes: Cracking the Case with Science and Forensics*, OUP USA (2013)

Pilbeam, Pamela, *Madame Tussaud and the History of Waxworks*, Hambledon Continuum (2006)

Pugh, Brian W., *A Chronology of the Life of Arthur Conan Doyle*, MX Publishing (2012)

Ramsland, Katherine, *Beating the Devil's Game: A History of Forensic Science and Criminal Investigation*, Berkley Publishing Group (2007)

Roughead, William, *Classic Crimes*, New York Review of Books (2000)

Sandford, Christopher, *The Man Who Would be Sherlock: The Real Life Adventures of Arthur Conan Doyle*, The History Press (2017)

Saxby, J. M., *Joseph Bell: An Appreciation by an Old Friend*, Oliphant, Anderson and Ferrier (1913)

Smith, Sir Sydney, *Mostly Murder*, D. McKay Co. (1959)

Tracy, Jack, *The Encyclopaedia Sherlockiana*, Avon Books (1979)

Wallace, Irving, *The Fabulous Originals*, Longmans, Green & Co. (1955)

Whittington-Egan, Richard, *Jack the Ripper: The Definitive Casebook*, Amberley Publishing (2015)

Wilson, John Gray, *Not Proven*, Secker & Warburg (1960)

Wood, Walter, *Survivors' Tales of Famous Crimes*, Cassell (1916)

Wormersley, Tara and Crawford, Dorothy H., *Bodysnatchers to Lifesavers: Three Centuries of Medicine in Edinburgh*, Luath Press Ltd (2010)

www.oldbaileyonline.org (for transcript of Monson's 1898 trial)

Acknowledgements

Firstly, my thanks to my agent, James Wills (and his assistant, Megan Carroll) and to Louise Dixon at Michael O'Mara, who commissioned the book. George Maudsley at Michael O'Mara coped admirably with editing yet another of my books, casting his expert eye over the text and improving it in countless ways. Your hard work, skill and patience is truly appreciated. Thanks also to my copyeditor, Howard Watson, for applying a final polish.

I am eternally grateful to all the individuals who took the time to share their knowledge and insights with me. Among them were Sheila McClue and Sue Thomson (descendants of Alfred Monson and John Comrie Thomson, respectively), Andrew Lycett, Jon Lellenberg and Daniel Stashower, Timothy Alborn, Martin Bagolley, Catherine Cooke, Cynthia Liebow, Robert Linford, Jan Bondeson, Eleanor McKay of the Argyll and Bute Library Service, Otto Penzler and Richard Rodger. Not to mention Val Wilson, who undertook expert research for me in Edinburgh when the arrival of a new baby kept me in London.

Nor would this book have happened without the British Library, or indeed Cubitt Town Library (long live the local library!) and Café Forever, which has become something of a second home. Most of all, thanks to my family for their ceaseless support over the years. My mum and dad gave early versions of the text a read and urged me on in the project. My two little ones, meanwhile, always ensure I have a smile on my face even at the end of the hardest day. And, as ever, thanks to Rosie, who not only accepts the vagaries of having a writer as a husband with good grace but positively encourages me to keep going! As Sherlock Holmes said of Irene Adler, she is always *the* woman.

Index

Aberdeen Weekly Journal 124, 137, 231

Academy 236

Ardlamont House:
    described 11
    Monsons' move to 62
    proposed purchase of 62–3, 66–7

The Ardlamont Mystery Solved (Monson) 192–5

Asher, Alexander (Sol.-Gen.) 137–8, 141, 144, 146, 162–3, 167, 168, 238 (*see also* Monson trial)
    closing statement of 168–71

Bell, Benjamin 97–8

Bell, Edith 97–8

Bell, Dr Joseph 153–4, 189, 212, 213, 219, 222, 238, 239, 240, 241
    academic career of 16–17, 19
    and ballistics 74
    and Bury case 82
    busy year for 96–7
    and Cecil death, *see under* Hambrough, Cecil
    and Chantrelle 80–1
    and close observation 74–6
    crucial to forensic science 69–70
    described 20–1
    Doyle dedicates volume to 25
    as Doyle mentor 20
    Doyle's correspondence with 25–6
    Doyle's rapport with 22–3
    in Doyle's thoughts 24
    and exhumation 95
    on fact and theory 144
    and footprints 77
    frustration of, with police 79–80
    and handwriting 76
    at heart of Doyle story 25
    as Holmes inspiration, *see under* Holmes, Sherlock
    influence of, on Doyle 26–31, 73
    and observation and perception 21–2
    and Ripper 81
    and Rose case 82
    and *A Study in Scarlet* 77
    and trial 146, 148, 155–7, 160, 161, 173, 179, 202–5 *passim*, 206–7, 209–10

Blair, John 102, 166, 184

Brown, Dr McDonald 99, 100, 153

Carmichael, Hugh 13, 85, 92, 101, 107

Chantrelle case 80–1, 179

Cheyney Court 42–3

Churchill, Robert 209, 224

Comrie Thomson, John (defence) 137, 142–3, 153, 158–9, 160, 167, 168, 208, 232, 238 (*see also* Monson trial)
    closing statement of 168, 171–7
    Monson's letter to 184–5

Crookes, William 70–1

Daily Chronicle 133
Daily News 185
Davis, Edward, *see* Scott/Sweeney, Edward
Day, Annie 126, 214, 218
Douglas, Lord Alfred 109, 236
Douglas, John 141
Doyle, Arthur Conan 19, 20, 22–3, 75, 129, 190, 209–10, 240–1 (*see also* Doyle works; Holmes, Sherlock)
Bell reviews book by 25
as Bell's assistant 154
Bell's correspondence with 25–6
first published story of 24
first single-volume collection of 25
and Parliament 240
as ship's surgeon 24
and short-story format 25
at university 16
US tour by 212
Doyle, Louisa 209
Doyle works (discussed) (*see also* chapter epigraphs):
'The Adventure of the Blue Carbuncle' 127
'The Adventure of the Dancing Men' 74
'The Adventure of the Dying Detective' 28
'The Adventure of the Empty House' 241
'The Adventure of the Lion's Mane' 74
'The Adventure of the Naval Treaty' 148
'The Adventure of the Noble Bachelor' 232, 234
'The Adventure of the Norwood Builder' 73

'The Adventure of the Reigate Squires' 74, 76
'The Adventure of the Yellow Face' 202
The Adventures of Sherlock Holmes 25, 74–5
'The Boscombe Valley Mystery' 13
'The Final Problem' 16, 129
The Hound of the Baskervilles 241
Micah Clarke 15
'The Problem of Thor Bridge' 74
'A Scandal in Bohemia' 144
The Sign of the Four 25
A Study in Scarlet 25, 28, 69, 73, 75–6, 77, 241
The White Company 15
Dunn, James 85

Eagle Insurance 34, 35, 36, 51, 52–3, 54, 55, 56, 60–2, 171–2, 225–6
Edinburgh, as hotbed of medical practice 16
Edinburgh Academy Chronicle 240
Edinburgh Evening News 187, 205
Edinburgh Medical Journal 17, 148
Edinburgh News 136
Edward VII 239
Edward VII (formerly Prince of Wales) 129–30, 239

Faulds, Henry 72
fingerprints 72–3
Fuller, Morris 53, 55, 58

Gaddesley Farm, Monson rents 44
Galton, Francis 72
Galway, Viscount 121–2, 191, 236
Glasgow Herald 187
Greet, Insp. Thomas 109

Hambleton, Dr 51–2, 58, 61, 109
Hambrough, Albert 33, 90, 125
Hambrough, Cecil:
  adultery claim concerning 230,
    233, 234–5
  Agnes protected by 48
  Agnes's court judgment against 60
  Ardlamont move of 62
  described 11
  doctor examines 86–7, 98–9
  exhumed 95, 98–9, 227
  fatal gunshot to 12–13, 85, 88, 94,
    98–100, 150–3, 154–5, 156–7,
    159–62, 167, 173, 223, 228
  financial schemes entered by 50
  and fishing 12, 83–4, 133
  found dead 12–13, 85
  funeral of 90
  grand life enjoyed by 48
  and guns 88, 91, 92–4, 101–2,
    103–4, 228
  health problems of 51
  and hunting trip 84–5 (see also
    Monson trial)
  inheritance of 224–5
  and insurance 54, 60–1, 63–6, 67,
    89, 91, 92–3, 94, 169, 171–2,
    180, 214–15, 223, 224, 226,
    228–29
  and Littlejohn's investigation
    98–102
  and military service 55–6, 57
  in Monson book, see Monson,
    Alfred: book by
  Monson charges concerning
    119–20, 132–3
  and Monson hypnosis 211
  and newspaper gossip 123–6, 133
  parents' death notice concerning
    237
  parents shunned by 56–8
  parents told of death of 88
  and proposed Ardlamont
    purchase, see under Ardlamont
    House
  and Tot 37, 62, 169, 171–2
  and trial, see Monson trial
  young life and family background
    of 32–5
Hambrough, Maj. Dudley 32–7
  passim, 48–58 passim, 60–1, 108,
  123, 124–5, 214–15, 224–5, 226,
  232, 233, 237
  and Cecil death, see under
    Hambrough, Cecil
  and insurance, see under
    Hambrough, Cecil
  and Monson's background 40
Hambrough, John 32, 33
Hambrough, Marion 34, 35, 87–9,
  237
Hanrott, R. C. 54, 56
Hay, Dr Matthew 102–4, 158–64,
  167, 173, 209
Heron Watson, Dr Patrick 99, 100,
  153–5, 173, 179, 203, 205, 219,
  234, 239
Herschel, William James 72
Hobson, Stanley 219
Holmes, Mycroft 26, 27
Holmes, Sherlock (see also Doyle,
  Arthur Conan):
  and ballistics 74
  Bell as inspiration for 19, 26–31,
    73, 153, 155
  Bell's criticism of 213
  and blood testing 73
  and dialect 76
  Doyle's fractious relationship
    with 15

Doyle's plan to kill off 15–16, 212, 240–1
forensics popularized by 72
and handwriting 76–7
high fame of 240–1
Littlejohn as inspiration for 13–14
and photography 74
and phrenology 127
and poisons 73
resurrected 241
Honour, Victor 217–18, 219, 220
Hotel Metropole 110, 230, 231–2
Huddersfield Chronicle 201

Isle of Wight 32, 90, 120, 171, 236

Jack the Ripper 81–2
Jerningham, Adolphus 59–60, 63
Jerningham, William 59, 60–1
Jones, Dr Harold 30

Kingsburgh, Lord (Judge) 137–8, 167, 204–5, 208, 238 (*see also* Monson trial)
summing-up of 178, 179–82, 187, 189

Laurie, John 82
Littlejohn, Harvey 239
Littlejohn, Dr Henry 18–20, 72–4, 80–2, 96–7, 212, 219, 222, 239–40, 241
academic career of 17–19
Bell's relationship with 29
and Cecil death, *see under* Hambrough, Cecil
checklist of 77–8
crucial to forensic science 69–70
and exhumation 95

as Holmes inspiration, *see under* Holmes, Sherlock
influence of, on Doyle 30–1
investigation by 98–102
knighted 239
'Original Sherlock Holmes' 240
press interview of 120–1
and trial 146, 148–53, 159, 160, 164, 173–4, 179, 202–5 *passim*, 206–7, 209–10
Liverpool Daily Post 240

Macmillan, Dr 86–7, 89, 91–5 *passim*, 109, 153, 166, 169, 228
and exhumation 98–9
MacNaughton, James 101, 102, 149, 152, 164
Macnaughton, Tom 92, 93–4, 98
Madame Tussauds, *see* Tussauds
Mair, Alexander 188
Mathers, Helen 190–1
Metcalf, Robert Ives 219
Middleton, Baron 122
M'Kellar, Donald 139–40
M'Lullich, John Campbell (Fiscal) 87, 92–5 *passim*, 106–7, 108, 169, 173, 195, 197, 199, 226
M'Nicol, Stewart 85, 140, 141
Monckton-Arundell, George 121–2
Monson, Agnes 113, 121–2, 123, 126, 132, 192, 214, 215, 218–19, 221, 229–33, 234–5, 236–7 (*see also* Monson, Alfred)
adultery claim concerning 230, 233, 234–5
and Alfred's wrath 48
background of 38
and Cecil death, *see under* Hambrough, Cecil
Cecil taken to court by 60

desertion alleged by 218
and divorce petition 230
and insurance on Cecil, *see under*
  Hambrough, Cecil
and proposed Ardlamont
  purchase, *see under* Ardlamont
  House
reunites with Alfred 41
at trial 138–9, 183
Monson, Alfred 12, 40–1, 43, 44,
  47, 52–68 *passim*, 83–90, 129,
  190–201 *passim*, 209–11, 213–33
  passim
Ardlamont move of 62
arrests of 95, 216
and Ballabrooie fire 216
bankruptcy of 47, 49, 58, 62
and 'baseness for gain' 235
and bathing machine 201
book by 193–5
and Cecil death, *see under*
  Hambrough, Cecil
at Cecil funeral 90
and Cecil's shunning of parents
  56–8
and Cecil's tutoring 11, 37–9, 40,
  47, 48, 52, 125
charges against 119–20, 132–3
and Cheyney Court fires 42–3, 68
Cheyney Court school closed by
  43
Comrie Thomson thanked by 185
conspiracy charges against 219
in custody 95, 131–2
defenders of, post-trial 236
desertion case against 218
and divorce petition 230
in Doyle correspondence 209–10
evidence eliminated by 101
an 'evil character' 205

and financial problems 43–7
  passim, 49, 52, 126, 213–14,
  215–16
and Fiscal 92–4, 95, 108
fraud charge against 45, 219–21
and hunting trip 84–5 (*see also*
  Monson trial)
and hypnosis 211
and insurance on Cecil, *see under*
  Hambrough, Cecil
Isle of Man move of 215
jailed for fraud 219–21
mother-in-law sues 218
new deceits of 217–18, 219
and perjury 199, 216
and proposed Ardlamont
  purchase, *see under* Ardlamont
  House
release of 236
and Scott's absence, *see under*
  Scott, Edward
suspicious character of 40, 42–3
trial of, *see* Monson trial
and Tussauds 196–200
uncertain ultimate whereabouts
  of 236
Wyvill name adopted by 215
Monson, Isabella 121–2, 191–2,
  213, 219
Monson trial 135–84 *passim*, 202–7
  passim, 209–12, 213, 230, 231,
  232, 235
closing statements in 168–77
defendant's statement in 141–2
exhibits in 149
importance of forensic evidence
  in 146
judge and counsel in, introduced
  137
judge sums up in 178–82, 189

jury in 139, 182–3, 185–8 *passim*
Monson's own thoughts on
    188–9
'not proven' verdict in 183, 186,
    187–8, 189
and parallel shooting incidents
    205–6
plea given in 139
press opinion on 183, 185–8
public debate about 188
review of 209
sermon concerning 188
transcript of 236
Monson, William 121
Morritt, Charles 192, 211, 237, 238
Mount Osborne Colliery 44
Mutual Life 65–6, 91, 93, 94–5, 107,
    214

Nightingale, Florence 17
Norgate, Percival 219
Norwich Union 219

Oxenbridge, Lord 90, 121, 191

Pall Mall Gazette 29, 79, 109, 153–4,
    155, 195, 202, 210
Peel, Robert 79
photographic evidence 74
Pipewell 33, 36
Prince, Mr 58, 60–1
Procurator Fiscal, *see* M'Lullich,
    John Campbell

Reichenbach Falls 16, 221, 241
Richards, Henry 60–1
Riseley Hall 39, 47, 48, 62, 230, 231
Rose, Edwin 82
Rosslyn, Earl of 217
Royal College of Surgeons 17

Royal Hospital for Sick Children 17,
    156, 212

Scotsman 149, 200, 219, 235
Scott/Sweeney, Edward 83–7, 193–
    7, 210–11, 224, 227–8, 237–8
absence of 106–18 *passim*, 169,
    174–5, 193, 195–6, 228
arrives at Ardlamont 11
and Cecil death, *see under*
    Hambrough, Cecil
declared outlaw 139, 196, 210
described 12
and disguise 112, 116, 194
evidence eliminated by 101
and hunting trip 84–5 (*see also*
    Monson trial)
in Monson book 193–5
trial references to, *see* Monson
    trial
Sketch 190, 195–6, 234
Spectator 185–6
Speedy, Tom 103–4, 167
Stanmore 33, 36
The Stark Munro Letters (Doyle) 209
Steephill 32–3, 34, 51, 53, 55, 60–2,
    171, 224–5
Steven, John 85–7, 89–90, 103
Strand 13, 15, 25, 28
and Holmes's Reichenbach fall 16
Sweeney, Edward, *see* Scott/
    Sweeney, Edward
Sweeney, George 110–11, 210, 224
Syme, Prof. James 16, 71

Tillard, Col. George 167–8
Times 238, 240
Tit-Bits 30, 75
Tottenham, Beresford Loftus 'Tot'
    197–9, 216, 225–6, 237

Agnes sells debt to 60
and Cecil death, *see under*
 Hambrough, Cecil
Cecil's allowance from 62
financial schemes entered by 50
Hambrough Snr grants mortgages
 to 52
Hambrough Snr, meets 36–7
and insurance, *see under*
 Hambrough, Cecil
and proposed Ardlamont
 purchase, *see under* Ardlamont
 House
rewards sought by 47
theft conviction against 198–9
Townsend, Sophie 33
Tussaud, John 198, 199
Tussaud, Louis 198
Tussauds 196–200

Ventnor 32, 33, 90, 95, 98, 226
Victoria, Queen 239

Wilde, Oscar 109, 236
Woodlands 38, 45, 46
Wright, James 83, 84, 92, 107